YOUNGER BRAIN, SHARPER MIND

YOUNGER BRAIN, SHARPER MIND

A 6-Step Plan for Preserving
and Improving Memory and Attention
at Any Age

ERIC R. BRAVERMAN, MD

Bestselling Author of *Younger (Thinner) You Diet*

RODALE

© 2011 by Eric R. Braverman

All rights reserved. No part of this publication may be reproduced or transmitted in any form or by any means, electronic or mechanical, including photocopying, recording, or any other information storage and retrieval system, without the written permission of the publisher.

Rodale books may be purchased for business or promotional use or for special sales. For information, please write to:
Special Markets Department, Rodale Inc., 733 Third Avenue, New York, NY 10017

Printed in the United States of America
Rodale Inc. makes every effort to use acid-free ♾, recycled paper ♻.

Illustrations by Alyssa Bieler
Book design by Christina Gaugler

Library of Congress Cataloging-in-Publication Data
Braverman, Eric R.
    Younger brain, sharper mind : a 6-step plan for preserving and improving memory and attention at any age / Eric R. Braverman.
        p.   cm.
    ISBN 978–1–60529–422–3   hardcover
    1. Brain—Popular works.   2. Brain—Care and hygiene—Popular works.
3. Self-care, Health—Popular works.   I. Title.
QP376.B739   2011
612.8'2339—dc23   2011036546

Distributed to the trade by Macmillan

4   6   8   10   9   7   5   hardcover

We inspire and enable people to improve their lives and the world around them.
www.rodalebooks.com

To my son, J. J. Braverman, for his great contributions toward a new world order for smarter people; to my daughter, Ellie, for all her assistance; and to my three smallest children, who live the Brain Advantage paradigm with me as "team DADS": <u>A</u>ri, <u>D</u>aniel, and <u>S</u>teven.

CONTENTS

Acknowledgments ix

Introduction xi

Part I: A Balanced Brain

Chapter 1: Brain Basics: What's Going On Inside Your Head........... 3

Chapter 2: The Causes of Cognitive Decline..................................... 23

Chapter 3: Identifying Personality and Mood Changes 32

Chapter 4: Identifying Memory Problems...................................... 48

Chapter 5: Identifying Attention Problems 63

Chapter 6: Identifying IQ Types 78

Part II: The Braverman Protocol

Chapter 7: Step One: Early Testing 87

Chapter 8: Step Two: Smart Lifestyle Changes 121

Chapter 9: Step Three: Diet and Nutrition for a Younger,
Smarter You 136

Chapter 10: Step Four: Exercises That Boost Your Brain............... 178

Chapter 11: Step Five: Natural Hormones
Jump-Start Quick Thinking 195

Chapter 12: Step Six: Brain-Balancing Medications...................... 215

Part III: Your Brain, Your Body

Chapter 13: Reversing Disease Makes You Smarter....................... 229

Chapter 14: The Daily Smarts.. 252

Appendix A: Answer Key for the
Braverman Brain Advantage Test 255

References.. 258

Index.. 270

ACKNOWLEDGMENTS

The creation of this book could not have been possible without the help of many individuals. I would like to thank my agent, David Vigliano, and my successful team at Rodale, led by Pam Krauss and Andrea Au Levitt. I would also like to thank my writer, Pam Liflander, for her unique skills, insights, and attentiveness in helping to get my ideas onto these pages.

I am grateful to my colleagues at the PATH Medical Center, Tatiana Karikh, MD, and Richard Smayda, DO, who have always been invaluable critics of my work. I am also fortunate to have a gifted team of medical and administrative personnel who have helped turn my research and ideas into successful work. Their skills are unsurpassed, and I am lucky to have them: Uma Damle; Victoria Gibbs; Melissa Dispensa; Anish Bajaj, DC; John Pillepich; Stanley Huang; and Preeti Pusalkar. I would also like to thank my medical staff members, whose loyalty and dedication to helping my patients cannot go unnoticed: Ellie Capria, RPA-C; Rosina Giaccio-Williams, RPA-C; and Dallas Worth, RPA-C.

And, finally, to my patients, the greatest teachers of all.

INTRODUCTION

In my experience, getting older has always meant getting better. Today, my 54-year-old body is stronger, leaner, and seemingly younger than ever before. I've mastered a healthy diet, so I can eat a full complement of delicious foods without worrying about gaining weight. I exercise daily, so I know that I'm maintaining strong bones, increasing muscular strength and mass, and all the while improving my metabolism. But most important, my mind is working optimally. I know this because I'm experiencing the three hallmarks of a balanced brain: I feel healthy, happy, and wise.

Overall good health cannot occur without a healthy brain; yet living without disease is only one aspect of staying young. In order for you to be able to enjoy and succeed in life for years to come, your cognitive functioning needs to remain at its peak even as you get older. A balanced, healthy brain ensures just that, so that you can continue to get smarter, remember, and stay focused and attentive.

Maturity and a calm, stable brain have also given me the ability to be a happier person. I can focus on the positive aspects of life instead of the negative, even during the most stressful times. While my days are demanding—running a busy medical practice and a brain research foundation, and raising five kids—I can manage it all without letting stress burn me out or creating anxieties. What's more, my positive attitude allows me to concentrate fully on making the right decisions for my patients, and particularly for myself, so that I can get ahead instead of dwelling on what is holding me back.

Research has shown that the old adage is correct, with a twist: Wisdom really does come with age, but only when you have a balanced, healthy brain. As a healthy brain ages, it begins to reorganize, and consequently, we literally act and think differently. Our judgment improves, and we can see new patterns and connections, or what author Barbara Strauch points out in her book *The Secret Life of the Grown-Up Brain* as the "interwoven layers of knowledge that allow us to instantly recognize similarities of situations and see solutions." Over the years I've also noticed that my healthy, fast brain has helped me become more empathetic to those around me. I can see different perspectives and resolve problems at home and in my medical practice. The insights I've developed about the human condition—what truly motivates and drives people— allow me to be a better communicator and a better doctor.

My goal for this book is to teach you how to balance your brain so that you can become happy, healthy, and, most important, wise. The key to your success will be keeping your brain young for the rest of your life. Education is the greatest ambition that the human race possesses, and your mandate is to take advantage of every opportunity to learn, which can only be possible if you can keep your brain as young as a 30-year-old's.

My patients have come to understand, as you will, that my "head first" approach to health care is the only way to avoid the ravages of aging, and I'm not just talking about the body. My patients come from all over the country for many reasons, but more often than not, they are beginning to worry about their aging brains, and what they can do to reverse or avoid a decline in cognitive health.

RECOGNIZING THE PROBLEM

One of the most distressing aspects of getting older is the thought of losing your mind. You may start worrying when you can't find your keys that you're heading straight toward dementia, the acquired deterioration in cognitive abilities that impairs the successful performance of daily living. You're probably afraid of becoming the stereotypical grandparent who forgets a grandchild's name, the postmenopausal woman who can't find her glasses, or the retired man who can't remember where he parked his car. These "senior moments" are all real signs that your brain is getting old and, sometimes, can actually be older than your chronological age.

A second problem is something I call the performance gap. As we get older, many of us experience an increase in familial or professional obligations: taking care of older parents at the same time that you are taking care of your own children, or achieving a higher status at work that often is accompanied by additional responsibilities. Unfortunately, these changes often occur simultaneously with a loss of brain power: We're asked to do more, yet at the same time our brain is actually doing less.

Business writer Dr. Laurence J. Peters first discovered and called this realization "the Peter Principle," which he defined as each person's ability to rise to their own level of incompetence. But now we know that the problem he identified is not apathy or sociology: It's biology. Research clearly shows that your brain—along with everything else in your body—changes as you age. These performance gaps begin as early as in your thirties and can increase to dangerous levels from ages 50 to 70. This means that at the time when we should be leading our lives the most intelligently, we are already losing our ability to reason and remember.

If you believe that you are experiencing even the subtlest changes in your memory and attention, you're not imagining things. The brain is like a superhighway for information, and an aging brain is like a highway after a jackknifed tractor trailer accident. Everything stops. Worse, the abuse the highway has taken over the years has caused it to be riddled with potholes. The brain actually atrophies in the same way that your muscles do when you don't exercise. Without the proper care, your brain literally cools, then shrinks and dries out. Just like a grape turns into a raisin, an aging brain loses cells and volume. When this happens, your brain processing speed and power begin to diminish, and you lose the ability not only to think clearly but also to rest effectively or stay calm. This is true for both men and women: We lose 7 to 10 milliseconds of brain speed for each decade, and there are 1,000 milliseconds in just 1 second. Since most of us think at a speed of only 100 milliseconds, a 20 percent loss of processing speed over 20 to 30 years is enormous, even if it is too small for us to evaluate on our own.

An initial change in brain speed results in a brain disease that is referred to as mild cognitive impairment, or MCI. Once the signs and symptoms of MCI begin to pile up, you will begin a downward crawl toward dementia and Alzheimer's disease. While these advanced stages can take between 15 and 20 years to develop, they always begin with

MCI. MCI can start during your thirties or forties. Today, 50 percent of all Americans between the ages of 80 and 85 are demented.

Yet even while we fear changes to our mental status, many people resign themselves to the fact that cognitive declines are expected shifts that occur with aging. While this is true, it doesn't have to be your destiny. The great design of the human body is self-repair, and the brain is no different. MCI is like a wound inside the brain, and just as you take care of a cut on your hand or a scraped knee, you can treat an aging brain and teach it to repair itself. The goal then for optimal brain health is to bolster and reverse impairments as early as possible, even before symptoms occur, in order to keep your brain young and your thinking fast.

I've written this book to show that you do not have to drift toward a life of forgetfulness. And you can close—and even jump over—the performance gap, just by retraining your brain. If you are already experiencing symptoms, rest assured they are reversible. Just as illness throughout the body can be reversed, so can imbalances in the brain. If you start taking care of your brain, it can remain healthy and vibrant throughout your life. The earlier you can reverse an aging brain, the better. With this new and innovative program, you will be able to add at least 15 smarter, happier, and more productive years to your life.

NEUROGENESIS IS THE ANSWER

When I attended medical school, we learned that many cells within the body have the ability to regenerate; entire organs are eventually renewed as old cells die off and are replaced with new ones. But the brain was held as the exception to the rule. We were taught that the brain was static, or unchanging, and that aging, drug use, and poor lifestyle choices killed off brain cells, which was why brain functioning declined as we aged. Worst of all, science was absolutely certain that these cells could not be replicated.

That assumption has been proven to be entirely false. Today, we know that the brain is plastic: It is just as alive as any other organ in the body, and it can repair itself and adapt to change. Not only is the brain malleable, it creates new neuronal connections every time we master concepts and information.

The fix for an aging brain, then, is simple: We have to stop brain atrophy, limit brain cell death, and maximize brain function and health. We do this by training our brains to create new, healthy brain cells to assist and achieve continuous repair. The process is called neurogenesis—the growth of new brain cells—and this exciting discovery has opened the door for a more positive attitude toward aging.

Neurogenesis teaches us that we can repair, recover, or even improve the aging brain. It is the process that fills the potholes and gets traffic moving smoothly once again. And when this happens, our thinking becomes more disciplined, focused, and confident, while our bodies and brains become more resilient to the damages we inflict through poor diet and lifestyle choices, or despite stressful or demanding environments.

The highest-functioning brains can maintain a continuous state of repair from age 30 onward, all through neurogenesis. This plasticity helps you to reverse or delay the impact of mental decline by up to 15 years. In fact, you'll become smarter in lots of other ways.

- Improved rapid visual information processing
- Enhanced learning
- Regained spatial recognition
- Reversed executive problems and low IQ
- Arrested memory decline

SIX STEPS TO A YOUNGER, SMARTER YOU

Over the last 30 years, I have developed a unique approach to enhancing all aspects of health by improving brain chemistry. Today, my nonprofit PATH Foundation is on the cutting edge of science, deciphering the complex codes of the brain to come up with new treatment options that allow us to continue to function at our very best throughout our lives. We've learned through PET scan technology that imbalanced brain chemistry is the largest obstacle to neurogenesis and is the cause of most medical problems that affect both the brain and the body. My preventive care approach doesn't wait until symptoms present themselves, because the more severe the symptom, the less likely that you will be able to

The Neurogenesis Equation

Your brain's cognitive energy is what keeps you thinking clearly and remembering. This processing speed is directly related to the number of brain cells firing off chemical messages. Just as Einstein's theory of relativity showed that energy was equal to an equivalent mass multiplied by the speed of light (squared), my PATH Foundation has discovered that cognitive energy equals the number of brain cells firing times the brain's processing speed, mathematically shown as:

Cognitive energy = voltage (number of neurons) × processing speed² (the speed at which they're fired)

reverse its impact. Instead, if we can correct illness early, you are much more likely to have a positive outcome.

My established protocol covers the same treatment options that my patients receive. It is a synergistic program that I've developed over more than 30 years of research and clinical experience for stimulating neurogenesis. By following this protocol, you too can actually get smarter as you get older. This book will teach you how to repair and grow your brain over and over again, by replenishing damaged brain cells with fresh ones and forcing the creation of new neuronal connections. Simply put, you can grow your brain back to full health and rewire your brain to reverse negative aging patterns of anxiety, poor sleep, and poor mood, so that you can increase your intelligence and creativity for the rest of your life. The core elements of my approach create a new standard for primary care, merging internal medicine and neuropsychology.

Part I explains how the brain works, and how to recognize if you're already affected by an aging brain. You'll be able to determine quickly if you are experiencing MCI, and learn how it is directly affecting your mood, memory, attention, and cognition, as well as your overall health.

Part II presents the Braverman Protocol, which will teach you exactly how you can build a better brain in just six simple steps.

Step One: Early Detection. Before you begin any program, you must determine your current brain health. Even if you are not experiencing the signs of MCI, it's important to define your cognitive baseline now, so that you can have a better, more educated understanding of how your brain changes as you age. I find that most people do not have established cognitive baselines, and they rely on their own memory to compare how their thinking has changed over the years. The problem with this, of course, is that they are coming to see me for problems associated with memory! The truth is that many forms of cognitive decline are too subtle for most people to recognize on their own, or they are mistakenly attributed to learning differences or aptitudes that we all do not share. That is why it is so critical to be able to thoroughly evaluate your brain health in a standardized format.

Step Two: Easy Lifestyle Changes. You'll learn to master technology to "de-spam" your brain and clear out the clutter in your head, so that you can begin to see improvements to your thinking right away. I have great strategies for staying on task and mastering new skills that anyone can follow. You'll also learn how to use technology to your advantage, instead of letting it overwhelm your mental inbox.

Step Three: Supporting Your Brain with Better Nutrition. You'll learn how personalizing your diet, including focusing on specific foods, teas, and spices, will enhance your particular brain chemistry as well as your cognition. I believe that your diet feeds the brain as much as, if not more than, it feeds the stomach. A great example is coffee. Heading out for a long drive? A little coffee is a good choice that will keep you awake. But if you drink coffee all day long, you'll end up nervous, irritable, and unable to sleep.

I also know that staying thin is one of the best ways to increase neurogenesis. Recent research shows that obesity is associated with brain atrophy. Just being overweight during middle age puts you at greater risk of having decreased cognitive abilities and suffering steeper cognitive declines in late life.

Vitamin and mineral supplements complete the effectiveness of a well-balanced diet and enhance neurogenesis in a natural, gentle way. However, don't take a handful of vitamins without first understanding which ones are right for you. My program highlights the best choices you can make once you understand how your brain works. You'll also learn why red wine—and its key nutrient resveratrol—may be the secret ingredient for restoring brain health.

Step Four: Brain and Body Exercises. Some of the brain exercises you will practice will help build memory and concentration, while others increase attention to detail. And while you are growing intellectually, you need to keep physically active so that your health can keep pace with your creativity. Studies have also revealed that exercise as simple as running can stimulate neurogenesis. Combined, these two strategies provide the means for your brain to continue working optimally as you age.

Step Five: Natural Hormones. Returning your body's natural hormones to younger levels is one of the easiest ways to boost your brain's power and speed. Ninety percent of all hormones are produced in or regulated by the brain. Our hormone levels peak when we are only 20. After that, the brain has to work harder as it tries to compensate for diminished production. Without the right levels of hormones, the brain can't process quickly or maintain its resilience.

Menopause occurs because of a severe decline in a woman's sex hormones and is the primary cause of dementia in women. Men experience their own loss of hormones during andropause, which also leads to dementia. However, a decline in the level of any hormone is neither irreparable nor permanent. You can reverse hormone-related aging and turn your brain back on by supplementing with bioidentical hormones.

Step Six: Medications. Lastly, prescription drugs have the fastest and most powerful impact on brain chemical imbalances. Numerous medications can be prescribed to help slow memory loss, control behavior problems, and improve sleep. However, my goal is always to use prescription drugs carefully, and for as short a time as possible. Once a prescribed medication has accomplished its goal, other, gentler alternatives can sustain it.

Part III addresses particular health issues that may be affecting your thinking. There's a fluid connection between how you feel and how you think, because the brain controls the body and impacts every aspect of your health. Subsequently, there are real physical predictors of mental impairment. Cognitive decline has been associated with almost every medical illness, including diabetes, bone loss, sickle cell disease, thyroid disorders, metabolic syndrome, and cancer. Because of this direct connection, it is important to take care of your whole body. The fix for these medical issues is straightforward: To restore your health, restore your brain chemistry.

Join me as we work together to build you a better brain, cell by cell, allowing you to close the performance gap as you learn how to replenish damaged brain cells with fresh ones, identify and reverse MCI and age-related dementia, and recover optimal brain function and performance. By doing so, you too can become healthy, happy, and wise.

Part I

A Balanced Brain

Chapter 1

Brain Basics: What's Going On Inside Your Head

The brain is the most remarkable organ in the body: It not only controls how you think, feel, and perceive, it manages all aspects of your health. It is responsible for how your body moves, digests, and ages. Most important, it generates the energy you need to fulfill these functions through the creation and dispersion of electricity.

Some say that the brain is like a supercomputer, but I imagine it more like the circuit box in your home. Whenever you want to turn on a light, you plug a lamp into an outlet, and electricity is transferred across the wires inside the walls directly from the circuit box to the lamp. The brain sends electric currents throughout your body in much the same way.

The brain's electrical activity typically begins with a stimulus: a thought, or a reaction from any of the five senses. When your brain receives the information from your sensory nerves, it, like the circuit box, sends electric messages down to the body in response. All the signals going to and from your brain travel through your internal wires, which are housed in your spinal cord. Together, the brain and spinal cord are called the central nervous system.

The smallest components of the central nervous system are billions of special cells called neurons. We are born with 100 billion neurons, and we now know that we can continue to produce them throughout our lives (this is where neurogenesis comes in). Every neuron has a gender as well as a nucleus (or head), arms called dendrites, and legs (or axons).

Each neuron has 10,000 axons and dendrites, which connect to other neurons to create your body's electrical network. Neurons come extremely close to one another but do not completely touch. The in-between space is called a synaptic gap. Each of us has 100 trillion of these neuron-to-neuron synapses. In this space, the axon of a neuron connects with the dendrite of another neuron. This connection activates the circuitry of the brain, literally flipping on a switch, which creates electricity and allows the electricity to pass continuously through them.

There are four measurements that determine the relationship between brain function and the creation and delivery of electricity. These are critical to maintain in order to build the most efficient and effective brain.

Voltage. Voltage measures your brain's power and output: the intensity at which it responds to any sensory stimulus—taste, touch, smell, sound, sight—and the brain's ability to process this information. Voltage determines your body's metabolism, or how fast it can convert food into fuel. It also measures the various states of consciousness, ranging from full alertness to deep sleep. Without proper voltage, you literally slow down—and so does your thinking.

The smartest brains rely on high levels of voltage. These people are quick thinkers with lots of cognitive energy and a healthy sense of curiosity, and they live with a sense of urgency. They pay attention to the details of life and can focus all their attention on completing a task, because there is always another accomplishment waiting for them to tackle.

Speed. The speed of your brain determines how quickly the electrical signals are processed. It is a measure of the intensity of how the brain is working. For example, the brain's electricity typically runs through the body at 60 cycles per second. Thinking occurs even faster, at only 2 to 3 cycles per second. The ability to maintain this rate determines your brain's "age," which might be very different from your actual age. As you can imagine, a younger brain is a faster brain. By increasing your brain speed, you can improve memory, IQ, and even behavior.

Balance. A balanced brain creates and receives electricity in a smooth, rhythmic flow. When the brain's electricity is generated and delivered evenly, you can achieve physical and emotional balance. You are in sync with others, have an overall sense of calmness, and possess a solid ability to handle stressful situations. However, when this same electricity is delivered in uneven bursts, you might feel anxious, irritable, or in pain. A balanced brain is the key to maintaining a happy, positive outlook on life, which allows you to become more empathetic and intuitive as you get smarter.

Synchrony. The brain's electricity moves as waves. There are four types of brain waves, each providing us with a level of physical as well as mental consciousness. The first type is *beta,* which travels at a rate of 12 to 16 cycles per second. When your brain is transmitting beta waves, you feel alert. The second type is *alpha,* and these waves travel at a rate of 8 to 12 cycles per second. When your brain is transmitting alpha waves, you feel creative. *Theta* waves travel at a rate of 4 to 8 cycles per second. When your brain is transmitting theta waves, you can feel drowsy. Last are *delta* waves, which travel at a rate of 1 to 4 cycles per second. When your brain is transmitting delta waves, you sleep.

These four brain waves always appear in some combination. You might feel alert and creative, or experience a deep sleep with extremely vivid dreams. True synchrony occurs when all four brain waves are coordinated throughout the day and night. When these brain waves get out of sync at night, you will not experience restful sleep; during the day, you'll find that your mind is wandering and your concentration is affected.

THE ELECTROCHEMICAL BRAIN

Each cell on the neuronal highway is programmed to produce, send, and receive a specific chemical, whose job is to activate brain cells to fire messages at each other by moving to various receptor sites within the brain's synapses. These receptors are like fingers on a glove: each one fitting only one part of your hand. When the receptors capture specific chemicals, your brain alters how your mind and body functions. The brain's chemistry generates the electricity, which then supplies power to the rest of the body.

Each chemical travels along a different path, resulting in a variety of physical processes as well as maintaining a high-powered, fast-moving, stable, and well-rested brain. The density of these chemicals is the key to your well-being: If there is an excess, the synapses are flooded and the signals can't get to the next neuron; if there is a deficiency, the nerve signals have nothing to travel on. Different parts of the body will react to brain chemical excesses and deficiencies by overworking or shutting down, leading to physical illness and cognitive decline.

There are four major brain chemical systems that travel on the neuronal highway: the catecholamine system, the cholinergic system, the GABAergic system, and the serotonergic system. Each of these is also related to the way electricity is distributed.

The key to boosting brain health is to balance the four categories of brain chemistry while you create new healthy brain cells.

- The *catecholamine system* features the brain chemical *dopamine,* which determines voltage. It is directly related to adrenaline, and the feeling you experience when you are excited. Dopamine controls bodily functions related to power, including blood pressure, metabolism, and digestion. Dopamine generates the electricity that controls voluntary movement, intelligence, abstract thought, goal setting, and long-term planning. A loss of dopamine results in decreased brain power, leading to fatigue, addiction, and a loss of attention.

- The *cholinergic system* features the chemical *acetylcholine,* which determines your brain's processing speed. This brain chemical family also acts as a lubricant and is necessary to keep the internal structures of the body moist so that energy and information can easily pass through each system. When your acetylcholine levels are high, you are creative and feel good about yourself. A loss of acetylcholine significantly decreases brain speed, resulting in "brain fog," which is what you experience when your thinking becomes disjointed. In extreme cases, it is linked to dementia and Alzheimer's disease, a type of dementia that occurs when the brain "forgets" how to take care of the body.

- The *GABAergic system* features gamma-aminobutyric acid, or *GABA.* This brain chemical is connected to electrical balance. It affects your stability and calmness. I like to think of GABA as the brain's natural Valium. When your GABA levels are correct, your mood is even and you can make good decisions. GABA is also involved in the production of endorphins, those "feel-good" hormones that are produced in the brain during a physical release, such as stretching, exercise, or even sex. A chemical imbalance of GABA causes headaches, palpitations, seizures, and anxiety.

- The *serotonergic system* features the brain chemical *serotonin*. Serotonin is connected to synchrony. It provides a healing, nourishing, satisfied feeling to the brain and body. Serotonin stimulates the growth of new neuronal connections, while the other brain chemical families ensure synaptic activity in existing neurons. When your serotonin levels are optimal, you can sleep deeply and think rationally. When they are out of balance, the effects include depression, sleep disorders, eating disorders, and sensory processing dysfunction.

Even when we are young, very few people are extremely high in only one brain chemical, or only low in another. Most of us are a combination of highs and lows. In fact, brain chemicals are synergistically related to each other. For example, dopamine and serotonin often work in conjunction with each other: When one is high, the other is low. Dopamine and acetylcholine are the brain's "on" switches, providing you with lots of energy. GABA and serotonin are the "off" switches—they help calm the body.

When your brain is balanced, you are creating the exact right amount of each of these chemicals, and you will feel energetic, creative, and calm, and will have the ability to reset your brain with restful sleep at night. But as get older, the structure of the neuronal highway gets worn down and becomes less efficient as both a chemical producer and transmitter. That's when you start to lose the speed of acetylcholine or the energy of dopamine. Without these, you will feel the low-serotonin blues, which lead to higher anxiety as GABA becomes imbalanced, which forces a low-serotonin inability to sleep. Dementia occurs when all the brain chemicals fail.

All these symptoms can contribute to your feeling older than your actual age, because they are literally aging your brain. And when that happens, you start to feel like you are losing your mind. This is why a youthful brain is perhaps the most crucial challenge of aging, and why you must keep your brain as young as possible throughout your life.

THE ANATOMY OF THE ELECTRIC BRAIN

The neurons that produce and receive the specific brain chemical families are located in particular regions of the brain. The brain is divided into three parts: the cerebrum, the brain stem, and the cerebellum. The cerebrum is further divided into two hemispheres that are linked by a thick band of nerve fibers called the corpus callosum. These hemispheres have identical areas that are designated as lobes. Each hemisphere of the cerebrum is divided into four lobes, and the cerebellum houses three. All of these lobes, in conjunction with the brain stem, control the automatic processes, such as breathing and digesting, and formulate our total health by managing all our other internal systems. Each lobe also directs mental functions: how we think, reason, create, and remember.

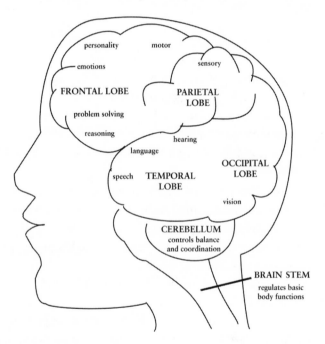

The Cerebrum

The cerebrum is what most of us think of when we picture the brain. It is covered by the cerebral cortex, which is the outer surface of folded bulges that increase its surface area and, therefore, increases the amount of information that the brain can process.

The cerebral cortex and the cerebrum together play a key role in memory, attention, perceptual awareness, thought, language, and consciousness. The largest part of the brain, the cerebrum, comprises both the left and right hemispheres of the brain, each of which contains four pairs of lobes. These lobes receive electrical currents from the central nervous system and translate them into specific chemical signals. Each pair is dominated by one of the four primary brain chemical families and associated with its corresponding measurement of electricity. A chemical surplus or deficiency within these lobes is what ultimately controls your thinking, your personality, and your health.

Frontal lobes. Every part of your body is connected to nerve cells that eventually lead to the frontal lobes. Through these connections the body receives the sensory signals associated with touch, including feelings of heat and coldness. The frontal lobes control your brain's voltage, or power. Beta brain waves are created in the frontal lobes from the neurons that produce dopamine and the other catecholamines. These lobes contain two parts, both of which are affected by levels of dopamine: The anterior (front) portion of the frontal lobe is called the prefrontal cortex. It is very important for developing and maintaining your cognitive functions and your ability to focus, as well as your personality. The posterior (back) of the frontal lobe consists of the premotor and motor areas. Nerve cells that produce movement are located in these motor areas.

Parietal lobes. Parietal lobes are the thinking factory of your brain. Seated just behind the frontal lobes, the parietal lobes control brain processing speed and help the brain recognize and react to sensory signals involved with sound, smell, taste, and visuospatial processing. The neurons here produce acetylcholine and its associated alpha waves.

Temporal lobes. Located just above the ears, the temporal lobes house the brain's ability to store memory and language. The neurons in these lobes produce the chemical GABA in the form of theta brain waves. These lobes assist in balancing the frontal lobes with the parietal lobes, orchestrating the connection between personality, movement, thinking, and action. While the frontal and parietal lobes are the leaders of the brain, the temporal lobes are the wings of creativity, stabilizing the brain.

Occipital lobes. These lobes, found at the rear of the brain, control vision. They also control your brain's ability to rest and resynchronize by producing the chemical serotonin and its resulting delta waves.

The Brain Conducts Energy
from the Outside

We walk by hundreds of people every day who aren't looking directly at us. But we always seem to notice when someone is looking directly at us. That connection occurs because the brain is both an energy provider and an energy conductor. When someone is staring at you, your brain will pick up on their electric energy, and you will involuntarily turn your head toward them.

The Corpus Callosum

The corpus callosum is like the Internet of the brain: It's the place where every brain cell has to connect so that the brain can work as a whole. This band of neuronal fibers is the electrical network between the right and left hemispheres, allowing the two sides of the brain to coordinate their tasks.

The left and right portions of your brain control the motor movement of the opposite side. For example, the left brain controls the movements of the right side of your body, and the right brain controls the left side. There are also predominant behavioral characteristics related to each hemisphere, and each of us favors one side or the other. For example, left-brained individuals tend to focus on thinking, analysis, and accuracy. They are usually extroverted and rely strongly on their verbal skills. The left-brained tend to be very logical, disciplined, and well organized, and they see things in terms of parts or sequences. Left-brainers usually have high levels of dopamine.

Right-brained individuals focus on feelings, intuition, and aesthetics. While they are social and active, they prefer to direct their energy inward. They are usually more empathic, intuitive, and subjective, and they see things in terms of a whole instead of the sum of individual parts. Right-brained individuals are also more impulsive and spontaneous, and they make decisions from an emotional place instead of a logical one. The right-brained are dominated by acetylcholine. Right-brainers are famous for their buoyant and contagious enthusiasm.

The corpus callosum allows us to mix the best aspects of our left and right brains. For example, in dreams we creatively process our fantasies along with real day-to-day events. Fact and fiction merge, connecting the right-brain emotions with left-brain processing of memory, uniting our entire consciousness. This ability to use both sides of your brain is called bilateralization, and it is not the weakest brains that do this, but the most robust ones. The higher your cognitive function, the more likely that you will learn to use both sides of your frontal lobes in order to solve problems and increase memory. Younger people typically use only the left side of the frontal lobe to learn a new word, and then switch to the right side of their frontal lobe to retrieve that memory. However, beginning in middle age, the smartest adults use the left side less for encoding and both sides simultaneously to do the harder job of recalling. By increasing your brain chemistry and creating new neuronal connections, you will automatically begin to use bilateralization as a strategy to protect your brain. This allows for more creativity as our brains become more densely wired. This neuronal integration is one way that as we get older, we are more able to reconcile our thoughts with our feelings.

The Brain Stem

The brain stem is the point where electricity is transferred between the brain and the body. The brain stem is the extension of the spinal cord into the brain, at a point called the thalamus. The brain stem is like the two-pronged plug found at the end of the cord attached to your metaphorical lamp. When the plug goes into the circuit box, the electricity stored in the circuit box follows the path of the cord into the lamp. One prong represents the parasympathetic nervous system; the other is the sympathetic nervous system. These two systems turn all the organs of the body on and off.

The Cerebellum

Located just below and behind the brain, the cerebellum controls balance and automatic movements such as arm and leg coordination. Animals with larger cerebellums than ours, such as cats, have incredible balancing ability.

Cerebrospinal Fluid

A healthy brain and spinal cord float in and drink from cerebrospinal fluid—what I call the ocean of life. Neurogenesis is completely dependent on cerebrospinal fluid to increase the production of brain cells and brain chemicals. New neurons are created and travel in this fluid and eventually settle in their particular locations. What's more, adequate hydration sustains cognitive energy with age by keeping the mind fast and powerful. Without this water, the brain would dehydrate, shrink, harden, and eventually die.

THE LIFE CYCLE OF MEMORY

The brain's life cycle shows that there are five unique electrical stages. The fetus acquires its electrical activity just 7 weeks after fertilization: This first stage is the spark of life. Immediately after birth, the child develops consciousness and begins to learn. As the baby grows new brain cells, its brain voltage is four to five times greater than that of adults; however, its brain's reaction time is significantly longer, causing the baby to experience "high-voltage dementia," in which the baby can't properly retain all the information it is exposed to. This second stage is also referred to as infantile amnesia, and we know it exists because very few of us have many memories from birth to age 4. At this stage the brain is very similar to one going through dementia, although it occurs at the beginning of life. Infants and toddlers can't organize their thoughts or recall information quickly. However, they have begun to develop emotional IQ, so they experience feelings and emotional connections, which also mirrors the experience of adults living with dementia.

Memory retention begins in the third stage, around the age of 5, and increases exponentially during puberty from the ages of 13 to 20. During this time, which I refer to as "blastoff of adolescence," teenagers experience a surge of 21 different hormones that transform them from children into adults. These same hormones also assist memory but make thinking, particularly decision making, scattered. This is important to remember, especially if you have children: When you are surprised at the decisions they make or their selective memory, what you are witnessing is not a personality flaw or the result of bad parenting: It's simply unstable brain chemistry. Yet the mental advantage adolescents have is clear.

This time of life is when we do most of our learning, and hormones play a significant role in allowing the brain to stay flexible and grow. This stage can be looked at as the opposite of menopause and andropause (male menopause), when hormone levels decline and memory and attention abilities wane.

In the fourth stage, the "consolidation of adulthood" takes place between the ages of 20 and 40, when the downpour of hormones subsides and brain chemical levels begin to stabilize. The brain reorganizes itself to function more effectively, and we are at our peak of mental performance. This is the time when people tend to establish their careers, start families, and generally settle down.

The fifth stage is a slow but steady functional decline. For women, this stage can begin as early as age 40, and their decline will be connected to their personal deficiencies of brain chemicals as well as declining hormones. Low-dopamine women will find that their attention wanders, and they may gain weight. Low acetylcholine will bring less creativity and a loss of cognition. Unbalanced GABA will lead to anxiety; low serotonin to depression. Women in this stage will also experience a loss of sexuality. Men tend to get another 10 years before they experience the same types of decline. Each decade thereafter, mild cognitive impairment (MCI) begins as brain speed and voltage are lost. By the time we are 70, many of us have reached what I call low-voltage dementia. Brain cells are no longer repairing themselves, memory retention is destroyed, and processing speed undergoes a very slow death.

It takes 50 years to "undo" the gains we made during the 7 years of puberty. However, you can halt—or even reverse—the life cycle of memory if you take care of your brain now. The goal is to return to the first 30 years of brain growth and retrain your brain to continue to repair itself as you learn. By doing so, you can continue neurogenesis well into your later years, all the while enhancing brain chemistry.

MCI OCCURS WHEN THE BRAIN AGES

All cognitive functions—your creativity, intelligence, and ability to remember, communicate, concentrate, or recall—are affected by the anatomy and chemistry of the brain, first by your brain's processing speed, and then by the presence and flow of its electrical energy. These functions naturally decline with age as brain cells die off, neuronal connections become short-circuited, and cerebrospinal fluid decreases. These underlying physical changes are mostly related to a deficit in the acetylcholine brain chemical family.

Unfortunately, you will notice that your body begins to age before you realize that your brain speed has changed. You might gain weight, have difficulty sleeping, or accumulate illnesses, yet meanwhile your brain has also been affected and is starting to tip toward dementia.

The gradual progressive cognitive decline associated with an aging brain exists on a continuum, just like the one that links minor allergies to severe asthma. Along this trajectory are three definite stages of cognitive decline. The first is now referred to as preclinical or pre-MCI. These cognitive changes are so mild that there is no evidence of a change in social or occupational functioning. The second stage is MCI, in which people might notice one or two small changes in their thinking and, without treatment, will remain that way for the rest of their lives. I've found that people in the earliest stages of MCI rarely exhibit severe symptoms, but may complain of mild problems performing complex tasks that they used to perform effortlessly, such as paying bills, preparing a meal, or shopping. They may take more time, be less efficient, and make more errors. However, when cognitive impairment is sufficiently great, such that there is interference with daily function, you may be diagnosed with the third and final stage, Alzheimer's disease or dementia.

We know with certainty that there is a preclinical phase at the start of this continuum, which is now called pre-MCI or "MCI due to Alzheimer's disease" (AD). During this stage there may be very subtle cognitive alterations that can be detected years before meeting even the most basic criteria for MCI and that also predict progression to AD or dementia. My most recently published scientific papers support these new guidelines: We have shown that pre-MCI stages can begin a full 20 years before significant symptoms occur. We now know that by the age of 40, 25 to 50 percent of Americans are already affected by MCI, even though less than 1 percent will show any symptoms. Again, this is why it is so critical to maintain that younger 30-year-old brain for the rest of your life.

The Continuum of Alzheimer's Disease

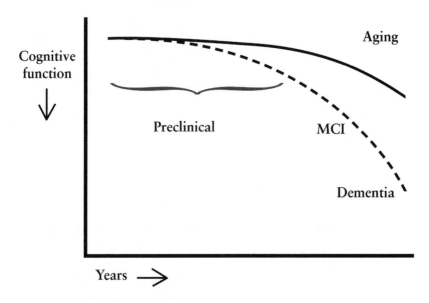

Cognitive function ↓

Aging

Preclinical

MCI

Dementia

Years →

The Warning Signs of MCI

Most people who are suffering from MCI can still function in daily activities but may be less efficient or accurate. The symptoms on this comprehensive list will be further discussed as you read on. For now, think of these as warning signs that something is wrong with the way you are thinking:

- Ability to remember things that happened years ago, but not something that took place a few minutes ago
- Agitation
- Anger
- Anxiety
- Changes in attention and concentration
- Commission errors (e.g., jumping the gun)
- Complex attention errors (e.g., cannot pull it together)
- Declining spatial perception
- Decreased creativity
- Depression
- Difficulty learning new tasks

- Difficulty retaining new information
- Difficulty with decision making
- Failure to recognize people
- Fear of being alone
- Fearfulness
- Forgetfulness
- Frustration
- Hoarding
- Inability to complete a task
- Inability to make decisions
- Inability to manage finances
- Jealousy
- Loss of normal emotional response
- Memory loss
- Mood swings
- Omission errors (e.g., missed stop signs)
- Paranoia
- Poor abstract thinking
- Poor judgment
- Self-neglect
- Slow response time
- Stunted intellectual growth
- Tension
- Unusual sleep patterns, or general lack of restful sleep

The standard progression of MCI symptoms usually affects the following areas. However, depending on your particular brain chemistry, you may notice changes in a different order.

Changes in Personality and Temperament

Depending on your brain chemistry, you may be more introverted than extroverted, intuitive instead of practical, a logical or a rash decision maker, organized or freewheeling. None of these types is better than another. However, if you always thought of yourself as one type, and now you are finding that you are thinking or feeling more like its opposite, you may be experiencing the first stages of cognitive decline. Neurological and psychiatric decline often occurs at the same time. Even the most subtle personality changes—especially increased anxiety, rigidity, or irritability—can be the first signs of MCI. Other signs to look for include a general loss of energy and mild depression.

It's critical to identify, repair, and reverse personality and temperament changes whenever you recognize them. First, the way you perceive the world has a direct impact on your motivation to continue taking good care of your health. What's more, maintaining a positive attitude allows you to be mentally resilient, even in the face of stressful or demanding environments: You'll be able to recover more quickly from life's adverse events, getting yourself back on track so that you can get over whatever obstacle you face and move on. These abilities allow you to become a more pragmatic, rationally thinking person, who can then make better decisions for every aspect of life.

Changes in Memory

Memories are the actual building blocks of all core domains of the brain. The brain's neuronal network develops as it is exposed to new stimuli, and memory is the recording of that information. Memory starts with the reception of information controlled by the parietal lobes and acetylcholine. It is followed closely by the processing of that information in the frontal lobes, which are powered by dopamine. All functions of the brain are really just complex memory processes that are regularly reworked into new learning and emotional growth. Memory is then the basis of our temperament, personality, and IQ, and subsequently, our ability to remember is affected by each of these.

Changes in Attention and Focus

Attention is the function of the brain that allows you to learn and remember. It is defined as the withdrawal from some tasks in order to

You Know You Have MCI When . . .

- You or someone in your family has noticed a change in your thinking or behavior
- Your thinking has changed relative to previous abilities during the past year
- You are experiencing difficulties concerning complex day-to-day activities

deal effectively with others. The human brain has limited attention resources: If we pay attention in one area, other areas must decrease. That's why you can listen to someone talking but lose your train of thought when an ambulance comes whizzing by. Or how you can focus so intently on a task that you don't realize how much time has passed. As we age, the ability to become distracted also increases. This is also associated with memory, but more closely aligned with attention.

Attention helps you organize information in your brain so that you can recall it when necessary, so without attention, memory storage is impossible. One way we memorize material is by focusing on its various differences compared with what we already know, so that we can remember them better.

DEMENTIA AND ALZHEIMER'S: THE END OF THE LINE

Recent studies have shown that the physical characteristics of Alzheimer's disease can be traced back to the changes that occur in the brain with MCI and even pre-MCI. A landmark 2006 study reported in the *Archives of Neurology* showed that after autopsies, the brains of most patients diagnosed with MCI showed changes in their temporal lobes that suggested a transitional state of evolving Alzheimer's disease. An earlier long-term study published in 2001 from Washington University in St. Louis reported that 100 percent of the individuals in the study who were originally diagnosed with MCI progressed to greater dementia severity over a 9.5-year period. What's more, the degree of cognitive impairment at baseline seems to dictate the severity of dementia later in life. This means that the longer you wait to reverse your cognitive

Symptoms of Declining Attention Are Linked to Declining Brain Chemicals

SYMPTOM	AFFECTED BRAIN CHEMICAL
Inconsistent attention, misplacing items	Dopamine
Carelessness, lack of attention	Acetylcholine
Impulsivity	GABA
Inability to grasp concepts quickly	Serotonin

decline, the more difficult it will become, and the more likely you will suffer from debilitating dementia.

Alzheimer's can be diagnosed if cognitive decline symptoms begin gradually, progressing over months or years. It commonly presents with progressive memory loss over time with associated slowly progressive behavioral changes, loss of language, impairments of visuospatial skills, and loss of executive function. Most important, these symptoms must impede functioning at work or in daily activities.

Alzheimer's is not really a disease, but a description of its symptoms. Nerve fibers surrounding the hippocampus, the brain's memory center, become tangled, and information is no longer carried properly to or from the brain. When this happens, new memories cannot be formed or stored, and memories formed earlier cannot be retrieved. Plaques composed of a protein-containing substance called beta-amyloid accumulate in the brain, further damaging nerve cells. This disease affects more than 5 million Americans and is the sixth leading cause of death in the United States. Yet only 50 percent of Alzheimer's sufferers are being properly diagnosed.

Not all people who experience pre-MCI and MCI will eventually develop Alzheimer's disease or dementia; however, everyone with Alzheimer's begins with the two earlier stages. While true Alzheimer's disease occurs at an alarming rate, most of my patients who think they are getting Alzheimer's disease are not. As one colleague pointed out, when you forget where you left your keys, you have a problem with your memory. When you forget what keys are, that's Alzheimer's disease. While MCI is reversible, Alzheimer's disease is deadly.

While the causes of Alzheimer's are still being sorted out—part genetics, part environment, part lifestyle choices, part disease-related, and part aging—its effect on brain tissue is clear. Alzheimer's disease damages and kills brain cells, virtually ending neurogenesis. It is typically diagnosed by the deposition of insoluble beta-amyloid protein plaques in the brain. These plaques cause healthy brain tissue to degenerate, as the beta-amyloid interferes with communication between brain cells, eventually causing cell death and a steady decline in mental abilities.

A second hallmark is neurofibrillary tangles. The internal support structure for brain cells depends on the normal functioning of a protein called tau. In people with Alzheimer's, threads of tau protein undergo alterations that cause them to become twisted. Many researchers believe this may also seriously damage neurons, causing them to die.

A last biological cause is decreased cerebral bloodflow, which is not directly related to either plaques or tangles. Studies have shown that individuals suffering from age-related cognitive decline show on brain imaging scans a decrease in cerebral bloodflow, while Alzheimer's patients have an even further decrease. Both types of patients exhibit vascular hypertension of the brain, which may contribute to this decreased bloodflow.

The following symptoms shows the typical progression of MCI and might be a sign that you or someone you love has the earliest stages of Alzheimer's disease:

- Verbal memory loss: repeatedly telling the same story, asking the same question, or giving the same request
- Unfamiliarity with daily tasks: difficulty getting dressed or preparing very simple meals
- Dysphasia: inability to come up with the correct word (i.e., "tip-of-the-tongue" syndrome)
- Confusing the concepts of "where" and "when": unawareness of one's location or date, inability to approximate time
- Confusion about the locations of familiar places (frequently getting lost)
- Compromised judgment, often leading to bad decisions
- Decreased awareness of personal hygiene
- Difficulty with abstract thinking: difficulty differentiating objects of similar sizes
- Placing objects in unsuitable places: putting a purse in the garbage or shoes in the refrigerator, or using dishwasher detergent as shampoo
- Extreme mood swings: going from joy to sadness to anger without any apparent reason
- Personality adjustments: personality disorder characteristics becoming more pronounced or new ones becoming obvious
- Lack of interest: avoidant behavior or increased thoughts of death, loss of spontaneity

REVERSE MCI BY ENHANCING BRAIN CHEMISTRY

Unfortunately, life is not always a series of perfect decisions. We've all made mistakes along the way: We may have eaten too much, partied too hard, lived too roughly. And because of this, we might not be as smart as we once were. Maybe your judgment has become impaired. You might be more tired than you should be, or lack the attention to get your job done to your highest capacities. But I'm here to tell you that the brain is resilient: You can get your cognitive functioning back to its highest levels, and even beyond. All you need is to learn how to repair and recover your brain at the earliest possible stage.

According to a 2011 study from the National Institute on Aging and the Alzheimer's Association workgroup, the current lifetime risk of AD or dementia for a 65-year-old is roughly 1 in 10 individuals. By following a screening and treatment program, like the one outlined in this book, you can slow the progression of this disease by as much as 50 percent and reduce your risk to 5.7 percent.

The key to sustaining a high level of brain performance and closing the performance gap is to keep your brain as young as a 30-year-old's for the rest of your life. We do this by replenishing damaged brain cells with fresh new ones in each of the different types of brain chemical receptor cells, creating new neuronal connections by constantly learning, and enhancing brain chemical production. Increasing dopamine and dopamine receptor cells stimulates working memory and enables you to push yourself toward accomplishments. Enhancing acetylcholine and increasing the number of acetylcholine receptor cells helps access memory and is responsible for improving processing speed and immediate memory function. Balancing GABA and creating more GABA receptors helps organize memory, particularly verbal memory, so that you can focus and gain mental stability. Increasing serotonin helps visual memory and perception, while increasing serotonin receptor cells gives you better mood, better sleep, and happiness.

The most exciting part is that when the brain is properly stretched, it can grow exactly the way you want. You can choose how you want to enhance your brain. You will learn how to push your brain to grow toward the functionality that you need. You can have clearer thinking, more memory, better attention, or all of these. The choice is up to you.

If you can stop the progression of this continuum, you can increase your brain processing speed right now. And by following the Braverman Protocol to enhance your brain chemistry, you increase your chances of living a younger, smarter life for years to come.

Chapter 2

The Causes of Cognitive Decline

A healthy brain processes information as a wave (via electrical impulses) and as a particle (via the brain chemicals) at a fast pace along the neuronal highway. Think of "the wave" that goes around a sports stadium during a football game. Every person in the stadium represents a single cell in the brain that passes along a ball of information to the next cell. As each person jumps to their feet and lifts their hands above their head, they pass a particle of information along. If the timing is off, the wave in the stadium simply stops. In your brain, if the cells cannot pick up all the particles of information, they get dropped and brain speed slows, the information delivery becomes unbalanced and out of sync, and your cognition begins to fade.

The difference between a resourceful mind and senility is only 100 milliseconds of brain speed. We react to light in 50 milliseconds, recognize sound in 100 milliseconds, and think in 300 milliseconds. By the time thinking slows down to 400 milliseconds, we can no longer process logical thoughts. The neurons no longer fire off information fast enough for the rest of the brain to respond, and new information will not become embedded in memory.

Typically, we lose 7 to 10 milliseconds—a tenth of a second—of brain speed per decade from age 20 on, which means that aging alone causes us to lose brain cells and processing speed. This minute change is very difficult to notice, even for the most tuned-in individuals, because aging occurs at a constant rate.

Imagine that you are sitting inside a windowless train, and the train is speeding along at 2,000 miles per hour. Now imagine that you are on the same train, but you are not moving at all. Would you feel any different? The answer is no. Without any external reference points, such as passing trees, and without acceleration, any constant speed will feel exactly the same to you—whether that speed is nothing or the speed of light. In a sense, our brain operates as if we are sitting in a windowless train travelling at the constant speed of aging. Without a reference point, no brain—not even a smart one—would be able to determine its own aging.

While we can't recognize a change in brain speed, many people do know that something has changed with their thinking. And if you sense that you are not as smart or quick as you used to be, you know it is an uncomfortable feeling. Some refer to it as "brain fog," because they know that they used to feel smarter but the thoughts are just not coming together as quickly. What's happening is that when brain processing

What's My Issue?

Depending on your symptoms and the level at which they present, you might be experiencing one of three separate forms of mild cognitive impairment, or MCI. While it's rarely clear how cause and effect are linked between the diagnoses, what is known is that multiple domain issues are a bigger problem than just losing your memory. Most people think that they are experiencing the first signs of MCI when they lose their memory, but as we now know, memory is often not the first domain of cognition to deteriorate. The diagnoses include:

- **Amnestic:** memory loss, increased forgetfulness

- **Non-amnestic, single domain:** loss of one aspect of cognitive functioning without forgetfulness

- **Non-amnestic, multiple domains:** loss of many aspects of cognitive functioning without forgetfulness

speed declines, you are literally thinking slower and remembering less. New information that you are presented with does not "stick" in your mind, and older memories are harder to recall. At the same time, a decline in brain chemical production causes brain cell death. Fewer neurons mean an additional decrease in the capacity to retain information.

What's more, not only does an aging brain think slower, but there is a separation between thinking and then doing. You know that you have things you need to do, but you can't quite figure out how to get them done, or you forget to take care of them. Once you bump into these problems repeatedly, you need to start rebalancing your brain.

THE CAUSES OF MILD COGNITIVE IMPAIRMENT

Aging is the number one cause of mild cognitive impairment (MCI). As you get older, your brain develops chemical imbalances. If you do not act to fix them, you are actually leaving your brain and your body open to get sicker.

What's more, there are hundreds of other reasons for your brain to tip toward dementia. Some of these factors are directly linked to specific brain chemical deficiencies that occur with aging or illness. Others are connected to lifestyle or environment.

Addiction. Any type of addiction, including to alcohol, street drugs (marijuana, cocaine, crystal meth, heroin, Ecstasy, nexus, ketamine, opium, Rohypnol, crack, hallucinogens, inhalants), overeating, gambling, or even shopping, is related to imbalanced dopamine, which you'll learn more about in Chapter 5. What's more, addictive substances directly cause cognitive failures. For example, alcoholics are notorious for experiencing blackouts, actual memory gaps that occur even when they are conscious. Most illegal street drugs tamper with memory, cloud judgment, limit attention, and increase forgetfulness.

Prescription medications. Many prescription medications affect cognitive abilities, even if you are not addicted to them. Some medications that reverse bad health and rebalance the brain can also cause brain fog, or worse. They may blur vision, increase fatigue, alter depth perception, make you see or hear things that aren't there, increase or decrease reaction time, and detract from focus and concentration. Common prescription drugs that affect thinking include medications that treat allergies, pain, diabetes, high blood pressure, cholesterol, ulcers, depression, anxiety disorders, and insomnia. Many of these are known to cause fatigue and daytime drowsiness. Tranquilizers, sedatives, and sleeping pills slow down the central nervous system, causing diminished reaction time, and impair your ability to concentrate. Antihistamines slow down reaction time and affect your overall coordination.

Compare the following list of drug types to your current prescriptions to see if what you are taking may be affecting your thinking, and then speak with your doctor to determine whether alternatives with fewer mental side effects are available:

- Alcohol-containing medications
- Amphetamines
- Antibiotics
- Anticholinergics
- Antidepressants
- Antidiarrheal medications
- Antihistamines
- Antinausea medications
- Antipsychotics
- Antiseizure medications
- Anxiety medications
- Barbiturates
- Blood pressure medications
- Blood sugar medications
- Caffeine-containing medications
- Pain medications
- Parkinson's disease medications
- Sedatives
- Sleep medications
- Stimulants
- Tranquilizers
- Ulcer medications

Over-the-counter medications. Decongestants can cause drowsiness, anxiety, and dizziness. Cold and cough medicines, antihistamines, pain relievers, diuretics, and remedies that prevent heartburn, nausea, or motion sickness can cause drowsiness or dizziness. What's more, combining prescription medications with over-the-counter remedies can also cause cognitive problems. Speak with your local pharmacist to determine if any of these remedies is affecting your thinking.

Parasites, bacteria, and viral infections. Parasites and other microbes enter the body and often excrete toxins to increase their chance of survival. These toxins change blood acidity, allowing the parasite to multiply in a perfect host environment. At the same time, toxic excretions can cross the blood-brain barrier and create inflammation in the brain, affecting your concentration and comprehension and creating brain fog. These microorganisms are often diagnosed as intermittent or chronic infections, HIV, tuberculosis, Epstein-Barr virus, Lyme disease, or cytomegalovirus (CMV).

Degenerative disorders. Serious illnesses associated with aging (including multiple sclerosis, neurodegenerative illness, Huntington's

Patient Profile: Lyme Disease and Memory

My patient Jennifer took great pride in her photographic memory. She could remember every trip she took as an airline flight attendant, down to the details of the outfits each passenger wore. But one day, it all unraveled. Jennifer began forgetting the simplest instructions or requests. She also began to feel achy, as if she had the flu. But when she came to see me, it was the middle of the summer, not the typical flu season.

Jennifer's anxiety increased with her symptoms. She told me that she couldn't remember the thread of a conversation, even if she was in the middle of it. She knew there was something wrong, but she thought that the cause was her stress from work. She worked on a private airplane and was dealing with people who expected world-class service all the time. But even though she was very good at her job, she had to take a piece of paper and write down what it was that they wanted to eat. Then she was finding that she also had to write down where the people were sitting and their names, because she couldn't remember.

I ordered a battery of blood work, and we discovered that Jennifer had Lyme disease, a common illness here in the Northeast that is transferred to humans through tick bites. Although dangerous, Lyme disease is very treatable, and more important, it is linked to short-term memory loss and deficits in attention, memory, processing speed, and executive function. Once we got her on the right antibiotics, Jennifer felt much better, and her memory returned.

disease, ALS, and Pick's disease), glaucoma, vascular diseases, stroke (the second leading cause of MCI), brain tumors, obesity, organ diseases (including endocrine, liver, and kidney), blood sugar imbalances, or hormonal loss can also affect your ability to think clearly. Anyone with a brain chemical imbalance will experience physical changes. Diseases of the body also affect brain function and will be explored in more detail in Chapter 13.

Physical trauma. This category can include recurrent head trauma, concussions, whiplash, battering, sports injuries, or injury due to child abuse, car accidents, or falling. Brain trauma has a cumulative effect: Each event builds on the previous one, directly affecting memory and cognition in both the short and long term. Even minor traumas add toward dementia. All the hits we received in our youth—from fighting with siblings to falling off a bike—pile up and later affect us, long after the physical bruises have healed. I can guarantee that everyone who is diagnosed with cognitive decline has experienced some of them.

For example, 75 percent of all people will have a mild concussion at some point during their life and will unknowingly develop severe brain chemical loss that will affect their thinking and personality. A concussion can be caused by a direct blow to the head, face, or neck, or elsewhere on the body, that leads to an impulsive force transmitted to the head. Concussions typically result in a rapid loss of neurologic function that is short-lived and resolves spontaneously. While your memory might be temporarily impaired, the physical structure of the brain remains intact. We know that this is true because in concussion, there are no abnormalities seen on standard neuroimaging studies. However, just because there is no structural damage, this doesn't mean that a concussion should be taken lightly. What's more, concussions and other head injuries also affect hormone levels, which regulate brain processing speed. Even minor whiplashes in which you don't lose consciousness can still affect your hormone production.

If you have been in an accident either recently or in the distant past that caused any of the following symptoms, let your doctor know. Even a fall, accident, or trauma that happened 10 to 20 years ago can be affecting your brain chemical balance today. Typically, you would experience symptoms immediately following the accident, but they may persist to some degree to this day.

The most popular misconception is that a recent concussion can be identified only if there was a loss of consciousness. Any of the following symptoms can be a result of a head injury and can contribute to cognitive decline, now or later:

- Amnesia (ranging from short-term blackouts to long-term loss of memory of a traumatic event)
- Behavioral changes (e.g., irritability)
- Depression
- Feeling in a fog

- Headache
- Increased emotionality
- Sleep disturbances or daytime drowsiness
- Slowed reaction times
- Unconsciousness

How's Your Sense of Smell?

Researchers at the University of California, San Diego, Medical Center found that people with Alzheimer's disease reported a decline in their sense of smell as much as 2 years prior to the beginning of mental decline. The rate at which the sense of smell is lost may predict how rapidly cognitive functioning is lost. Smokers, who have a decreased sense of smell, are at greater risk of missing this signal.

Psychiatric disorders. Anxiety, depression, schizophrenia, panic attacks, and other similar disorders are conditions resulting from an unbalanced brain. In the next chapter, we will discuss how they affect cognition or simultaneously occur with a cognitive impairment. These conditions exacerbate cognitive decline and at the same time are its earliest symptoms.

Sleep disturbances. Insomnia and other sleep disorders are serotonin-related conditions resulting from an unbalanced brain. In the next chapter, we will discuss in more detail how they affect cognition. And just as with the psychiatric disorders above, it's interesting to note that these conditions exacerbate cognitive decline and at the same time are its earliest symptoms.

Toxic exposures. Lead, aluminum, arsenic, cadmium, and mercury can affect brain speed, IQ, memory, and attention and alter personality and temperament. And it's not just current exposures that you have to worry about: Past exposures from as early as childhood can still be affecting your health and how you think. For example, an exposure to lead before and immediately after birth can damage short-term as well as long-term memory. This disruption of neuronal activity can alter the developmental processes of synapse formation and result in a less efficient brain with cognitive deficits by which you might still be affected. Chronic exposure to lead may result in poisoning that presents symptoms including fatigue, depression, and confusion. Other heavy metals, such as mercury, aluminum, cadmium, and tin, affect chemical synaptic transmission in the brain and the peripheral and central nervous system. The brains of people with Alzheimer's disease have been found to contain higher-than-normal concentrations of mercury, to which their primary exposure was dental fillings.

The good news is that through simple blood work and, if necessary, neuroimaging such as PET scans and MRIs, you can determine quickly and easily whether you are carrying a toxic load. Even better, you can treat these problems with naturopathic programs, including making small changes to your diet (more on that in Chapter 8).

The table below shows how you may have been, or may continue to be, exposed to the most dangerous heavy metals.

CHEMICAL	EXPOSURE
Aluminum	Cookware, antacids, antiperspirants, aluminum cans, kitchen utensils, paints, toothpaste, baking powder, cheese, flour, table salt, sea vegetables, dental fillings, tobacco
Arsenic	Poison, pigments, dyes, preservatives, insecticides, wine, well water, coal burning, shellfish, treated lumber, car exhausts, detergents, pesticides, weed killers
Cadmium	Water from galvanized pipes, evaporated milk, shellfish, cigarette smoke, sewage sludge, paint, pigments, air pollution
Lead	Car exhaust, canned food, hair dyes, newsprint, tap water, crayons, lead crystal, lead paint, lead pipes, tobacco, cosmetics
Mercury	Dental fillings, vapor lamps, seafood, polluted water, skin-lightening creams, sewage sludge, batteries, fluorescent lights, plastics, tobacco smoke, fish

Vitamin and mineral deficiencies. People with MCI are often deficient in thiamin (vitamin B_1), niacin (B_3), pyridoxine (B_6), vitamin B_{12}, nicotinic acid, and zinc. Low levels of these and other vitamins, minerals, and antioxidants in the diet can contribute to cognitive difficulties such as poor judgment or memory loss. Recent studies show that the progression toward Alzheimer's can be slowed or even reversed by taking the proper amounts of antioxidants, either through making better food choices or through supplementation. Chapter 9 outlines a nutritional supplement regimen that can correct this problem depending on your brain chemical deficiency. It's also important to know that excessive alcohol consumption depletes the body of crucial vitamins and minerals, which is why it's virtually impossible to try to balance good habits with bad ones.

Addressing these causes of MCI may help you achieve real cognitive change right away. The next few chapters will explore the specific cognitive problems surrounding MCI, and how brain chemistry imbalances affect your thinking. Identifying which phase or area you are experiencing problems in will help you tailor the Braverman Protocol to suit your individual needs, so that you can get younger and smarter with relative ease.

Chapter 3

Identifying Personality and Mood Changes

The earliest symptoms of mild cognitive impairment (MCI) and pre-MCI are highlighted by changes in personality and temperament. You might notice that you just feel "off," or not like yourself. This is typically followed by a sense of anxiousness, about either your health or other issues in your life. Unfortunately, anxiety can lead to a cascade of mental health symptoms, including insomnia. Without proper sleep, you begin to feel even more anxious or even blue, and without treatment, you'll quickly find yourself sliding into depression. Together, the personality changes of increased anxiety and depression create more damage to the brain, inducing what many refer to as "brain fog." This can manifest as an inability to get things done, overall confusion, or just a feeling of mental slowness.

For example, you might have noticed that it is very hard to concentrate—or remember—when you are anxious or depressed. You may feel that when you have "too much on your plate," you become easily irritated, restless, or forgetful; or when you're feeling blue, you might not have the physical or mental energy to solve problems or finish tasks. For example, the "tip-of-the-tongue" syndrome of forgetting things is really more a symptom of anxiety than of MCI. Anxious people are often the first to notice a memory problem because they are so worried about their health.

Anxiety initially produces an increase in brain speed. Think about how you feel when you have a deadline looming: You might find that you are better able to focus, and for longer periods of time, when you know that you have to get a job done. Or you might feel like you have a million great new ideas racing around in your head. This type of stress increases the dopamine-related chemicals adrenaline and cortisol, resulting in that jittery feeling when you can't calm down, no matter how hard you try. Many people can use this extra energy to rise to the occasion, staying up later than usual and blocking out other distractions in order to finish their projects.

Afterward, they are surprised to have "crashed" in exhaustion. But what really happened is that an increase in these dopamine-related brain chemicals causes a decrease in the calming power of GABA. After a while, this extra energy creates a different kind of anxiety that gives way to a loss of dopamine energy and mental quickness. You might also find that you can't "keep it together," and you start acting emotionally immature. Now you've created a vicious stress loop, rewiring your brain and negatively impacting neurogenesis.

In a 2009 article appearing in the journal *Science*, researchers at the Life and Health Sciences Research Institute at the University of Minho in Portugal found that chronically stressed rats lost their cunning and instead resorted to familiar routines and rote responses, like compulsively pressing a bar for food pellets even though they weren't hungry. When their brains were more closely observed, it was found that the dopamine regions associated with executive function—including decision-making and goal-directed behaviors—had shriveled, while the GABA sectors linked to habit formation had expanded. The chronically stressed rats were no longer producing more dopamine; in fact, they were producing less. Because of this, they had cognitively conditioned themselves to "go through the motions" of life, repeatedly doing the same tasks over and over instead of trying something new. In other words, they created a neuronal pathway that stunted their creativity and their mental energy.

I find that people react in the same way. When we get stressed, we either get caught in a rut or return to some old pattern that we had created earlier in life to self-soothe (food, shopping, crying, etc.). When the brain is too heavily focused on staying on task, it loses its ability to grow and stretch to allow for new memories that come from new learning and experiences. When you have "too much on your mind," the stress you may be feeling is your brain chemicals fighting for the chance to grow and remember.

I just went through a phase of tremendous stress in my life, and when it was over, I realized that I had let my GABA levels go too far down. I was feeling anxious and irritable and had lost my focus and intensity. In retrospect, had I been taking better care of my brain, I could have been balancing my GABA better by following my own six-step protocol, and subsequently better managing my stress. However, it's never too late: I'm back to working to rebalance my brain to correct my temperament, and I can see that positive changes are already taking place.

Stress Kills Brain Cells

According to my colleague Dr. Daniel Amen, long-term exposure to stress hormones like cortisol has been found to kill cells in the hippocampus involved with memory, learning, and emotion. In fact, people who are chronically stressed have smaller hippocampal regions, which may result in an inability to continue learning as they age.

ANXIETY AND BRAIN CHEMISTRY

GABA orchestrates the infrastructure of the brain's stability. When your brain is not producing enough GABA, your electricity is generated in bursts. This is called a brain *arrhythmia*. But when a *dysrhythmia* occurs, these bursts lose their orchestration, and you may begin to feel restless, anxious, nervous, or irritable. The signals in your brain are coming through as constant chatter instead of a smooth, even flow.

As soon as the brain loses its balance, its stability is lost. You may complain more regularly that you don't feel well, or develop a chronic pain that never goes away. Or your thinking can be affected in any of these ways:

- Difficulty concentrating
- Global memory problems
- Impulsivity
- Inability to think clearly
- Inconsistent attention patterns
- Irritability and/or hostility
- Poor verbal memory
- Restlessness

Stress and the Glutamate-GABA Relationship

According to Harvard professor Dr. John Ratey, roughly 80 percent of the signaling in the brain is carried out by two brain chemicals that balance each other: glutamate, which begins the signal transmission, and GABA, which limits its activity. Glutamate excites cells to higher states of activity so that they can receive and process information. It allows neurons that haven't communicated to make a connection, thereby increasing neurogenesis and facilitating learning and memory. Every time we learn something new, glutamate is released. And every time glutamate is released, GABA must be there to funnel it in the right direction.

However, when you are stressed and your GABA is unbalanced, too much glutamate can be released. Instead of increasing learning, an abundance of this brain chemical actually kills off neurons, and the process of neurogenesis halts. Without these neurons, the chemical signals

||||||||||||||||||||||||||||||||||||||||||||||||||||||||||||||||||||||||||||||||||||||||||||||||||

THE BRAVERMAN ANXIETY TEST

If you can answer "true" to five or more of the following statements, you may be experiencing a GABA imbalance:

1. I'm nervous and jumpy. T/F
2. I have trouble finding "the right word." T/F
3. My patience is diminishing. T/F
4. I feel shaky. T/F
5. I need a drink to relax. T/F
6. My ability to focus comes and goes. T/F
7. When I read, I find I have to go back over the same paragraph a few times to absorb the information. T/F
8. I am a quick thinker but can't always say what I mean. T/F
9. I have chronic aches and pains. T/F
10. Sex is a chore. T/F
11. I overeat when I'm stressed. T/F
12. I'm often constipated. T/F

||||||||||||||||||||||||||||||||||||||||||||||||||||||||||||||||||||||||||||||||||||||||||||||||||

can't be caught, and information literally gets lost. And during times of high stress or anxiety, this neuronal loss makes you feel more rigid and set in your ways, instead of being encouraged to think "outside the box." You lose the ability to compare the situation you are facing with older memories that can actually help you. Worse, you can't recall the coping

Patient Profile: Sylvia Couldn't Concentrate

Sylvia was a 45-year-old woman who came to see me because she was scared that she was heading toward dementia. She told me that she woke up tired every day and found herself drinking coffee and smoking cigarettes to stay awake at work. She had a very stressful job as an elementary school principal, and she was worried that she was unable to keep on top of all the details regarding her students like she used to. She was losing her focus, couldn't remember names or places, and was continually misplacing her glasses. Sylvia had a family history of Alzheimer's disease, so she was particularly anxious that she was heading down this same path.

First, I suggested that we start off by determining her cognitive baseline and doing a complete mental and physical health exam, including Brain Electrical Activity Mapping (BEAM), to see exactly what problems she was experiencing. The BEAM revealed that she was low in both dopamine and GABA. This made perfect sense: She was self-medicating her lost dopamine energy with coffee and cigarettes, and her anxiety was very high. Her blood tests revealed that she was low in estrogen and was already experiencing some of the signs and symptoms of menopause. Otherwise, her health was fine. Her main problems proved to be her anxiety and nervousness—the fear of developing Alzheimer's, rather than actually having it.

I treated Sylvia with bioidentical estrogen therapies, dopamine-boosting nutrients, and GABA dietary changes. We talked about her smoking and started her on the NicoDerm patch. I didn't treat her for memory loss, because that wasn't her problem. Instead, I made her less anxious and improved her hormonal profile. After just 1 week of this treatment, her memory and attention returned.

mechanisms you have at your discretion, including help from friends or family. Before you know it, the stress cycle starts again.

DON'T LET STRESS GET YOU DOWN

I know that every day is a stress-management challenge. One of the easiest ways to decrease stress and increase your ability to cope during stressful times is to increase your production of GABA. By following the Braverman Protocol, you'll be able to do this quickly and naturally. In the meantime, here are some easy behavior modifications you can make to immediately decrease the stress in your life.

1. **Laugh.** Studies show that laughter can reverse serious disease, and it certainly reduces stress. Get yourself to smile and chuckle, and you can basically reduce the burnout of everyday life.

2. **Get out in the sun.** Getting a few minutes of exposure to natural light is crucial because vitamin D, which we manufacture from the sun, helps to improve your mood. When your brain is out of sync, vitamin D is like a natural steroid. It raises the adrenaline levels in your brain.

3. **Reminisce.** Open a photo album and flip through some cherished moments. You can recapture both the memory and the emotion of happiness and the sentimentality and feeling by reliving old memories. Plus, you'll see just how good your memory really is when you are in a more relaxed setting.

4. **Clean up.** Sitting amongst clutter all day can weigh you down. Everyone at times feels overwhelmed. And even if life is very busy, we can artificially convince ourselves that it's not so cluttered by cleaning up. And if you can remember where everything goes, you're in good shape.

THE SLEEP FACTOR

It's hard to get a good night's sleep when your GABA levels are unbalanced and you are anxious. But that is only one reason why you might not be sleeping well. As you get older, the quality of your sleep normally

Make Time for You

People who have high levels of GABA are nurturers, who derive pleasure from taking care of others. However, they often feel disappointed that no one is taking care of them. People who have low GABA levels can't even take care of themselves and are left feeling like anxious wrecks. Either extreme needs to take a break. See if you can put aside 1 hour each day to calm down: listen to music, quietly read, take a walk, or even pray.

deteriorates, even if you are getting the same number of hours of shut-eye. This can be caused by declining serotonin levels.

When your serotonin levels begin to wane, your brain cannot modulate the energy created by the dopamine system. So instead of being active during the day and rested at night, your brain goes into overdrive all day long just to keep you functional and motivated. Meanwhile, your production of sleep-inducing delta waves increases, blocking alertness (dopamine), creativity (acetylcholine), and playfulness (GABA), and leading to feelings of depression. At night, they limit your ability to sleep soundly and restoratively because your brain is literally too wound up to override the excess dopamine state. The epitome of this experience is called general adaption syndrome, which we more commonly refer to as the fight-or-flight syndrome: the adrenaline rush we feel when we are forced into survival mode. Unfortunately for those with poor sleep, they experience this as their constant state.

Disrupted sleep hinders your ability to achieve the proper amount of REM (rapid eye movement) sleep, which is the deepest, most restorative sleep phase. A lack of this type of sleep is one of the great age accelerators, further aging your brain and affecting your thinking. Without REM sleep, the brain cannot reboot overnight to get ready for the next day. Worse, it creates its own stress cycle that's hard to break. When you do not achieve a deep-sleep state, all your fears, phobias, obsessions, compulsions, and blues become exacerbated, which keeps you up all night worrying about them. The popularity of sleep aids like Lunesta shows just how much the brain changes as you age. Remember back to when you were a child, or how your own children sleep: They don't need Lunesta. But your older, unbalanced brain does. Poor sleep patterns include a difficulty falling asleep, recurrent waking in the middle of the night, or waking up and being unable to go back to sleep. You might be plagued with night terrors or nightmares. You may wake up frequently to go to the bathroom, or you may never get to sleep at all, tossing around all night long.

Many chronic insomniacs have come to me believing that they are becoming demented. In some respect it's true: Their lack of sleep is affecting their thinking. Without proper serotonin levels, you simply can't sleep, which affects your cognition in a variety of different ways. First, your reaction time can become slower. It takes longer to learn new information or retrieve memories. You may experience overwhelming confusion, fail to make mature decisions, or even respond inappropriately.

There is also a correlation between a lack of REM sleep and the onset of depression. This is referred to as psychomotor retardation: the slowing down of thought, speech, and affect, and a reduction of physical movements. The lack of proper sleep leading to these symptoms makes some people feel depressed because their fatigue and lack of motivation affects their physical and cognitive performance, as well as their mood. You may find that without sleep you can't appreciate activities that were once pleasurable, or you find the world boring in general. However, once we restore the ability to sleep, you'll find that your memory and other cognitive functions, such as reaction time, concentration, and attention, as well as your good mood, return very quickly.

My protocol is to treat insomnia by enhancing the brain chemicals that can improve sleep, specifically GABA and serotonin. These allow the brain to shut off at night, so that the brain increases its ability to transform serotonin into melatonin, another brain chemical that helps synchronize the brain to be awake during the light hours of the day and to become tired when it is dark. The brain measures light and dark through the pupils of the eyes, which are linked to the secretion of melatonin in the pineal gland. The best news is that when you enhance your serotonin, you will master sleep, which is a cornerstone in helping you to bring back all the other diminishing brain chemicals. You'll be able to master brain stability with more GABA. You can master addiction and brain energy with more dopamine, and possibly achieve thinness as an added benefit. You'll master creativity and faster thinking because you'll be able to produce more ace-tylcholine. Best of all, you'll be able to pull all these components of health together to create the new paradigms to live smarter.

An Additional Dilemma: Sleep Apnea

Sleep apnea is a common medical condition many people don't realize they suffer from unless they are literally in bed with a light sleeper. It is a disorder that affects sleep and results in dozens or even hundreds of "mini-awakenings" that fragment the sleep cycle, yet are so subtle that the person may be able to remain asleep through them. The result is that those with this condition may believe they slept straight through the night but, in fact, were roused constantly, leaving them tired in the morning.

During sleep apnea, the person momentarily stops breathing. When the brain realizes that it isn't getting enough oxygen, it forces the person to wake up and take a breath, creating multiple sleep interruptions. Unfortunately, the brain's constant vigilance means that it never gets enough downtime—again, inefficient sleep does not allow you to achieve enough REM phase sleep. At the same time, the brain is losing brain cells because of the lack of oxygen. The result is that during the day, the brain is slow, making retrieving information or acquiring new skills more difficult.

If you've been told that you snore loudly, or you know that you frequently wake up at night, wake up tired in the morning, or suffer from daytime sleepiness, talk to your doctor about an easy test you can perform at home to determine whether you have sleep apnea. This test measures your heart rate, oxygen level, airflow, and breathing patterns while you sleep. Depending on the results, your doctor may be able to prescribe a therapy without further testing.

Sleep Creates Memory Consolidation

Another important function of sleep is referred to as memory consolidation. According to Robert Stickgold, professor at Harvard University, your brain needs to be fully rested to take in the maximum amount of information. Memory circuits can get fatigued along with the rest of your body, and when this happens, you don't learn as well. Then, once you do learn something new or when you respond to stimuli, the memory you create is

Patient Profile: Catherine Needed More Sleep to Think Better

When Catherine came to see me in 2009, she told me that she had "come to the end of herself." At 62, she just couldn't sleep and was always exhausted. She had always prided herself on being alert and intelligent, but she was beginning to feel as if her brain wasn't cooperating. She had cloudy thoughts and confusion and had difficulty planning and processing her days, which was making her anxious and depressed. There were times when she couldn't remember what she was going say, and she was even having problems making the to-do lists that she had come to rely on. Catherine thought that her quality of living was declining because she couldn't focus on finishing her work, which left her little free time to do anything else.

After thorough testing, I was able to link all her issues to her brain chemical imbalances. I had Catherine increase her dopamine and acetylcholine through nutrients and light dosages of medications so that she would be able to feel more alert. But I also had a suspicion that something else was keeping her up at night, because I noticed that when she listened to me, she kept her mouth slightly open. This was a sign that her breathing was off, so I sent her home to complete a sleep study to determine whether she had sleep apnea.

When Catherine came back to my office the following week, I told her that her take-home sleep test revealed that she had severe sleep apnea. She told me that her husband was always on her case because of her snoring, which seemed to be getting worse with age. I told Catherine that this was very common, but that sleep apnea was far more serious than snoring. I gave her the name of a good dentist who could create a mouthpiece she would wear at night when she slept that would allow for better breathing.

A month later, Catherine came back to my office, looking like a much healthier woman. She told me that she was getting better sleep than she had in years and felt restored mentally and physically each morning. Best of all, the clarity in her thinking returned once she was able to sleep through the night.

not in its final form, or one that is most stable and useful to you, until you literally sleep on it. During sleep, memories are consolidated and moved into long-term memory storage as the neuronal connections are strengthened. I take that to mean that sleep increases neurogenesis.

In his book *The Harvard Medical School Guide to Achieving Optimal Memory,* Dr. Aaron P. Nelson reported on a landmark 2003 study published in the journal *Nature,* which showed that people remember more once they've slept on new information. In the study, participants were given a word list and then asked to recall the words throughout the day. Most of the participants were able to recall the words at first, but as the day went on, they could recall fewer and fewer. However, the next morning they were retested with the same words, and their recall improved: Something had happened during sleep that made these memories more accessible. What was learned was that sleep provides the ability for the brain to assemble fragments of information and translates them into long-term recallable memories.

THE ONE-TWO PUNCH:
DEPRESSION AND COGNITIVE LOSS

Both dementia and depression are associated with atrophy of the hippocampus. A loss of brain cells in this area causes gradual damage,

A Nightcap Doesn't Lead to a Good Night's Sleep

Alcohol and salty snacks (think wine and crackers) are an enticing nighttime snack because they boost serotonin and GABA. Choosing them before bed is actually a form of self-medication for anxiety and depression. But while your brain might feel momentarily better, even one glass of wine can prevent you from getting a good night's sleep. Alcohol also suppresses deep sleep, causing sleep fragmentation and contributing to sleep apnea. The salty snacks aren't great for your blood pressure, or your waistline. Instead, try relaxing before bed with at least a half hour of exercise, meditation, yoga, or prayer.

which in turn leads to memory loss and, eventually, dementia. Depression can be viewed as the natural consequence of dying brain cells combined with a loss of voltage, or brain power. Without reversing this brain cell loss and brain electrical loss, you will experience significant changes to your thinking as well as your temperament.

To my mind, there is no gap between dementia and depression. MCI is marked by depression, and those with depression are slowly becoming demented. Left untreated, both lead down the same path: Untreated depression leads to Alzheimer's. Untreated memory loss leads to depression. However, the news on treating depression is quite remarkable when

|||||||||||||||||||||||||||||||||||||||||||||||||||||||||||||||||||||||||||||||||||||||||||||||||||||||||||||

THE BRAVERMAN DEPRESSION TEST

Like cognitive impairment, depression is another symptom of ineffective brain performance. While the fix is the same, you might want to get to the bottom of whether your thinking is affecting your mood, or your mood is clouding your thinking. If you answer "true" to more than five of the following statements, don't hesitate to talk to someone—your spouse, a friend, a doctor, or a spiritual leader—about clinical depression. Choose the answer that best reflects how you felt over the past week.

1. I cry very frequently. Y/N

2. I often wish I were dead. Y/N

3. It is not easy falling asleep (takes more than half an hour). Y/N

4. I feel like it takes a huge effort to work or perform activities. Y/N

5. I can't sit still. Y/N

6. I'm afraid that something bad will happen. Y/N

7. I've lost my appetite. Y/N

8. I'm frequently worrying about my health. Y/N

9. I feel that my life is empty. Y/N

10. I'm bored most of the day. Y/N

11. I prefer to stay at home, rather than going out and doing new things. Y/N

12. Most people are happier than I am. Y/N

|||||||||||||||||||||||||||||||||||||||||||||||||||||||||||||||||||||||||||||||||||||||||||||||||||||||||||||

Patient Profile: Talia Improved Her Mood and Her Memory

Talia first came to see me a few years ago, primarily because she wasn't sleeping. At the time, she was a 55-year-old nurse who was working at a busy hospital. When she came into my office, I saw a haggard woman with a dazed look on her face who was about 35 pounds overweight. Talia told me right away that her lack of sleep was affecting her thinking. She told me that at first she couldn't remember simple things, like where she put her car keys. Within a few weeks her memory got worse: She lost the whole car. She reached the end of her rope when she couldn't remember where she was supposed to be during the day; she had to write everything down. This was especially painful for her because she used to pride herself on having such a good memory. Yet now she was writing the simplest little tasks down on a piece of paper. When she came home from work, she had notes in every pocket.

What's more, her lack of sleep was throwing her diet out of whack. She gained weight because she was craving carbohydrates to keep her energy up during the day, even though as a nurse, she knew she wasn't eating properly. And with every pound she gained, she became more irritable and felt less and less like herself. She decided to come to see me because she just didn't like the person she was becoming.

The first question I asked Talia was to determine how long this lack of sleep had been going on. I was shocked to find out that she had lived

it comes to reversing MCI. The brain can experience neurogenesis while treating depression with either antidepressants or nutritional supplements. That's why we call antidepressants "brain salts," because they preserve your brain and allow for the growth of new brain cells, therefore stopping dementia.

MCI Checklist: Emotional Changes

Depression and anxiety are not the only mood changes you may have experienced, although they are usually the most pronounced. Remember,

this way for the past 5 years. Then I asked her to describe her sleep and tell me how a typical night went. Talia told me that in the past 5 years she hadn't slept for more than 3 hours a night. During the day, she worked 13-hour shifts and would come home ready to go to bed. Yet when she fell asleep at 8:30 to 9:00, she would be up again at midnight and wide awake for the rest of the night.

I told Talia that she should never have waited so long to seek help. No one could manage to stay stable with only 3 hours of sleep a night. I asked her what were the three most important changes that she wanted to make, and she knew the answer right away. First, she wanted to sleep; second, she wanted to lose weight; and finally, she wanted to get smarter. The connection was completely clear to me, so I told her, "Once you sleep, you will get smarter."

After a full-body checkup and a battery of cognitive testing, it was clear to me that she was suffering from a severe serotonin deficiency. I immediately started her on the Braverman Protocol to enhance this brain chemical. In just 3 weeks, she was able to retrain her brain so that she was sleeping soundly 7 hours every night.

Six months later, Talia came back to my office beaming. The weight she'd gained had dropped right off her frame—she lost 38 pounds. But best of all, her memory returned. She told me that her mind was much sharper and that she could finally make it through the day without writing notes to herself. I was thrilled to hear her say that her life had changed 100 percent since she'd started my program.

personality and mood changes are not psychological, but are part of the dynamic process of a changing brain. The loss of cells, loss of neuronal insulation, loss of water and blood supply, loss of hormones, loss of nutrients, and loss of mental stimulations, along with exposure to electromagnetic fields, pesticides, toxins, and so forth, can affect your personality. Unless you reverse these losses, you will not be able to retrieve your previous levels of happiness or positive mood.

The following checklist relates to other personality changes you may have seen in yourself or are continuing to experience. Check any of the symptoms if you think there has been a change for the worse over the past year. If possible, record when you first noticed that something had changed. If you check five or more of these descriptions, you need to start the Braverman Protocol right away.

- ☐ Tendency to become easily upset or rattled
- ☐ Increased suspiciousness
- ☐ Decreased emotional responsiveness
- ☐ Diminished initiative or growing apathy
- ☐ Focusing exclusively on yourself
- ☐ Inappropriate sexual behavior or comments
- ☐ Increased stubbornness
- ☐ Lack of emotional control
- ☐ Lack of regard for feelings of others
- ☐ Uncontrollable laughter during inappropriate situations
- ☐ Withdrawal from friends and family

Mood changes are among the easiest brain reversals that you can make, because they appear during the mildest brain chemical deficits. On top of that, I can't emphasize enough how important good mood is to learning. According to a *New York Times* article, maintaining a positive mood lowers the brain's threshold for detecting weaker or more remote connections, making it easier to find solutions to problems, including solving puzzles. In one 2010 study conducted at Northwestern University in Chicago, researchers instructed college students to solve word-association puzzles after watching a short comic routine. The students solved more of the puzzles, and significantly more by sudden insight, compared with when they were shown a scary or boring video. In another 2010 study from the University of Toronto, researchers found that people who were able to maintain positive moods literally saw more detail in every picture they were shown, thereby taking in more information and enhancing their learning experience.

Other studies portray a more negative picture, but they confirm what you've learned in this chapter. In a study reported in the journal

Neurology, people who tended to experience psychological distress were more likely to develop Alzheimer's disease than those who had better coping skills. Those individuals who routinely experienced negative emotions such as depression and anxiety were twice as likely to develop Alzheimer's as those who did not. This is why we must do everything in our power to maintain a positive outlook on life, which you will be able to achieve by following the Braverman Protocol.

Once you determine whether you are suffering from anxiety, insomnia, or depression, you can begin the Braverman Protocol and rebalance your brain. By treating these issues, you might see remarkable differences in your memory and attention right away. However, if these are not apparent causes of your symptoms, read on to see exactly how—and why—your memory and attention may have changed.

Chapter 4

Identifying Memory Problems

Memory is central to the entire function of the brain. A declining ability to remember typically occurs when there is a loss of brain processing speed. This is defined as the rate electrical signals are transmitted. Losing brain speed is directly related to a loss of the brain chemical acetylcholine, which regulates our ability to process sensory input and access stored information—essentially, acetylcholine is all about memory.

Very few people have naturally high levels of acetylcholine, but you can recognize those who do right away: They have a distinct creative flair. They are keenly aware of their surroundings and have the ability to keep long-lasting relationships that are based on fond, shared memories. People who are high in acetylcholine are able make friends easily because they are both intuitive and empathetic: They "get" other people and their motivations. What's more, acetylcholine people are smart. They have a strong immediate memory, and many can remember things from just a single exposure. They excel at school, are quick witted, and are generally fun to be with.

LOSING BRAIN SPEED

As we get older, our levels of acetylcholine naturally decrease. The brain's production of this powerful chemical declines, or if you have an excess of acetylcholine, your brain is speeding along so quickly that you are literally burning it up. When you don't have enough acetylcholine, you'll begin to slow physically and emotionally, as well as deteriorate cognitively. Slower brain speed causes an information bottleneck, allowing for fewer memories to cross over from short-term working memory to long-term memory. The result is that they will get lost in the process. Without treatment, a typical 85-year-old is able to remember only one-half the number of words that he or she knew at age 18.

Losing your brain speed is one of the most aggressive age accelerators, quickly making everyday tasks unmanageable. The first thing you may experience is a general absentmindedness—you become forgetful. You can't remember where anything is or where you are supposed to go. Without the ability to store new memories, you quickly forget old ones, and your intelligence falters. The brightest people I know constantly tell me that, as they've gotten older, they have difficulty learning new skills or thinking through problems. Many of my patients have told me that they can no longer visualize once-familiar objects, people, or places, and they lack the concentration necessary to recall information. Many tell me that they simply "blank out" when they are trying to remember, even midway through a sentence or, worse, a task.

This type of forgetfulness does not mean that you are losing your mind, or your memories. Studies have shown that as we get older, much of what we learn is not lost; it's just at the bottom of the brain's memory pile. For the most part, memory loss does not mean that you are no longer storing new memories. The problem is that you are having difficulty retrieving them. As Barbara Strauch says in her book *The Secret Life of the Grown-Up Brain,* it's like trying to find the right book in a well-stocked library.

Memory loss does progress beyond forgetfulness and will change for each individual at different rates. For example, before the age of 60, you should not be experiencing more than once every few months a failure to recognize places you've been. Yet 40 percent of people have other symptoms of a declining memory by age 50, such as losing their train of thought, and some experience a decline in overall memory as early as age 20. This means that their brains are aging faster than the rest of their bodies, or that some of the other factors we discussed in Chapter 2 are affecting their thinking.

What's more, memory loss can also lead to a myriad of other symptoms, some of which are linked to anxiety, insomnia, and depression, which we discussed in the previous chapter. The cyclical nature of mild cognitive impairment (MCI) makes the experience even more frustrating. You may suffer from:

- Agitation
- Anxiety
- Apathy
- Attention difficulties
- Depression
- Difficulty driving
- Disorientation
- Easy frustration
- Excessive and inappropriate flirtatiousness
- Explosive spells of anger
- Falling
- Fearfulness
- Impulsivity
- Inconsistency
- Insomnia
- Irrational decision making
- Neglect of household chores
- Neglect of self-care
- Restlessness
- Social withdrawal
- Suspiciousness
- Trouble understanding the spoken and written language
- Wandering

The following chart shows typical mental changes in relation to a loss of brain speed in milliseconds. Your brain speed should peak at a value of 300 milliseconds plus your age if your brain is in good health. For example, an ideal brain speed of a 30-year-old is one that can process information in 330 milliseconds (msec). As you can see, at age 30, a small change in brain speed is a small problem. But at 50, a similarly small change in brain speed presents a much bigger problem. When you lose brain speed, it takes longer for you to make mental connections and have physical reactions. By lengthening your reaction time by just 7 milliseconds, you might recognize a slowing down of your thinking, even if your baseline is faster than average.

The goal of my program is not just to reverse memory loss, or increase brain speed back to age-appropriate levels. To feel younger and smarter, you need to increase brain speed beyond what you've already experienced. You need to maintain a brain speed of no greater than 330 milliseconds or lower, or what is normal for a 30-year-old brain, for the rest of your life.

Typical Brain Processing Speeds

CHRONOLOGICAL AGE	BRAIN SPEED (IN MSEC)	COGNITIVE STATE
Age 30	320	Vibrant
Age 30	330	Normal
Age 30	350	Slight changes in memory
Age 50 and beyond	380	Noticeable changes in memory
Age 50 and beyond	390–400	Significant dementia

When you think faster, you can react more effectively to everyday situations. High performing brain speed allows you to access information you already know and absorb and process new information more effectively. Quick thinking makes it easier to switch from one task to another, to multitask with less stress, and to solve problems in creative new ways. You'll also find that you are more deeply in touch with your emotional life, which makes you more empathetic and intuitive.

Being in touch with your emotions and the emotions of others not only makes you seem smarter, it actually improves your memory. This is because memory and emotions are stored in the same part of the brain: the prefrontal cortex. Unless you get more intuitive, you can't get smarter. My research and my experience with patients have shown that sensory types—those who are influenced only by what they can see, hear, touch, taste, and smell—are more likely to have dementia later in life. I believe this is because their rationally thinking brains don't get exercised by an imaginative life. They can't think beyond what they experience. Without this type of thinking, their brains literally get stuck and don't ever expand with new neuronal connections that come from deeply understanding new ideas.

Intuitiveness requires a vision of life that's beyond the here and now. One way to become more intuitive is to shift your focus away from the present. That means you have to begin to embrace the intangible parts of life, whether it's through spirituality, literature, art, science, or self-reflection. It doesn't matter if you believe in God or if you believe in atomic structure. Both are concepts that require you to step away from the rational and embrace the infinite possibilities of your imagination.

Empathy skills increase when we learn to see things from other perspectives. But without acetylcholine, this transformation in reasoning cannot happen. By following this program, we will increase our acetylcholine levels and become more empathetic.

THE FOUR TYPES OF MEMORY

There are multiple forms of memory, and some are more important than others. There are actually four distinct types of memory, each ruled by one of the brain chemical families. When memory begins to decline, you lose these capabilities in the following order:

Verbal (auditory) memory. This type of memory is necessary for decoding sounds, words, sentences, and stories. Verbal memory involves the ability to absorb and retain verbally presented information. For example, being able to listen to a set of instructions and then later recall exactly what was said demonstrates good verbal memory. But if you cannot remember a joke someone recently told you, then your verbal memory is affected. In a 2006 study from Columbia University, researchers found that deficits in verbal memory strongly predicted a later progression to Alzheimer's disease. The temporal lobes, which are regulated by GABA, store verbally presented information. A loss of verbal memory can be diagnosed as an immediate loss (when you forget something you heard right away) or a delayed loss (when you can recall information right away but then forget it after more than 30 minutes).

Visual memory. This involves the ability to absorb and retain information such as faces, colors, shapes, designs, your surroundings, pictures, and symbols. People who can drive to a location after being there only once demonstrate excellent visual memory. The occipital lobes do the visual and sensory training. A loss of visual memory can be diagnosed as an immediate loss (when you forget something you just saw) or a delayed loss (when you can recall information right away but then forget it after more than 30 minutes).

Immediate memory. A short-term stage—lasting only 30 seconds—this type of memory occurs when a stimulus is presented, but before the record is transferred to long-term memory. It comprises verbal and visual memory and is an indication of one's learning capabilities and basic alertness. If your immediate memory falters, you cannot absorb new facts or information. When this type of memory is affected, you might be able to remember what happened to you back in high school but will have difficulty remembering what you ate for breakfast. Immediate memories are briefly stored in the parietal lobes, which are regulated by acetylcholine.

Working memory. The most important form of memory, this is the ability to absorb information from stimuli, retain it, and connect it to information you have already learned. Working memory connects patterns and concentrates on broad areas of information: what I call "bandwidth memory."

People who are intuitive and introverted typically have the strongest working memories, because they have a high ability to concentrate, learn a broad range of concepts, and create paradigm structures they can live by. Working memory is what distinguishes us from chimpanzees: It is actually the most important function of the human brain because it determines how we think. It involves synthesizing old and new data that we've recorded from visual, auditory, and immediate memory; cross-referencing it throughout the brain; and then pulling up the right information when we need it. When we get overloaded with the different pieces of information, the brain will begin to dump older memories, and working memory will become less efficient. However, you'll know when your working memory declines, because you'll feel as though you've lost access to the information you need. It's like sitting at a desk that's covered in papers: You know the information you're looking for is on different pieces of paper in that pile, but you just can't assemble them in the right order, or make sense of them.

LONG-TERM MEMORY CORRELATES
WITH WORKING MEMORY

If you are initially able to absorb and retain information, you will also be able to store it for an extended period of time. Working memory is also critical to executive function, the mental activity involved in planning and regulating behavior. Executive function is the central organizing function of the brain and is what's called upon during goal-oriented activities, such as driving, or even eating.

The frontal lobes, which are regulated by dopamine, handle motor control, concentration, problem-solving skills, planning, retention of knowledge, and initial registration—all functions of working memory. Because working memory is the last to decrease, many people do not realize when their other domains of memory have been significantly affected. If their working memory is still intact, they can still process information even if their personality has changed, or if one of the other memory functions has declined.

Working memory also puts together the past, present, and future. It's using your entire past and your vision of your entire future, and bringing it into the present. That's the definition of maximum intellect.

MCI Checklist: Vision

Some people with MCI begin to have problems understanding visual images and spatial relationships. Check any of the following symptoms you may have experienced over the past year. If possible, record when you first noticed that something had changed. If you check four or more of these phrases, you need to start the Braverman Protocol and see an ophthalmologist (eye specialist) immediately.

☐ Change in vision

☐ Difficulty determining color and contrast

☐ Difficulty judging distance

☐ Difficulty reading

☐ Inability to recognize faces in photographs

MCI Checklist: Daily Living

Check any of the following symptoms if there has been a significant change over the past year that has affected how you manage your day-to-day tasks. If possible, record when you first noticed that something had changed. If you check eight or more of these phrases, you need to start the Braverman Protocol right away.

☐ Consistent problems recalling recent events

☐ Constantly asking for information to be repeated

☐ Difficulty handling financial affairs (e.g., balancing checkbook, handling small sums of money, paying bills)

- [ ] Difficulty performing household tasks independently
- [ ] Difficulty preparing meals, eating, or getting dressed
- [ ] Difficulty remembering a short list of items, like a grocery list
- [ ] Difficulty remembering appointments or important birthdays
- [ ] Difficulty with driving, following directions to get from one place to another, finding familiar streets, or finding your way around a location you've been to before
- [ ] Excessive use of reminder notes or to-do lists
- [ ] Forgetting the correct season, month, or year
- [ ] Forgetting recently learned information
- [ ] Losing or misplacing common items daily
- [ ] Problems with judgment (e.g., falling for scams, buying inappropriate gifts for others)
- [ ] Reduced interest in hobbies/activities
- [ ] Trouble learning how to use a new tool, appliance, or gadget (e.g., DVD player, computer, microwave, remote control)

Specific Memory Functions

There are different memory functions that work by linking the different types of memory: verbal, visual, immediate, and working. These functions are related to the long- and short-term storage of information. They include:

Episodic memory. Experiences that bind the "what, where, and when" aspects of events. These are the most common deficits of memory loss.

Procedural memory. Acquisition and later performance of cognitive and motor skills.

Prospective memory. The ability to remember to perform an action in the future, such as remembering to go to an appointment or to take a medication.

Semantic memory. Facts and general knowledge about the world.

HOW MEMORIES ARE MADE

Creating memories takes place over four stages: registration (exposure and acquisition), retention (storage), stabilization (consolidation), and retrieval (decoding and recall). For every sensory experience we face, the brain has to notice it, store it, match it to other knowledge or previous exposures, and then be able to call upon it when necessary.

Although memories are stored in the prefrontal cortex, they are actually broken up into different bits of information rather than stored as one whole event. The brain distributes incoming information into different networks of highly specialized neurons that only respond to certain types of input. For example, your memory of reading this book will be broken down into:

- what the book physically felt like (or what the pages looked like, in the case of an e-book)
- the act of reading it
- the act of learning something new
- the ability to tell someone what you learned

The visual of the book is stored in the occipital lobe; the title and the lessons you learned are stored in the parietal and temporal lobes. Once you finish the book and reflect on it, your memory of the book is pulled from all these sites to form one single memory. Not only that, the memory of reading the book will be related to your memories of reading all the other books you've ever read.

According to Dr. Aaron P. Nelson, of the Harvard Medical School, each time you have a conversation, learn something, or see something new, the neuronal pathways of your brain are reconfigured. Some connections are strengthened, while others are weakened to make room for additional information. These changes underscore some memories and cement them into long-term memory, and at the same time erode others.

The key to keeping new experiences in your memory is a simple four-step process:

Step One. Make each new exposure the most sensory experience possible by focusing your attention. Because each of the senses stores information in specific and unique parts of the brain, a fully sensory experience guarantees that some part of the new memory will be stored in long-term memory in a way that is easily recalled.

Step Two. During the exposure, make a mental note connecting what you are experiencing with something that you have already experienced. For example, if you are taking a walk with your partner in the park, try to remember another walk you shared, or another park you've visited.

Step Three. Delve into your emotions during the event. Discover how the experience makes you feel at that moment.

Step Four. Replay the experience in your mind about an hour later, and then a day later. Talking about it with others encourages you to organize the information in your brain so that you become more fluent with it, especially if it is a set of instructions. Or, record your thoughts on a piece of paper. Sometimes the simple act of jotting down notes is all your brain needs to move a memory into long-term storage.

Memory Loss Is Not Getting Lost in the Details

The majority of all memory lapses are losing names: those of friends and acquaintances, famous people, and those not truly germane to everyday life. Generally speaking, forgetting names is a normal part of mental functioning. We have only a limited storage for memory.

Memory is manipulated by perception, feeling, and experience, which is why most individuals can rarely continue to remember the events of childhood accurately. As we age, we remember events of long ago differently than what might have actually occurred. Memories of traumatic childhood events are frequently distorted. False memories can easily occur, and the reality of a memory is extremely difficult to establish unless it has been recorded. For example, if you ask someone to recall a childhood event when he or she is 55 and then again at age 70, the answers will vary greatly.

Perception is colored by past experiences, associated memories, and concurrent social inputs. For example, how you remember a trip to New York City depends on your feelings, experiences, and beliefs about the city that were created prior to, and even after, the visit. Some people know New York to be a city of tall buildings, and they may selectively remember the skyscrapers; others who may perceive it as a crowded city of exciting cultural events will remember the fun they had at a museum or Broadway show.

If you asked 10 of your friends to watch an event together and report on the details, including shapes, colors, and sizes, all 10 will have slightly different "takes," because they all perceive things uniquely. Clinically depressed people often describe colors as faded, conveying a sense that the world looks washed out, even though their capacity to recognize and distinguish specific colors is unchanged. So if someone recalls an event differently than you do, it doesn't mean that you're marching toward dementia. They aren't, either. However, if you can't recognize a friend you see at least once a month, then you do have something to worry about.

If you do need help with keeping track of the details, here are some of my best tips to help you get started before you begin to balance your brain chemistry.

1. Look people in the eye when they are talking to you. Don't be shy to ask them to repeat themselves if you don't understand what they are trying to tell you. Sometimes just hearing something twice is all you need to make the neuronal connection stick.

2. The same applies to written material: The second time's the charm. Rereading instructions is a good way to create and retain a memory.

3. Repeat aloud what you just heard or read. Some people are auditory learners and retain information when they hear it rather than read it.

4. Minimize interruptions by prioritizing people and events. We have to work aggressively to de-spam our environments so that we can focus on the task at hand and then remember what we've accomplished.

5. If you are trying to connect a name that goes with a face, you just need to examine a person's face discreetly when you are introduced. Try to pinpoint an unusual feature (their ears, hairline, forehead, eyebrows, eyes, nose, mouth, chin, complexion, etc.). Then create an association between that characteristic and the name in your mind. This trick is called chunking. The association may be to link the person with someone else you know with the same name or same physical feature. Or it could be a word that rhymes with the name of the person or the defining feature.

Brain Speed Meets Brain Structure

Besides governing brain processing speed, acetylcholine is also the building block for myelin, a fatty substance that insulates the nervous system, keeping it moist and strong. Myelin surrounds neurons just like the rubber

Patient Profile: Asher Prevented Dementia with Early Detection

Asher came into my office in a panic. Though it wasn't yet noticeable to his family and friends, he knew very well that at age 54 his forgetfulness was getting in the way of his performance at work. He was forgetting where he put things and was frequently at a loss for names of people he recognized. He found this particularly troubling because he was an accountant and was known in his office for having an excellent memory for details involving his clients. Asher was afraid that if word got out that he wasn't as smart as he used to be, he might be out of a job.

I explained to Asher that some forgetfulness is normal at any age. However, we needed to identify his brain's age and determine if he had already lost brain processing speed. After he took the Braverman Memory Test, we did a thorough medical checkup, including Brain Electrical Activity Mapping (BEAM). I was able to establish that he was experiencing a loss of brain processing speed: His 54-year-old brain was functioning like it was 72.

Asher immediately started following the Braverman Protocol for low acetylcholine to improve his brain speed. A change in diet included the foods and nutrients that naturally increase choline, the building block for acetylcholine. I also asked him to do more physical exercise and take time each day to read some science fiction, to get out of his rational-thinking brain with a new boost of imagination.

Asher came back 2 months later with a big smile on his face. Even before we did follow-up tests, he told me that he felt that his memory was better than it had been in years. His scores on his memory and attention tests put him at a cognitive peak for a man his age. What's more, he found that he really enjoyed reading again, even though he hadn't read a novel since he was in college. I was proud of Asher because he is a prime example of how early detection and a few small changes can add many smarter, higher-functioning years to a person's life.

THE BRAVERMAN MINI MEMORY TEST

By testing your brain speed early and often, you can catch MCI and an acetylcholine deficiency while you can still remember to take the tests. This little quiz is a quick assessment of your memory. There is a longer, more complex test that begins the Braverman Protocol in Part II of this book. If you score in the lowest category on the test here, start boosting your acetylcholine and sharpen your cognitive skills by following the Braverman Protocol now so that you won't have to worry about dementia in your later years.

STAGE 1

- Memorize these words: banana, boat, firefly
- Memorize this name and address:
  Jamie Mackintosh
  3375 Broad
  Pittsburgh, PA

STAGE 2

- Count backward from 60 by sixes. See how far you can get in 60 seconds. Record your answers; then check your math. Give yourself a point for each correct answer (out of a possible 10 points for a perfect score).

coating surrounding electrical wires, creating a membrane barrier that coats and protects each brain cell. This insulation increases each cell's conductivity and reaches its maximum thickness during middle age. With the right amount of myelination, your neuronal circuits fire more rapidly, allowing the neurons to recover faster after signals have been sent, giving brain cells "greater bandwidth," and boosting their processing capacity. Excellent myelination is like the newest cable or DSL connections compared with the Internet service you used to receive on your dial-up modem.

There is some evidence that women produce more myelin than men do. As myelin increases, it builds connections that help us think faster. Myelin also thickens with use. When new neuronal connections are

- Spell the following words backward aloud, having someone else write down your answers. Give yourself a point for each correct answer: WORLD, DRAMA, MOVIE, PLATE, CHEESE, CAMERA, ENVELOPE, TABLE, PHONE, LIZARD

- Without looking back, write down the three words you were asked to remember at the beginning of the quiz. Give yourself one point for each correct answer.

- Without looking back, write down the name and address you were asked to remember at the beginning of the quiz. Give yourself one point for each of the following: correct name (first and last), correct street address, correct town and state.

SCORE

26: perfect score, no impairment

20 to 25: mild impairment

14 to 19: moderate impairment

13 or below: severe deficit

made as you master a task, the myelin coating becomes heavier.

While animals such as dolphins and elephants have bigger brains and more gray matter—the stuff that is made up of all the neuronal connections—humans have more white matter, or myelin sheathing. Some researchers believe that it is the amount of white matter alone that has allowed us to develop language.

The decay of myelin leads to cognitive decline and memory loss when the messages that brain chemicals carry get disrupted as their pathways lose their lubrication. Without the proper amount of myelin and acetylcholine, the brain can short-circuit. You may notice this if you have ever been in the middle of a conversation and suddenly your mind went blank. However, you can reverse this decline and restore memory simply

Smokers Experience Great Memory Loss

We unknowingly mess with our brain speed by the way we choose to live. Smokers do not remember names and faces as well as non-smokers do. A 2004 study in the journal *Neurology* showed that over a 5-year period, memory decline for smokers was five times worse than that of nonsmokers. If you are a smoker, it's never too late to quit or reverse damage. The same study found that former smokers exhibited less memory loss than current smokers.

Nicotine is an effective stimulant that can improve thinking temporarily, but in the long run it destroys acetylcholine and your ability to remember. Nicotine also damages your lungs, which serve a critical function for memory by providing oxygen to the brain.

You must quit smoking now. But don't replace one bad habit with another. Don't justify eating more or drinking more because you're trying to quit smoking. Instead, get professional help. There are great medications out there, such as varenicline (Chantix), that your doctor can prescribe to help end your addiction to cigarettes once and for all. Other medications that can help defuse your appetite for nicotine include Wellbutrin, Effexor, and natural testosterone.

by increasing the amount of acetylcholine your brain produces. By following the Braverman Protocol, you will retrain your brain to run faster and smoother with more myelination.

Memory loss is probably the first aspect of MCI that you will be able to pick up on your own, especially if you are an anxious person. But don't despair if you notice it: Memory loss is reversible. By following this program, you'll be able to increase all four components of memory and achieve an even higher level of working memory than you had before. The key will be to increase your acetylcholine levels. When you do so, you'll find that you're more creative and better able to relate to others. You'll be able to draw on your years of experience in relationships and apply what you've learned to the people in your life today.

Yet memory may not be the only cognitive problem you are facing. In the next chapter, you'll be able to determine if your attention is waning, and what types of errors you may experience.

Chapter 5

Identifying Attention Problems

The dopamine family of brain chemicals delivers your brain's voltage, or power. Voltage is the intensity at which the brain responds to a stimulus and the effectiveness of its ability to process the information that monitors your physical and mental health. Your brain's power determines your ability to stay focused, stay on task, concentrate, and get a job done. It also controls your working memory, which we know is the most closely linked to attention.

People who naturally have high levels of dopamine are also likely to have high traditional IQs. With lots of dopamine, you can quickly master any skill or information presented to you, because you have intense focus and concentration. You are more likely to be highly extroverted. While that's fun at a party, it might be holding back your thinking: Your fear of being alone and an inability to close out the world leave you with less time to be truly introspective and intuitive.

A dopamine deficiency occurs when your brain is either burning too much dopamine or not producing enough. Typically, you produce less dopamine as you age. Without enough dopamine, you cannot maintain enough voltage, so everything about you literally slows down. When dopamine production wanes, you begin to lose your mental intensity. You may find that it takes more time and effort to get things done. Your concentration may wander, your thinking and decision making are not as quick, or your intensity at work is diminishing. Frustrated, you begin to put off tasks that you know are important. Your abstract thinking, which was once your hallmark but is now poor, may lead you to take out your anger on your friends, family, or colleagues.

You may even sleep a little longer but still wake up tired. You may start reaching for a stimulant, like coffee or another caffeinated beverage, just to get yourself going in the morning. The coffee supplies the fix you need to feel like yourself, but the effect is temporary. So you reach for more throughout the day, because otherwise you can't sustain your usual level of performance. Those experiencing a dopamine deficiency might be the first to notice that they are falling into the performance gap and will be the most affected: Those typically able to sustain a high level of output at work will notice when they are no longer effective or can't keep up with their coworkers.

Low-dopamine sufferers often feel sluggish, even cranky. In response, you may have an instinctive, often subconscious urge to bring the fire back. Besides craving caffeine, you may find that you are attracted to foods that will deliver an energy boost: high-sugar, fast-digesting carbohydrates. These foods successfully boost dopamine production, so in effect you are doing the right thing. However, these foods will also cause you to gain weight, which you are especially susceptible to. Without dopamine, both your brain's metabolism and your body's have slowed down.

The following chart is an approximate voltage meter and shows what happens to your thinking when your brain's electrical power begins to fail. The chart highlights that just a very small change in voltage has a major impact on your cognitive abilities, mood, and psychological state.

Declining Brain Power Leads To . . .

- Attention deficit disorder
- Decreased alertness
- Distractibility
- Failure to finish tasks
- Failure to listen and follow instructions
- Forgetfulness
- Hyperactivity
- Impulsivity
- Poor abstract thinking
- Poor concentration, especially with numbers

VOLTAGE	CONDITIONS
20	Superior energy and concentration
10	Normal energy and concentration
9	Fatigue, mild memory loss or cognitive deficit
8	Insomnia, panic disorder
7	Obesity, moderate obsessive-compulsive disorder, mild depression
6	Moderate addiction, major depression
5	Borderline personality disorder, chronic fatigue
4	Chronic depression, violent behavior
3	Attention deficit disorder
2	Alzheimer's disease
1	Schizophrenia
0	Coma

LOSING FOCUS VERSUS ADULT ATTENTION DEFICIT DISORDER

Attention deficits were once thought to be associated mostly with children, but we now know that attention problems not only continue into the adult years but can reveal themselves in more of us as we age. What's more, attention decreases are one of the first signs of mild cognitive impairment, or MCI, and can begin as early as age 30. If you failed more than two of the attention parameters in the Braverman Mini Memory Test in Chapter 4, your brain has slowed down by at least 20 milliseconds, putting you at great risk for attention-related accidents and further mental decline.

There are four core forms of attention errors:

Omission. This is a lack of response to a stimulus, such as not answering a direct question; running a red light or a stop sign or slamming on the brakes when driving; or missing social cues.

Commission. An inappropriate response to a stimulus. Some examples are talking over someone in conversation; noticing the red light but walking into traffic anyway; jumping the gun in decision making; and impulsive buying or behaviors.

Reaction time. This is an unusually long delay in response timing to a stimulus, such as forgetfulness; not immediately removing your hand that is touching something hot; watching yourself bleed before addressing a wound; or driving too slowly or hesitating to change lanes.

Variability. An inconsistent response to a stimulus. Examples include yo-yo dieting; erratic highway driving; highly distracted thinking; and impulsive behaviors.

Most adult attention problems are very different from those that children are often burdened with. Adults are very infrequently hyperactive and instead are making attention errors because they are slowing down: errors of omission and commission. These errors in large part lead to the fifth leading cause of death in the United States: accidents due to declining attention.

Attention is really a subcategory of memory, and when it goes in adults, they forget things, they jump the gun, and they are unable to take visual and verbal information and process it into thinking. A good example of this is an aging politician who can still remember 1,000 faces or memorize a 1-hour speech but can no longer synthesize his ideas into a coherent policy or strategy.

Depending on our particular brain chemical deficiency patterns, family histories, and personalities, each of us can feel less attentive in different ways. Men seem to make more anxiety-related commission errors. Women make more omission errors, which can be linked to depression. People over 65 most often make commission, omission, and reaction time errors. They make fewer variability errors because that is related more to excessive levels of dopamine and hyperactivity, rather than a deficit. However, it's important to keep in mind that just because you feel less focused doesn't mean that you are no longer smart—the truth is that people with above-average intelligence or high levels of creativity are among the first to notice a change in their attention.

Declining attention is very different from adult attention deficit disorder (ADD), a clinical diagnosis given to those who have never had the ability to focus clearly. It was previously thought of as a childhood syndrome that disappeared as children matured. However, we now know that ADD kids grow up to become ADD adults.

The problems associated with adult ADD are much the same as those of an age-related loss of brain power or processing speed; the difference is that you might have always had them. If you are distracted, impulsive, bored, or addicted to certain types of behavior, and in the past you did not have these issues, you probably are suffering from MCI. However, if you have had these same symptoms all your life, you may be suffering from adult ADD.

MCI Checklist: Attention

Are you losing your ability to focus? Almost 50 percent of all adults perform poorly on attention tests. This checklist mimics the results of the computerized screening for attention deficit, called TOVA (Test of Variable Attention). Check any of the symptoms below if you think there has been a pronounced change in your behavior over the past year. If possible, record when you first noticed that something had changed. If you check six or more of these descriptions, you need to start the Braverman Protocol right away.

☐ Accident prone

☐ Avoids new situations and meeting new people

☐ Consistent forgetfulness of tasks, even after instructions have been given

☐ Easily "gets off task," e.g., when interrupted by a phone call while shoveling snow in the driveway, completely forgets to finish until hours later

☐ Easily angered or low tolerance for frustration

☐ Feeling slow when processing information

☐ Frequent interruption of thought

☐ Frequently (daily) loses or misplaces items

☐ General feeling of distractedness

☐ Has difficulty concentrating on work or other tasks requiring sustained attention

☐ Has difficulty organizing material to complete a task

☐ Has difficulty sticking to a single activity

- [ ] Has difficulty waiting in line
- [ ] Impulsivity (e.g., jumping the gun)
- [ ] Loses track of time
- [ ] Low self-esteem, even while appearing confident to others
- [ ] Misses stop signs
- [ ] Needs instant success to keep interest level up
- [ ] Not attending to tasks quickly
- [ ] Often acts before thinking
- [ ] Procrastinating

MCI Checklist: Communication

People with MCI may have trouble during conversations. Check any of the following symptoms if there has been a negative change in behavior over the past year. If possible, record when you first noticed that something had changed. If you check four or more of these symptoms, you need to start the Braverman Protocol right away.

- [ ] Difficulty finding the right word (dysphasia)
- [ ] Difficulty following or joining a conversation
- [ ] Difficulty initiating a conversation
- [ ] Losing train of thought in the middle of a conversation
- [ ] Repeating questions, stories, or statements
- [ ] Struggling with vocabulary
- [ ] Using words incorrectly

Reversing Impulsive Behaviors

One common trait of adults with ADD is impulsiveness, reacting without thinking first. This can be seen in the following behaviors:

- Agreeing to complete something before thinking about whether it is feasible

- Interrupting during conversations or speaking out of turn
- Making rash or quick decisions
- Not stopping to check details
- Reckless spending habits

Impulsivity or variability errors are hard to control. Most require a plan that has been detailed in advance. First, see if you can identify your particular type of impulsive behavior. For example, do you spontaneously shop when you are feeling frustrated or upset? Do you interrupt others on a consistent basis, creating problems in relationships? Do you find yourself always trying to "fix" your life because you have made poor decisions? Next, try the following strategies to combat impulsive behavior.

For impulsive shoppers, keep a list handy that is divided into "wants" and "needs." For items that are in the "want" column, put off purchasing for at least 1 week, then go back to the list and reevaluate. Chances are you might not even remember why you wanted the item in the first place.

Try to take 24 hours before making big decisions. If someone asks you for a favor, getting back to them the next day will allow you to decide if you really can make the commitment they require. Then, write down two "pros" and two "cons" for each decision. This can help you to slow down and look at the decision from different viewpoints.

Tips to Stay on Task

Whether you have ADD or just waning attention, these simple tips can keep you focused:

- Make a list of tasks to be accomplished each day, and don't try to take on too much.
- Use sticky note pads for important reminders. Then stick them wherever the task needs to be completed, or where you will be most likely to notice them.
- Keep an appointment book or planning calendar to track appointments and deadlines. If you like gadgets, a BlackBerry, a PDA, or even your home computer makes this type of tracking more fun.

- Carry a notebook so you can write down ideas or things you'll need to remember as the day goes by. Smartphones usually have this feature as well.

- Set up systems that are meant to keep you organized at home and at work.

- Break down large projects or tasks into smaller, manageable steps.

- Follow a daily routine that's consistent.

- Reward yourself when big projects or tasks have been completed. Choose something other than food—something that is meaningful, tangible, and concrete that you can look at often to remind yourself of your progress.

- Don't be too hard on yourself—getting organized is challenging for everyone. And remember, no one is perfect.

ADDICTIONS AFFECT BRAIN POWER

The long-term damage of drug and alcohol addiction is directly related to cognitive decline, as it both kills off brain cells and disrupts brain chemical production. Chronic intoxications from alcohol and drugs are directly linked to dementia. In a paper I published in *The American Scientist* in 1996, we discovered that frequent exposure to addictive behaviors decreases the number of dopamine receptors in the brain. With fewer receptors, lower levels of dopamine are activated, leaving more intense cravings and increased stress. This loss of dopamine begins the cycle of addiction.

All of us are vulnerable to the addiction cycle when we experience a dopamine deficiency. Earlier in my career, I worked with Dr. Kenneth Blum, professor of pharmacology at the McKnight Brain Institute at the University of Florida College of Medicine; Dr. Ernest P. Noble, former head of the National Institute on Alcohol Abuse and Alcoholism; and Dr. Nora D. Volkow, current head of the National Institute on Drug Abuse. Our research proved that dopamine genetics predicts a very high predisposition for various addictions. I have also conducted studies that showed that a dysfunction of the D2 dopamine receptors in the brain can lead to addiction, aberrant substance-seeking behaviors, and aggression. What's more, we found that there is a correlation between adult ADD and adult drug abuse. In many instances, people who suffer from inattention have the same dysfunctional D2 receptors and are prone to addictive behaviors. In fact, the dopamine D2 receptor gene is present in 49 percent of children with ADD.

Disturbances in the dopamine "reward system" are associated with addictive behaviors. Anything you enjoy doing but can't seem to rein in can cause a release of dopamine. When this happens, you will initially feel that surge of excitement, or "rush." This is true whether you are addicted to drugs, alcohol, shopping, or sex. But if you are already low in dopamine and you abuse drugs or alcohol, you'll feel less and less satisfied with each exposure.

Worse, now that you've experienced a good rush, you crave the experience again. So not only do you become addicted to the substance, you become addicted to dopamine, even as your brain produces less and less. This is exactly how the addiction cycle begins.

The catch is that the brain can't keep up with demand. Instead, it strives to reach homeostasis, or balance, so that each time you are exposed to the addictive substance or behavior, the brain releases less dopamine, not more. When this happens, the euphoric feeling doesn't come back at all. Yet low-dopamine people will still continue to drink or smoke, in hope of its returning. Unfortunately, these addictions affect every part of your health, including your thinking.

Addiction is almost always a self-medication model. Some people choose cocaine or caffeine because they have a stimulating dopamine effect. Others choose alcohol, marijuana, narcotics, or even pain pills such as OxyContin for their calming GABA effect. If you or someone you love is battling addiction, I'm here to tell you that you can do better by following this program and balancing your brain chemistry in a healthy, less destructive way.

In order to break this cycle, you need to learn how to increase dopamine in a more balanced approach: first choosing foods, then nutrients, and sometimes even medications, so that alcohol, drugs, or shopping doesn't become your only source of a dopamine rush. By increasing levels of dopamine, you'll be able to help yourself break the cycle of addiction and gain control over your life. You will also be able to create new brain cells to replace the ones you've destroyed in the past. Remember, addiction is serious and will sometimes require professional help. If you believe that you have an addiction, especially to drugs, alcohol, or nicotine, talk to your doctor to find the right programs that address your particular health issues.

Even if you don't fall completely into the dopamine addiction cycle and you think you can manage your vices, think again. Even if drinking at low levels, older adults are more likely to experience impaired motor skills, making driving especially dangerous. Sleep disorders and the risk of injury from falls increase as we continue to drink as we get older. I believe that for men, more than 14 drinks a week, or more than four drinks on any given occasion, is too much. For women, more than seven drinks per week or more than three drinks per occasion is considered hazardous drinking. So if your weekly consumption is greater, let your doctor know so that together you can create a plan to get your drinking under control.

What Is One Drink?

Each of the following is considered one drink:

- Beer or wine cooler: 12-ounce glass, bottle, or can
- Malt liquor: 8.5-ounce glass, bottle, or can
- Table wine: 5-ounce glass
- Fortified wine (port, sherry): 3.5-ounce glass
- Cordial, liqueur, or aperitif: 2.5-ounce glass
- Distilled spirits, brandy: 1.5-ounce shot

TECHNOLOGY IS CHALLENGING OUR ATTENTION

Researchers claim that our ability to focus is being undermined by bursts of information from e-mail, text messages, constant phone calls, and other electronic disruptions. I believe they're right: Who doesn't jump when they hear the ping of a smartphone telling them a new e-mail's just come in? Who doesn't take a cell phone call the minute the phone rings? It's no wonder we aren't getting anything accomplished when we are fully entangled. What's happening is that we aren't fully engaged.

This quick reaction to incoming information plays to a primitive impulse to respond to immediate opportunities and threats. The stimulation provokes a dopamine release similar to a response to any other type of addictive behavior. Not only is our attention level affected, so is our level of addiction. Without electronic stimulus, the most wired among us report that they are simply bored.

Some believe that it is impossible to multitask any two activities adeptly, namely driving and talking on the phone. I believe that this is not really the case. We can drive and listen to the radio. And our internal bodies are multitasking machines, constantly doing many things at the same time. However, heavy multitaskers have more trouble focusing and shutting out irrelevant information.

It's the information overload, not the multitasking, that's the culprit. I find that too much information, even when you are completing only one task at a time, causes distraction. A study at the University of California, Irvine, found that people interrupted by e-mail reported significantly increased stress compared with those left to focus. And a 2011 *Newsweek* article pointed out that e-mail aside, exposure to excessive information on any given topic has harmful cognitive effects, particularly in our ability to make smart decisions. Researchers proved that when people are faced with an overwhelming array of choices, they are apt to make no decision at all or simply choose the last one they were presented with, even if other choices were noticeably better.

The science behind these findings is remarkably simple. First, remember that the prefrontal cortex is the same location used for decision making and emotional control, and that these functions are almost always intertwined. This area houses working memory and can hold only seven different pieces of information at any given time. Any more must be processed into long-term memory, which is why we have to "study" for a test: We are preparing our long-term memory with all the facts we'll need to recall. When more than seven units of information are presented, the brain instinctively struggles to figure out what to keep and what to put into storage. The last information learned takes precedence: You'll be able to recall that first and will be swayed by that information when making a decision.

(continued on page 76)

Patient Profile: Tessa Went Back to School Once She Could Focus

Tessa was 46 years old when she first came into my office. While she appeared to be relaxed and in control of her emotions, I could see immediately that she was living with a secret. Her face was puffy, and she had incomplete eyebrows and a receding hairline. She told me that she had been a nurse who enjoyed working in a hospital setting, but had had to leave 13 years before because she couldn't handle the workload and the pressure. Tessa broke down when she told me that her declining attention had begun when she was only 34.

Once she left the workplace, Tessa thought it would be a good idea to get an advanced degree so that she could someday return to the hospital. She told me that she had always been a very academically oriented person. However, she found the schoolwork to be a constant struggle, and she couldn't find the time to study while raising her children. Worse, she suffered from panic attacks during the exams, even though she knew the subjects well enough to teach them herself. Tessa also told me that over the years, her kids would tease her that she was forever getting lost, even when she was driving to places she had been to many times before. She constantly felt stressed when she started a conversation because she couldn't remember what she was talking about by the middle of a sentence.

At the same time, Tessa noticed that her energy was slipping. She didn't have the desire to exercise anymore, even though she was a lifelong runner who still held a high school track record and had run 13 marathons in her thirties, including qualifying for and completing the Boston Marathon. Lifting weights was torture because her muscles ached all the time. She had even tried tae kwon do in an attempt to firm up but instead had found that she wasn't getting any stronger. Her eating habits were not the problem. She was following a low-carb organic diet and taking professional-grade supplements. Still, her energy was plummeting and her anxiety was skyrocketing. Right before she came to see me, she had gotten on her home scale to find that her weight was climbing upward toward her pregnancy weight, even though she was doing "all the right things." The last thing she told me was heartbreaking: "I tried to accept all of these as the inevitable consequence of years passing, but I was only 46. It didn't make sense to be so uncomfortable and stupid at such a young age."

First, I assured Tessa that none of her decline was something that she would have to live with 1 more day. Thirteen years was enough. Immediately we began the Braverman Protocol to get her intellectual functioning back. Brain Electrical Activity Mapping (BEAM) quickly showed that she was 80 percent deficient in three of the four brain chemical families and 50 percent deficient in the fourth. I reorganized her diet to include high-nutrient proteins and more herbs and spices, and set out a plan that included both conventional and holistic medicine. Over the next year, I was determined to return her to optimal health, not just "normal lab values." And now I'm happy to report that Tessa is, in my view, a new person. Her body returned to her training weight: 110 pounds with 20 percent body fat. Her hair is full and shiny, her eyebrows make a complete arch, and her face is radiant with health.

Best of all, her memory is profoundly improved, including an increase of 26 points in immediate auditory memory. Tessa recently called to tell me that she had been accepted to a family nurse practitioner program at one of the top nursing universities in the nation based on her interview skills. For the first time in more than a decade, she had reactivated her nursing license and completed a fellowship in anti-aging and regenerative medicine. She was also excited to report that she would be beginning a master's degree program in metabolic and nutritional medicine. Her only regret was waiting so long to take care of herself.

Create a Technology Plan

In order to protect yourself from making bad decisions because of excess information, Sharon Begley, the author of the article, suggests that you sort through your information before you try to process it. For instance, instead of reading and responding to text messages and e-mails as they come, deal with them in batches—this will give your brain time to respond appropriately to their urgency rather than their immediacy. If you can turn off the auditory signal that a new message has come in, you'll find it much easier to let the messages go unanswered until you are ready to deal with them.

When you are faced with a glut of information, edit down your pool of resources before you contemplate the information they provide. That way you won't be swayed by an overload, and you will force yourself to make your decisions based on only those most reliable sources. This technique has always served me well. I make a practice of filtering out all the extraneous information—especially when it's negative—so that I can stay focused and true to my work in order to get the best results.

Getting smarter also means that you have to prioritize your attention, which begins by completely de-spamming the brain and getting rid of the extraneous white noise that's clogging up your thinking. Technology has made so many types of information instantly accessible that it has become the norm for people to let their ears and eyes wander,

Your Stuffy Nose Is Clogging Your Brain

With increased pollution and the products from the global village arriving at your door every day, there is no such thing as an "allergy season." Whenever your sinuses are clogged, you are literally taking in 50 percent less air, which means that there is almost a 50 percent reduction in dopamine production in your brain. This instantly upsets your whole rhythm, sending you into overdrive looking for a stimulant that is full of carbs and sugar. The lesson here is that clear sinuses are critical to your thinking. Talk to your doctor about the medications and treatment options you might need to keep breathing freely.

as if they were constantly on the lookout for the next big thing to record and upload. As a result, people take in too much information, and their brains become overloaded with disconnected sounds and images: in a word, spam. I notice that many people can listen to two or three conversations at a time. Their auditory processing is so good that they can be on a cell phone, or two, and still talk to the person in front of them. But what I also find is that they aren't really connected to any of the conversations.

I know that it's hard to tear yourself away from your cell phone, iPod, or iPad, but you have to, especially when there is a real human being in front of you waiting for your attention. Practice what I call "ear control" and focus first on the person you're in conversation with that you can actually see. Tell the one on the phone that you'll get back to them as soon as you can focus solely on their needs. Not only will you be able to have more focused concentration, everyone will appreciate the fact that they have your complete attention, even if it is only for a short time.

THE POSITIVE SIDE OF AN AGING BRAIN

As we age, we are at the height of our neuronal connections, which gives us wisdom. By adding increased attention to greater wisdom, you will have the capacity to make the best decisions possible for yourself and your family. You will be able to deeply dissect problems and reach meaningful solutions, whether you are refinancing your mortgage, thinking of making a career change, or juggling business and family life. What's more, you'll have the energy to tackle new problems and situations in an efficient way that will allow you to leap over the performance gap, instead of falling into it.

Chapter 6

Identifying IQ Types

Your intelligence quotient, or IQ, is not just a measurement of how smart you are: It quantifies different aspects of how your brain functions. The concept of IQ was first introduced by the French psychologist Alfred Binet in 1904. The "quotient" refers to Binet's definition of IQ as a person's mental age divided by their chronological age. This quotient was then multiplied by 100 to make it a whole number. Today, IQ tests use a "deviation IQ" rather than a ratio IQ. Test takers are compared with other people their own age. The average IQ is still 100, but deviations from the average are assigned a number, which corresponds to a percentile rank. Most IQ tests consist of subtests measuring various qualities, including factual knowledge, short-term memory, abstract reasoning, visual-spatial abilities, and common sense.

It used to be thought that there was only one type of IQ, and that your intelligence could not change after the age of 16. We now know that neither of these premises is true. There are many different ways to measure and qualify intelligence. And, in order to become smarter as an adult, you need to be able to increase—and eventually master—every type of IQ. What's more, your dominant IQ type can be greatly modified by improving your memory and attention functions.

All types of IQ depend on maintaining the total health of the brain. Otherwise, even the best brains and highest IQs will fall with age. Even people as brilliant as Albert Einstein will still notice a decline in their intelligence by the time they are 60, even though they could still function as geniuses because they have overdeveloped certain patterns in order to function.

TYPES OF IQ

There are four main categories of intelligence, and each corresponds to one particular brain chemical family. Each type of intelligence develops during the earliest years of school and can change throughout your life. It's quite common for people to be highly developed in one area and deficient in another, or for one type of intelligence to develop when you are older, later than others. As you read through the following descriptions, see if you can determine what your greatest IQ strengths are, what they used to be, and how your current cognitive state is affecting the way you think.

A noticeable decline in any of these four areas is a definitive hallmark of a loss of brain speed and should act as a warning signal that you need to start retraining your brain. When memory and attention are not at peak levels, all areas of intelligence will diminish. If you were high in abstract IQ, memory loss can affect your ability to remember trivia and important factual information you used to readily recall. If you were high in emotional IQ, poor mood will not allow you to relate well to others. Thought confusion will decrease both creative IQ and common sense IQ, as you will lack the ability to pull disparate pieces of information together to complete "the bigger picture." Lastly, attention errors will affect your common sense IQ, because you will lose the ability to react to situations quickly.

Abstract or traditional IQ. This is your ability to master schoolwork, including arithmetic, spelling, reading, and writing. Abstract IQ is governed by the brain chemical dopamine. The typical geniuses, like Einstein, have high abstract IQs because they are able to synthesize facts, recognize patterns, and create new paradigms. They are motivated by intellectual rewards: the feeling of accomplishment that comes with getting an A on a test. If you score high on the typical IQ test, which solely measures abstract IQ, you will likely have high working memory along with high attention. Many doctors I know have high abstract IQ and high working memory, but don't have the social skills that come with good verbal and visual memory. They are interested in solving problems rather than creating deep relationships. However, when this type falters—and it will be the last part of your intelligence to go—you will find that you have difficulty with things that used to come easily to you, like balancing your checkbook or writing a grocery list.

Creative IQ. This is the ability to incorporate new ideas into established ways of doing things, leading to a change in viewpoint. Individuals with high creative IQs are also empathetic, because they can see multiple perspectives. This type of IQ is governed by acetylcholine, and when this chemical is abundant, you have the ability to produce or construct things very easily, because you have high attention and strong visual and verbal memory. Many politicians I know have enormous creative IQ and low working memory: They are able to remember faces extremely well, they can develop strategic ideas, and they are excellent people pleasers with high levels of empathy. However, without acetylcholine, you may find your creative IQ diminishing. You won't feel the passion in life as you used to and won't be motivated to pay attention to the details.

Emotional IQ. First brought to public awareness by author Daniel Goleman, emotional IQ includes the ability to be sensitive to others and to sustain long-term relationships. A loss of emotional IQ may be occurring if you find that you would rather be alone because people annoy you, when you used to be extremely social. It is governed by the brain chemical GABA, which is one reason why women, who typically have more GABA than men, have better emotional IQs. When emotional IQ declines, or was not fully developed, not only can your personality turn people off, but you will not be able to deal with others with empathy. And you can't have sustained relationships without the ability to see others' perspectives. For example, low emotional IQ people have poor verbal and visual memory, although they have high working memory. This means that they will have a hard time remembering faces or listening to long stories.

Common sense or perceptive IQ. An ability to see things for what they really are, this expertise is governed by serotonin. These people are often thrill seekers who can keep a low profile and seem mellow most of the time, but are able to jump into action when necessary. Many firefighters I know have extremely high common sense IQs. People who thrive in a multitasking environment also have high common sense IQs, along with high levels of attention, because they can focus on many chores at the same time. A loss of this ability may lead you to make poor decisions or form unrealistic conclusions about others.

The Meaning of IQ Numbers

Fifty percent of people the world over have abstract IQs between 90 and 110, while only 25 percent have lower scores. Another 25 percent have higher IQs.

IQ SCORE	DESCRIPTION
55	Mild mental retardation
70	Borderline
85	Low average
100	Average
115	High average
125	Superior
130	Very superior/gifted
145	Genius

TYPICAL TRAITS OF HIGH IQ

The following questions are often used to assess gifted or high IQ individuals. I've modified the list to show how I believe the questions reflect the four domains of IQ. If you can answer yes to 15 of the 20 questions, consider yourself gifted. You can also use these questions as a prompt to determine if you used to exhibit any of these traits but no longer do. This would be a very clear sign that you are suffering from mild cognitive impairment, or MCI.

1. Is your vocabulary better than those of most of your friends or colleagues? (Abstract)

2. Can you recall information quickly? (Abstract/Perceptive)

3. Do people accuse you of reading too much into a story or movie? (Perceptive/Creative)

4. Do you like to figure out how things work? (Abstract/Creative)

5. Are you interested in discussing your opinions on topics such as politics, race relations, and religion? (Abstract)

6. Do you always think you're right? (Abstract)

7. Do you think you know more than others? (Abstract)

8. Do you normally figure things out before someone explains them? (Abstract/Creative/Perceptive)

9. Are you a perfectionist? (Abstract)

10. Are you creative? (Creative)

11. Do you express your opinion a lot? (Emotional/Creative)

12. Do you feel comfortable engaging in conversation? (Emotional)

13. Are you sometimes skeptical when you hear statements from government officials or "experts"? (Perceptive)

14. Are you sensitive to beauty? (Creative)

15. Are you self-critical? (Abstract)

16. Do you come up with original ideas and solutions? (Creative)

17. Do you like to solve puzzles? (Abstract/Creative)

18. Are you normally energetic? (Emotional)

19. Are you witty? (Creative/Abstract/Emotional)

20. Do you have a good sense of humor? (Creative/Emotional)

A BALANCED BRAIN CAN IMPROVE ALL DOMAINS OF INTELLIGENCE

The secret of building a resilient brain is to maintain and raise abstract IQ and at the same time develop the other IQs that you may not have had before. For example, I'm naturally an abstract IQ person: I thrive in a school environment, and I still have a deep passion for research and new learning. But as I get older, I'm learning that there is more to a full and balanced life than being "right" all the time. I'm concentrating on retraining my brain to develop my emotional IQ so that I can be a better parent and a more empathetic doctor. I do this by working hard every day at changing my temperament and by balancing my brain by following my own protocol.

We all know some people who are extremely creative or perceptive, which are IQ types that seem inherent. All four types of IQ are, in fact, directly related to your brain chemistry and biological temperament. In my book *The Edge Effect*, I explained how each of us is governed by a dominant brain chemical, which not only affects the ability to focus and remember but also governs how we learn and in what type of IQ we are most dominant.

The challenge of aging is the ability to shift from one type of IQ to another and become a master of all four domains. Increasing any type of IQ and changing your temperament are the pinnacles of total brain health and can come about only when you are able to maximize all your efforts to enhance your brain chemistry. You can choose where you want to take your brain. Raise your dopamine and become more extroverted; raise your acetylcholine and become more intuitive; raise your feeling and intimacy capacity by raising serotonin; and raise your organizing capacity with GABA. This is the true test of becoming younger and smarter.

My goal for you is to become the best of the best: a person who is both intelligent and relational. Intelligent means improving your memory and enhancing your attention so that you can relate to the past, live in the present, and plan for the future. Relational, or having the ability to pay attention to people, involves living in the present and having high emotional IQ. Learning from the past involves high common sense or perspective IQ. Maintaining a focus on the future involves setting and meeting your own goals, which requires high creative IQ.

In today's fast-paced world, mastering only one domain of IQ is no longer enough. If you have only great emotional IQ, then you've got nothing interesting in your head; if you have great abstract IQ, you can't deal with people. All types of IQs need to be balanced in order to enhance memory, attention, mood, and relationships. By following this program, you can have the mind of the most creative thinkers, as well as the character of the most socially astute people.

Neurogenesis Leads to New Thinking

The best way to develop new neural pathways is to harness a fuller sense of imagination. If you can maintain an open, creative, and imaginative childlike mind, you'll be more receptive to new learning. Education broadens and expands your horizons; allows the application of the knowledge you already have to generate bigger, better ideas; and increases all types of intelligence.

IMPROVE YOUR INTELLIGENCE BY INCREASING YOUR BANDWIDTH

In researching this book, I uncovered lots of ways to improve memory, including memorizing a phone book. But in today's world, that skill is no longer required. I want you not only to be able to remember more, I want you to get smarter. Memorizing a phone book isn't going to get you there. You have to have a wide range of interests in order to be smarter.

You can do this by reading and learning a variety of different subjects. Go out of your comfort zone and take on science, politics, history, literature, the Bible, or spiritual texts. Learn another language using Rosetta Stone software, or take a class and meet new people trying to accomplish the same thing—that way you'll be raising your emotional IQ as well as your abstract IQ. It doesn't matter what you learn, as long as you are stretching to master something new. That is what keeps the brain flexible so that you can maintain the ability to learn and grow.

You might be interested in increasing your intelligence even before your memory or attention has faltered. Or you might have noticed that you are not as smart as you used to be. The smartest people I know are able to take their enhanced memory and attention and create new paradigms because they are constantly learning. Education broadens and expands our horizons.

Reaching the highest levels of a balanced brain by attaining every type of IQ won't happen overnight: It is a whole life mission. This journey has been well documented over time. It's called The Path in Christianity, Ha Derech in Judaism; in Buddhism it's called the Eight Noble Paths. In my office, it begins by balancing the brain. And the only way you can change is by commencing your journey by following my program. Let's get started.

Part II

The Braverman
Protocol

Chapter 7

Step One: Early Testing

Every time you see your doctor, he or she checks some, but not all, of your vital organs. Doctors will always check your heart, your lungs, and your weight. A woman's breasts and pelvis might be examined 60 times over the course of her life; a man might have 60 prostate exams. All these results are recorded in your chart and then compared to last year's results to see if there has been any change. Yet year after year, your doctor disregards the most important organ in your body: your brain. Without a brain checkup, you can't pinpoint if and when change is occurring. And without a cognitive baseline, you'll never know how much power, processing speed, balance, and synchrony you've actually lost, and you will never be able to repair your brain, or get smarter.

A full brain health checkup is the first step in the Braverman Protocol. It is the only way that we can start an effective early prevention program that includes detection and treatment of mild cognitive impairment, or MCI, and possibly delay the onset of dementia. This type of health assessment enables me to recognize the first and most subtle shifts in brain chemistry and electricity.

Each of us has a unique brain, and there are various ways to determine how it is functioning. There are complex and amazingly accurate imaging techniques, as well as my own tests and quizzes, that can help you determine whether you have a brain chemical imbalance or are experiencing the earliest stages of MCI. This chapter will help you create your first cognitive baseline, so that you can assess your symptoms as well as your treatments to see if you are getting younger and smarter.

ASSESSING BRAIN HEALTH

In my medical practice, I offer the latest technology for early diagnostics. With these tools, I can help my patients identify whether they are experiencing problems with their general health and cognitive status before real physical symptoms occur. Because the brain and body are so intimately connected, I begin to diagnose many areas of the body by starting with the brain.

While anatomical deviations within the brain can be assessed with an MRI or CT scan, these tests cannot pick up subtle changes in brain chemicals or the transfer of electricity. Instead, my practice is based on the work of Dr. Clark Randt, the founding neurologist at NYU Medical Center. He was the first director of life sciences for NASA and a pioneer brain researcher. He was possibly the first to conceptualize mild cognitive impairment through his 24-hour recall memory tests. I've been able to take his good work and update it for the 21st century. My brain assessment focuses on Brain Electrical Activity Mapping, or BEAM, for assessing brain electrical transmissions. BEAM accurately measures the four individual brain waves. It then provides a status report of your brain chemistry as the electrical impulses are converted into pictures showing colored bursts that represent actual electrochemical transmissions. When your brain is in harmony, the image looks like a full-spectrum rainbow; when there are deficiencies or excesses, one color may dominate the picture. From these pictures, we can make intelligent decisions about which of the four brain chemical families need to be addressed, and later, we can accurately assess the effectiveness of treatment.

A BEAM exam measures the brain's voltage and processing speed and assigns it a "P300 value." This number represents how fast you are thinking. The P300 wave is an event-related potential that measures synaptic speed during an electroencephalography (EEG) test. It measures voltage as compared with brain cell mass. The presence, magnitude, topography, and time of this signal can measure processing speed, power, and quality of your brain's electrical signaling.

The P300: A Brain Speedometer

My most recent research involving P300 data from a large and diverse patient population indicates a direct relationship between delayed processing speed, as measured by P300, and brain hypometabolism, or the overall slowing down of brain function, as detected by PET scan. Hypometabolism was most severe in patients with both enhanced processing latency and memory complaints. This provides evidence that changes in processing speed underlie the processes of aging, including cognitive decline. I believe that the P300-evoked potential component of the EEG may provide a readily accessible early window on cognitive decline well in advance of the irreversible changes leading to dementia.

These measurements can reliably predict just how many years away from dementia you may be—it's like a stress test of the brain.

The P300 is an easy-to-administer test that takes just 10 minutes and is well suited for use as a screening tool in any primary care physician's office. My vision is that we're all going to have laptop brain-health checkups, similar to how your doctor can readily test for coronary heart disease with electrophysiological testing (as elicited by an exercise treadmill).

PET Scans Are Detecting Dementia

BEAM testing is the gold standard for determining your brain chemical makeup. Now, recent advances in PET (positron-emission tomography) scan technology have made PET scans another excellent method that is even more sensitive for accurately identifying Alzheimer's disease and early dementia. PET scans are noninvasive, accurate, and fast, offering lifesaving information that helps physicians detect and diagnose diseases so that they can quickly begin treatment.

PET is a medical imaging tool that detects disease on the cellular level by producing digital pictures and measuring the functionality of different organs, including the brain. By using PET scans, I can detect disorders before anatomical changes are visible. These scans can separate the diagnosis of Alzheimer's disease from other MCI processes or chronic depression. The PET scan is a phenomenal marker of brain metabolism indicating neuronal degeneration in MCI and likely progression to dementia, and can catch subtle changes as long as 10 years before noticeable symptoms manifest. A healthy brain on a PET scan is hot: It looks like it is on fire. When the brain temperature goes down, your brain begins to fizzle, and you will lose your sizzle.

PET works by using small amounts of a radioactive tracer, which chemically attaches to glucose in cells. The tracer then emits radiation as the glucose metabolizes the tracer, and its level is then detected by the scanner. The scanner records these signals and transforms them into images. While PET scanning has been effectively used as a tool to identify early-stage cancers, it had many limitations when used to detect Alzheimer's disease. The biggest obstacle was the dye, which had a half-life of only 20 minutes. However, PET scanning became much more economical and accurate in late 2010, when Dr. Daniel Skovronsky and his Philadelphia-based team at Avid Radiopharmaceuticals announced that they had developed a dye that can show the hallmark plaque buildup during a PET scan more accurately. Before this discovery, plaque buildup could be confirmed only through autopsy. What's more, this new dye can last for more than 2 hours.

These findings are significant because in the past, a full 20 percent of people with dementia received a diagnosis of Alzheimer's and yet, upon autopsy, did not have plaque buildup. Unfortunately, with such a high rate of misdiagnosis, many people are still mistakenly told that they have Alzheimer's and, worse, are not treated for other conditions that may be causing MCI.

All this good news about PET scans comes with a very large price tag. This type of testing is expensive. However, while the PET scan is amazingly helpful in seeing patients in mild cognitive impairment states that are damaged already, with the P300, I can predict who's going to get a bad PET scan at a fraction of the cost.

MRI Detects Silent Disease

Magnetic resonance imaging (MRI) is often used to study how aging affects structural changes in the brain. MRIs can show structural lesions in white matter that can cause dementia and Alzheimer's as well as small areas of dead tissue that result from silent strokes, which we in the medical community refer to as silent infarcts. Studies have shown that there is increasing structural damage with each passing decade after the age of 50. By the age of 70, 50 percent of people have suffered from these silent infarcts, making them far more common than stroke, with respect to both prevalence and incidence. Two recent studies—the Cardiovascular Health Study and the Rotterdam Scan Study—reported a 30 to 40 percent higher prevalence of silent brain infarcts among women than men.

Silent brain infarcts do not present with stroke-like symptoms; however, they are associated with subtle neurological deficits. The two studies mentioned above both concluded that people with silent brain infarcts had worse cognitive ability and greater depression. Worse, the presence of silent infarcts more than doubles the risk of later stroke or dementia.

Routine MRI screening is expensive, but the clues it yields to your overall health are priceless. However, by following this program, you will be able to make your brain more resilient without the expense of early detection. Better still, you'll have peace of mind knowing that as you age, you will be less likely to experience this type of silent disease.

DEFINE YOUR COGNITIVE BASELINE WITH YOUR DOCTOR

In order to enhance processing speed, we need to first determine your current cognitive baseline so that you can recognize the changes you will experience and understand what problems look like. Until BEAM and PET testing are reasonably available to everyone, you can use the following combination of tests to determine whether you have begun to experience MCI. While neuroimaging like BEAM and PET is ideal, 80 to 90 percent of the time, I can achieve similiar results with the following series of checklists and tests.

There are several standardized tests that I use in combination in my office every day to determine cognitive function. The first is a computer test known as TOVA: the Test of Variable Attention. Many doctors can administer this test right from a regular computer. TOVA is an objective, neurophysiological measure of all areas of attention. It takes roughly 20 minutes to complete. A computer measures your responses to either visual or auditory stimuli. These measurements are then compared with a standardized battery of results. Originally developed to accurately diagnose attention disorders such as adult ADD, it is equally effective in determining MCI.

Another strong indicator is the Wechsler Memory Scale (version IV is the most recent), which not only determines verbal, visual, and delayed recall memory, but also can quantify your attention/concentration. This is a standardized series of tests that you can take at most doctors' offices as well.

The CNS/VS is a series of computerized, standardized tests that can be performed in your doctor's office or on the Internet. They provide the necessary testing for memory, attention, reaction time, judgment, and brain injury following a concussion.

The Wechsler Adult Intelligence Scale (WAIS) is an IQ test that many physicians and psychologists rely on to test many types of intelligence in adults as well as adolescents. It does not test for emotional intelligence.

The Mini Mental State Exam (MMSE) is a structured test of mental status that takes about 10 minutes to complete. It determines global cognitive function by testing orientation, word recall, attention, basic calculation, language, and visuospatial registration. It is a widely used and reliable method of screening for Alzheimer's disease, but it is less reliable in determining MCI, because the questions are very basic. I use it in my office along with other testing for best results.

The General Ability Measure for Adults (GAMA) is a second type of IQ test. It is a self-administered, timed test that uses abstract designs, shapes, and colors to help measure intelligence. It is most useful for people who do not test well on other types of IQ tests, including the WAIS, and to test for abstract IQ.

My latest research conducted through my PATH Foundation has shown that by calculating an individual's P300 speed and comparing it with the results of TOVA and CNS/VS memory tests, we've been able to accurately predict more than 80 percent of PET scan results at a fraction of the cost. We can also predict the success rate and reversal of an aging brain's metabolism, returning quicker attention and better overall general memory to my patients than through the standard approach most doctors follow.

Ask Your Doctor

If you believe that you are having problems in one of the following specific domains of MCI, ask your doctor to administer the following test or tests. If he or she isn't able to, it may be time to find a new doctor.

DOMAIN	TESTS
Learning (auditory/verbal memory)	Wechsler Memory Scale, CNS/VS, WAIS
Delayed recall (verbal memory)	Wechsler Memory Scale, CNS/VS
Linguistic function	MMSE
Global cognitive functioning	CNS/VS
Verbal IQ	WAIS
Performance IQ	Wechsler Memory Scale
Abstract IQ	Wechsler Memory Scale, GAMA
Attention	TOVA, GAMA
Processing speed	TOVA
Reaction time	CNS/VS, TOVA
Judgment	CNS/VS, TOVA

DEFINING YOUR COGNITIVE BASELINE AT HOME

While the tests mentioned above are some of the best ways to determine cognitive impairment, I've devised other criteria you can use right now. First, you have to determine how your brain is functioning presently. You can begin to determine your cognitive baseline by assessing your overall health. On my Web site, www.pathmed.com, you can find two important assessments, my Brain Quiz and my Age Print Quiz. The Brain Quiz is a true/false test that can quickly determine if you are experiencing any brain chemical deficiencies: It will verify the results from the quizzes and checklists from Part I of this book. The Age Print Quiz will show you which parts of your body are aging faster than others, so that you can address and reverse health concerns that may be contributing to premature aging of your brain and your body.

Another great test on my Web site is my Nature Quiz, which allows you to see how your brain chemistry is affecting your personality and temperament, which then affects your IQ level as well as your IQ style, memory, and attention. Together, these additional tests will provide you with a total picture of your brain health. I think that it is best to start with those tests if you are experiencing illness as well as MCI. However, if MCI is your biggest health issue, start with the following test: the Braverman Brain Advantage Test. This is a comprehensive memory and attention test I've created exclusively for my patients. Research studies have shown that tests like this one are useful for identifying those MCI patients who have a high likelihood of progressing to Alzheimer's disease or other forms of dementia within a few years. This evaluation will show exactly where your deficits are and should verify your results from the shorter tests and checklists in Part I. This quiz should take no longer than 15 minutes to complete. The tests vary in degree of difficulty, and each assesses a different segment of your cognitive function. Then, use your scores to help you personalize the Braverman Protocol for your own use.

Keep in mind that low scores in particular segments of the test may indicate individual learning differences and naturally occurring individual aptitudes rather than cognitive decline. For example, you may have always retained information better when you could see information rather than hearing it. In this instance, a low score on a verbal aptitude checklist may not mean that you are experiencing MCI. However, the good news is that if you can identify your learning style, you can also improve your weaker modes of learning just by following the protocol.

The Braverman Brain Advantage Test

Test One: VERBAL MEMORY

Please carefully read each of the following stories one time. The test would be even more effective if you could have someone else read them to you slowly. After each story, answer the questions. Do not read the questions before you read the story, and do not reread any part of the story to answer the questions.

STORY #1

Stephanie Appel is an 8-year old Girl Scout whose goal was to earn the Cookie Badge from her Girl Scout troop. She has been working to sell cookies to her other classmates at her school, Boardman Elementary School. One of Stephanie's classmates bought five boxes of Thin Mints. At the next Girl Scout meeting on Tuesday, November 19, Stephanie received the Cookie Badge. Her parents were so proud of her that they took her out after the meeting for her favorite dessert: a sundae with 2 scoops of cookies-and-cream ice cream with hot fudge.

Questions for Story #1

1. What is the Girl Scout's name?

2. How old is she?

3. What school does she attend?

4. When did she receive her Cookie Badge?

5. Who was her customer?

6. What kind of cookies did the customer buy?

7. What month was the next Girl Scout meeting?

8. What day was the next Girl Scout meeting?

9. What happened at the next meeting?

10. How were Stephanie's parents feeling about her?

11. What did they take her to get after the meeting?

12. How many scoops does Stephanie like?

The correct answers can be found in Appendix A.

STORY #2

Thomas Morgan was walking to work on a Friday as he passed a brick building that was under construction. Seven men were there tearing the building down. As he turned onto Madison Avenue, he heard what sounded like puppies crying. The man went back to the construction site and saw two puppies huddled in a corner. The puppies were a shade of brown that reminded the man of his morning coffee. He couldn't leave the puppies at the construction site, so he picked them up and took them to work. At the end of the day, he dropped them off at an animal shelter.

Questions for Story #2

1. Was the story about a man or a woman?

2. What day was it?

3. Where was he walking to?

4. What did he pass on his way?

5. What was the building made of?

6. What was happening to the building?

7. How many men were working on it?

8. What street did he turn onto?

9. What did he hear as he turned the corner?

10. What did he find at the construction site?

11. How many were there?

12. What color were they?

The correct answers can be found in Appendix A.

STORY #3

Wendy and Steven Murphy have owned the Have a Healthy Smoothie Shop on the corner of River Street and Stanwich Street for the past 17 years in rented space. In February, the building was sold and the new landlord decided to increase the rent by more than $500 per month. Wendy and Steven decided the rent was too expensive and found a new store to rent. Their new shop will be open for business in August after blueberry season is finished, so that they will have plenty of fruit to work with.

Questions for Story #3

1. What are the names of the store owners?

2. What was the name of the store that they owned?

3. Where was the store located?

4. How long had the store been at that location?

5. Did they own the building where the store was?

6. What happened to the building?

7. What did the new landlord do?

8. When was the rent increased?

9. How much was the rent increased?

10. What did the proprietors do in response to the rent increase?

11. Are they renting the new space?

12. What month will they be open for business again?

The correct answers can be found in Appendix A.

Scoring: Give yourself one point for each correct answer.

Total Number of Correct Answers: _____

Range:

> 1–9: Poor Verbal Memory
> 10–18: Fair Verbal Memory
> 19–27: Good Verbal Memory
> 28–36: Excellent Verbal Memory

Test Two: VISUAL MEMORY

For this quiz you'll need a deck of playing cards. Shuffle the deck and randomly pull out 20 cards and leave them facedown. Then turn over the first 10 cards and memorize them in 1 minute, writing them down on a piece of paper. Then shuffle them with the 10 remaining cards and put the paper away. Turn each one over and circle "yes" if you have seen that card before and "no" if you haven't. Set those cards aside; do not shuffle them back into the deck. Compare your answers with the first sheet of paper.

Card 1:	YES	NO	Card 11:	YES	NO
Card 2:	YES	NO	Card 12:	YES	NO
Card 3:	YES	NO	Card 13:	YES	NO
Card 4:	YES	NO	Card 14:	YES	NO
Card 5:	YES	NO	Card 15:	YES	NO
Card 6:	YES	NO	Card 16:	YES	NO
Card 7:	YES	NO	Card 17:	YES	NO
Card 8:	YES	NO	Card 18:	YES	NO
Card 9:	YES	NO	Card 19:	YES	NO
Card 10:	YES	NO	Card 20:	YES	NO

Scoring: For each right answer, give yourself one point.

Total Score: _____

1–4: Poor Visual Memory
5–11: Fair Visual Memory
12–14: Good Visual Memory
15–20: Excellent Visual Memory

Test Three: **IMMEDIATE MEMORY**

You will need a stopwatch or other timing device to complete this test.

Look over these pictures carefully for the next 30 seconds. Turn the page and write down the names of the 20 animals you saw.

1. _____

2. _____

3. _____

4. _____

5. _____

6. _____

7. _____

8. _____

9. _____

10. _____

11. _____

12. _____

13. _____

14. _____

15. _____

16. _____

17. _____

18. _____

19. _____

20. _____

Scoring: For each right answer, give yourself one point.

Total Score: _____

1–4: Poor Immediate Memory
5–11: Fair Immediate Memory
12–14: Good Immediate Memory
15–20: Excellent Immediate Memory

Test Four: **WORKING MEMORY**

You will first read a sequence containing one letter and one number. Then you will cover the entry and write the sequence, putting the number first, before the letter. For example, H-5 would be 5-H, and 5-H would be 5-H. Eventually, you will see a sequence with more than one number. Continue to put the numbers first before the letters, but in lowest to highest order. For example, 2-G-4 would be 2-4-G. Finally, sequences with multiple letters need to be placed in alphabetical order after the numbers. For example, 2-F-1-A would be 1-2-A-F.

After two incorrect answers, please stop and grade your performance.

1. K-4 ___-___

2. T-3 ___-___ .

3. 8-P ___-___

4. G-T-1 ___-___

5. P-5-8 ___-___-___

6. W-9-B ___-___-___

7. Q-6-2-H ___-___-___-___

8. Z-5-1-J ___-___-___-___

9. 4-M-3-Y ___-___-___-___

10. 5-F-2-K-9 ___-___-___-___

11. V-8-D-1-P ___-___-___-___-___

12. 6-U-2-4-C ___-___-___-___-___

13. B-3-N-9-L-6 ___-___-___-___-___

14. J-5-X-2-T-8 ___-___-___-___-___

15. 5-S-8-Z-7-F ___-___-___-___-___

16. G-4-K-9-C-3-B ___-___-___-___-___-___

17. 4-L-2-H-9-A-I ___-___-___-___-___-___

18. 5-7-8-Q-E-G-Y ___-___-___-___-___-___

19. D-7-W-4-B-8-S-6 ___-___-___-___-___-___

20. 1-L-6-X-2-Y-C-8 ___-___-___-___-___-___-___

Scoring: For each right answer, give yourself one point.

1–4: Poor Working Memory
5–11: Fair Working Memory
12–14: Good Working Memory
15–20: Excellent Working Memory

Total Score: _____

Test Five: **ATTENTION**

I call this test the Written TOVA, because it identifies problems with attention just as successfully as the electronic TOVA test described earlier. For each question, rate your answer on a scale. Answer these questions as either true or false.

Omissions

1. I am distressed by the disorganized way my brain works.   T/F
2. I often fail to finish things I start.   T/F
3. I have difficulty sticking to an activity.   T/F
4. I have trouble going through established channels and following proper procedures.   T/F
5. I often avoid, dislike, or am reluctant to engage in tasks that require sustained mental effort (such as paperwork).   T/F
6. I tend to fall asleep or become tired while reading.   T/F
7. I have difficulty awaking (I need coffee or other activity before feeling fully awake).   T/F
8. I have trouble following a plan.   T/F
9. I start many projects but always seem to get sidetracked.   T/F
10. I have difficulty keeping track of what I do with my time.   T/F

Commissions

1. I am impulsive, either verbally or in action—as in impulsively changing plans, enacting new schemes, or altering career plans.   T/F
2. I have a short fuse and experience periods of extreme irritability.   T/F
3. I am an impulsive spender.   T/F
4. I have an internal feeling of anxiety or nervousness.   T/F
5. My irritability tends to build, then explode, then recede.   T/F
6. I have trouble falling asleep due to too many thoughts at night.   T/F

7. I am frequently restless with lots of nervous energy.　T/F
8. I find myself saying impulsive things that I later regret.　T/F
9. I get very upset by minor annoyances.　T/F
10. I have difficulty organizing my work.　T/F

Variability

1. I have a sense of underachievement, of not meeting my goals, regardless of how much I have actually accomplished.　T/F
2. I often juggle many projects simultaneously but don't follow through.　T/F
3. I find it difficult to read written material unless it is very interesting or very easy.　T/F
4. Especially in groups, I find it hard to stay focused on what is being said in conversation.　T/F
5. I move about excessively during sleep.　T/F
6. I often engage in thrill-seeking activities, including the potentially dangerous ones.　T/F
7. I am always "on the go."　T/F
8. I have inconsistent work performance.　T/F
9. I tend to put things off.　T/F
10. I have difficulty getting organized.　T/F

Reaction Time

1. Many things upset me.　T/F
2. I tend to misjudge the impact I have on others.　T/F
3. I have frequent feelings of demoralization or that things won't work out for me.　T/F
4. I feel tired and have little energy, which makes it difficult to concentrate.　T/F
5. I feel that things always go wrong no matter how hard I try.　T/F

(continued)

6. I don't enjoy the activities I used to.   T/F

7. I have lost interest in sex or am experiencing sexual
   difficulties.   T/F

8. It takes longer than before to make decisions.   T/F

9. I sometimes feel sad or blue.   T/F

10. I become easily upset.   T/F

Scoring:

Any section with more than 4 "true" responses indicates the earliest signs of declining attention in that particular domain. Any section with more than 6 "true" responses indicates a more significant loss.

Test Six: **EXECUTIVE FUNCTION TEST**

You will need a stopwatch or other timing device to complete this test. Test A consists of 25 circles numbered 1 to 25. Draw lines to connect the numbers in ascending order. In Test B, the circles include both numbers (1 to 13) and letters (A to L). Draw lines to connect the circles in an ascending pattern, but with the added task of alternating between the numbers and letters (i.e., 1-A-2-B-3-C, etc.).

In both tests, connect the circles as quickly as possible, without lifting your pen from the paper. Use a stopwatch to determine how quickly you can connect the "trail." If you make an error that you immediately recognize, don't worry; just continue to finish the trail.

TEST A

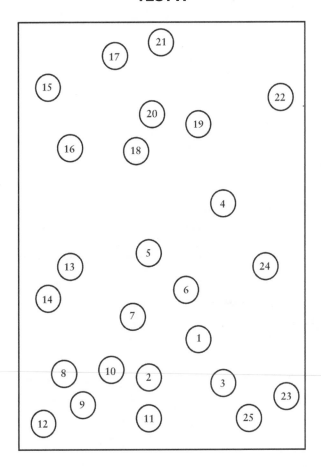

TEST B

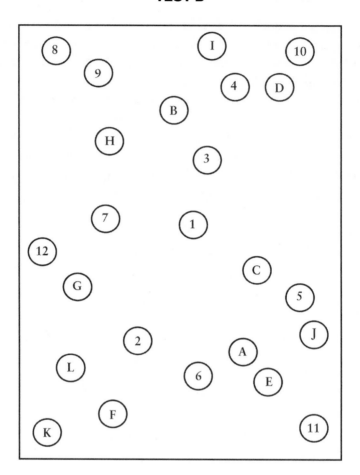

Record your time in seconds: Test A: _____

Test B: _____

Compare your score to the following table:

	AVERAGE ATTENTION SCORE	DEFICIENT ATTENTION SCORE
Trail A	29–77 seconds	>78 seconds or longer
Trail B	75–272 seconds	>271 seconds or longer

Test Seven: IQ/PARADIGM PATTERN RECOGNITION

The ability to recognize patterns and paradigms is the secret to continued and enhanced intelligence. In this test, the task is to point out the connection between words in two- and three-word sequences. For example, the answer to the word pair "computer-brain" could be "two entities that process information."

1. train-bicycle _____

2. watch-ruler _____

3. hand-foot _____

4. cry-smile _____

5. eat-sleep _____

6. blue-green _____

7. rabbit-cat _____

8. pen-pencil _____

9. DVD-video _____

10. grass-trees _____

11. orange-lemon _____

12. turkey-chicken _____

13. house-apartment-trailer _____

14. roses-lilacs-daisies _____

15. English-French-Japanese _____

16. cinnamon-basil-thyme _____

17. corn-broccoli-asparagus _____

18. bees-fireflies-cicadas _____

19. whales-cows-dogs _____

20. running-swimming-bicycling _____

(continued)

Scoring: Compare your answers to the key in Appendix A. Give yourself two points when the answer is correct and one point for a partially correct answer. When the answer is wrong, award zero points.

Total Score: _____

1–8: Poor paradigm skills
6–16: Fair paradigm skills
17–24: Average paradigm skills
25–32: Good paradigm skills
32–40: Excellent paradigm skills

Test Eight: LEFT BRAIN/RIGHT BRAIN TEST

Answer the following questions as truthfully as possible. For each question, circle either "A" or "B" for the answer that is most like you.

1. When I'm in a group of people:
   A) I am the one who enjoys having one-on-one conversation.
   B) I am the one who introduces others and is social with everyone.

2. When it comes to looking at a picture:
   A) I tend to look for details and facts.
   B) I tend to look at the overall creative picture.

3. Before I speak:
   A) I tend to think it through.
   B) I say the first thing that comes into my head.

4. When it comes to working with others, it is more important to be:
   A) Logical
   B) Empathetic

5. I tend to be:
   A) Objective
   B) Subjective

6. I enjoy being:
   A) Sequential and planned
   B) Random and unplanned

7. I tend to see things in:
   A) Parts
   B) Whole

8. When cooking a recipe:
   A) I follow the instructions.
   B) I tend to improvise.

9. Most of the time:
   A) I would prefer to do something on my own.
   B) I enjoy being with other people.

(continued)

10. I like to make most of my decisions based on:
    A) Thinking or logic
    B) Personal values or feelings

Scoring: If seven or more of your answers are As, then you're left-brained. If seven or more of your answers are Bs, then you are right-brained. If you answered with almost an equal number of A and B answers, then you use each side of your brain equally.

Test Nine: **DELAYED RECALL**

This test draws on the verbal memory (Test One), visual memory (Test Two), and immediate memory (Test Three) tests.

PART A

Story #1

1. What flavor ice cream did Stephanie order?

2. Was it in a cup?

Story #2

1. Where did Thomas Morgan take the puppies?

2. What did he do with them at the end of the day?

Story #3

1. Will the new store be having specials on salads?

2. What will their feature fruit be?

See Appendix A for correct answers.
Scoring: For each right answer, give yourself one point.

Part A Total Score: _____

PART B

Pick up the pile of 20 playing cards you used in Test Two. Turn each one over and circle "yes" if you have seen that card before, and "no" if you haven't. Compare your answers to the first sheet of paper.

Card 1:	YES	NO		Card 11:	YES	NO
Card 2:	YES	NO		Card 12:	YES	NO
Card 3:	YES	NO		Card 13:	YES	NO
Card 4:	YES	NO		Card 14:	YES	NO
Card 5:	YES	NO		Card 15:	YES	NO
Card 6:	YES	NO		Card 16:	YES	NO
Card 7:	YES	NO		Card 17:	YES	NO
Card 8:	YES	NO		Card 18:	YES	NO
Card 9:	YES	NO		Card 19:	YES	NO
Card 10:	YES	NO		Card 20:	YES	NO

Scoring: For each right answer, give yourself one point.

Part B Total Score: _____

PART C

Write down the names of the 20 animals you identified in Test Three.

1. _____   11. _____

2. _____   12. _____

3. _____   13. _____

4. _____   14. _____

5. _____   15. _____

6. _____   16. _____

7. _____   17. _____

8. _____   18. _____

9. _____   19. _____

10. _____   20. _____

Scoring: For each right answer, give yourself one point.

Part C Total Score: _____

Add together scores from Parts A, B, and C: _____

> 1–9: Poor Delayed Recall: Major deficiency
> 10–19: Fair Delayed Recall
> 20–29: Average Delayed Recall
> 30–39: Good Delayed Recall
> 40–46: Excellent Delayed Recall: No deficiency

UNDERSTANDING YOUR SCORE

Your scores determine your cognitive functioning. If most of them were in the "excellent" range, you are clearly in great shape. Your memory and attention are strong, as are your intelligence and executive functioning.

If most of your scores were in the "good" range, then you may be experiencing the most subtle form of pre-MCI. Scores on cognitive tests for individuals with pre-MCI and early-stage MCI are typically only 1 to 1.5 standard deviations below the mean, as compared with healthy individuals of the same age and education. However, don't use a high score as an excuse not to move forward. Small changes are the easiest to correct, which means that there is no better time to start balancing your brain than right now. Many of my patients are able to achieve a perfect score after following the Braverman Protocol for 30 to 60 days, and there is no reason why you should not reach the same results.

If the majority of your scores were in the "average," "fair," or "poor" ranges, then you need to get working on your cognition right away. The "average" range is a good indicator that you are experiencing MCI. The "fair" range shows that your symptoms might be more pronounced, putting you in a category called moderate (instead of mild) cognitive impairment. If your scores were in the "poor" range, you might be suffering from severe cognitive impairment.

Following the "steps of care" approach, try to increase your brain chemical production and stimulate neurogenesis first through the lifestyle, diet, and exercise components of the protocol. Give yourself at least 2 weeks to see results. If there is no change in your thinking, or your scores were in the "good" or "average" range, the next step would be to incorporate nutritional supplementation. Again, this may take a few weeks to see significant changes. The next step is natural hormone therapies, followed by medications. These two options are critical to incorporate right away if your scores were in the "fair" or "poor" range.

The left brain/right brain challenges are analyzed differently because they are personality/temperament questions. In Chapter 10, there are some easy exercises to help you bend your nature more toward a middle ground.

Now it's time to get to work. The following chapters outline every aspect of the Braverman Protocol. Once you start to balance your brain, you will begin to feel younger and smarter. A balanced brain that is working optimally will allow you to increase mental energy, better mood, better memory retention, better focus and attention, and even better sleep.

Chapter 8

Step Two:
Smart Lifestyle Changes

Every preventive medicine program begins by making small changes that can improve your life, and the Braverman Protocol is no exception. I tell my patients all the time that every positive change they choose to make is a step in the right direction, motivating them to take on more and stretch to reach their goals. I also know that it's impossible to change your brain if you are upset and anxious. So just as the first signs of mild cognitive impairment, or MCI, appear as personality changes, those will be the first that we will reverse.

This chapter introduces a handful of therapies that everyone can incorporate while following the program. They are all meant to get your mood back on track and lessen anxiety, so that you will be in the best mental state to incorporate the larger lifestyle suggestions for diet and exercise. The easiest ones to incorporate have been listed first, but don't disregard them because you've heard about them before. Sometimes small, easy-to-accommodate changes are all you'll need to get your brain back on track.

These therapies are also tailored to help you relax so that you can be less stressed and have a better night's sleep. Lack of sleep is one of the largest obstacles to restoring health, because it is one of the biggest lifestyle issues that affect both the brain and the body. Without at least

7 consecutive hours of sleep, you cannot properly rest and reset your brain for the next day. Instead, stress, anxiety, and depression build, which affects not only your mood but also your thinking.

You've probably heard of some of the many ways to help achieve better sleep, and all of these tips are valid. I recommend that you sleep in a completely dark room, and that you use your bedroom for sleep only, not as a home office or entertainment area. That means removing the television and the computer from the bedroom and making sure that you log off from all electronics—including the television—at least an hour before bedtime. Your last meal should take place at least 3 hours before you go to bed, and try not to snack after dinner. Stay well hydrated throughout the day, but limit nighttime beverages, especially caffeinated ones. Many of my patients also find that while a beer or a glass of wine makes them tired in the evening, it doesn't promote solid sleep throughout the night.

Luckily, an overstressed brain is reversible. These easy lifestyle changes yield dramatic results in improving your thinking, no matter what you scored on the Braverman Brain Advantage Test. By following any or each of these suggestions, you'll begin to take better control of your mood so that you can focus on the things that matter most: creating a balanced brain and a healthy body.

TREAT YOURSELF TO A MASSAGE

Massage therapy is no longer exclusive to the rich and famous: You can easily find good massage therapists working at local spas and gyms, medical clinics, hospitals, nail salons, and even airports. Massage can also be performed by several types of healthcare professionals, such as a physical therapist, occupational therapist, or chiropractor. Ask your doctor or someone else you trust for a recommendation. Most states regulate massage therapists through licensing, registration, or certification requirements. You can even learn how to do self-massage or engage in massage with a partner.

Massage is the general term for manipulating your skin, muscles, tendons, and ligaments by pressing and rubbing. Massage therapists use their hands, arms, and fingers in a range of movement from light stroking to deep pressure techniques to alleviate stress points in the body. A massage session may last from 15 to 90 minutes, during which you should feel calm and relaxed. Some studies have found massage helpful for relieving stress; controlling blood pressure; and managing anxiety and depression, pain, and stiffness, all of which affect your mood and personality.

There are many different types of massage, but the ones I find most effective for relieving stress are as follows:

Aromatherapy massage. This combines massage with one or more scented plant oils, or essential oils, to address specific needs. The therapist selects oils that are relaxing, energizing, stress reducing, or balancing, depending on your particular needs. One of the most common essential oils used in aromatherapy massage is lavender. Aromatherapy massage is particularly suited to stress-related conditions.

Deep-tissue massage. Slower, more forceful strokes are used to target the deeper layers of muscle and connective tissue.

Hot stone massage. Smooth stones that have been heated are placed on certain points on the body to warm and loosen tight muscles. This therapy is gaining in popularity among those who have muscle tension but prefer a lighter massage.

Sports massage. Similar to Swedish massage, but it is geared toward helping prevent or treat injuries for both serious athletes and regular folks.

Swedish massage. A gentle massage technique, this is the most popular. It uses long strokes, kneading, deep circular movements, vibration, and tapping to help you relax and reenergize.

Trigger point massage. This massage focuses on sensitive areas of tight muscle fibers that form after injuries or overuse.

Some forms of massage can leave you feeling sore the next day, but the actual massage shouldn't be painful or uncomfortable. If any part of your massage doesn't feel right or is painful, speak up right away. And before a massage therapy session starts, a good massage therapist will ask you about any symptoms and your medical history. Then they should perform an evaluation through touch to locate painful or tense areas and to determine how much pressure to apply.

PRACTICE QUIET MEDITATION

Meditation, chanting, and prayer have calming effects, which allow the brain to slow down, rebalance, and resynchronize so that you can think more clearly. However, the belief in an afterlife, reincarnation, or a

Aromatherapy Is Another Option

Calming and comforting, aromatherapy involves the delivery of a scent either by inhalation or through skin application via massage. Certain odors can lift our spirits like a natural antidepressant. Studies show that lavender and eucalyptus can calm the senses. I've found that both hand lotions and aromatic oils that are based on some of the acetylcholine-producing herbs such as peppermint and lemon balm make me feel both relaxed and alert, which is good for creating a younger brain. I also find that when my patients don't want to take pills, a cream form of the same nutrient can be just as effective when it is used like a massage cream before bed.

Supreme Being isn't a prerequisite for reaping the rewards of spiritual practice. Two of the best techniques I've used with my patients were developed independently by a doctor and a pharmacist.

One meditative technique that I particularly like is called the relaxation response. It was pioneered by Harvard physician Dr. Herbert Benson in the 1970s. Designed to elicit the opposite reaction from the fight-or-flight response of an adrenaline rush, the relaxation response can produce a state of deep relaxation in which our breathing, pulse rate, blood pressure, and metabolism are decreased. Training our bodies on a daily basis to achieve this state of relaxation can lead to enhanced mood and reduced stress.

The relaxation response technique consists of the silent repetition of a word, sound, or phrase while sitting upright with eyes closed for 10 to 20 minutes. This should be done in a quiet place free of distractions. I recommend practicing for 20 minutes before you go to sleep (be sure that this is at least 2 hours after you have eaten your last meal, to allow your body to fully digest your food).

Dr. Benson prefers sitting to lying down in order to avoid falling asleep, but I tell many of my insomnia patients to do this lying down as a way to achieve deeper sleep. Whatever you choose, the first step is to consciously relax each of your muscles starting with your feet and progressing up to your face. Then inhale through your nose and exhale through your mouth for 10 breaths before you begin your chant.

You can choose to focus on any word or phrase you like. You can use a sound such as "om," a word such as "one" or "peace," or a word with special meaning to you. Choose a word from your religious background or one that instantly brings a peacefulness to your mind. Repeat the word or phrase slowly and clearly, either out loud or in your head. Try to breathe deeply after each repetition of the word. Intruding worries or thoughts should be ignored or dismissed to the best of your ability by focusing on the repetition. It's okay to open your eyes to look at a clock while you are practicing, but do not set an alarm. When you have finished, remain seated, first with your eyes closed and then with your eyes open, and gradually allow yourself to reenter the everydayness of your world. While the relaxation response requires some practice, I have found that anyone can learn it and benefit from it.

A second popular meditation technique is visualization. French pharmacist Émile Coué first popularized the belief that the mind is capable of creating a state of relaxation in which positive thinking can help reduce physical and mental symptoms.

Visualization requires you to connect with your imagination in a quiet place where you can be alone. It can be as simple as daydreaming, remembering past memories, or self-talk. Lie down or sit comfortably in a quiet space with your eyes closed. Then consciously relax each of your muscles, starting with your feet and progressing up to your face. Then inhale through your nose and exhale through your mouth for 10 breaths before you begin.

Use as many senses as possible to imagine a peaceful scene, such as walking through a forest. In your mind, listen for birds, feel a cool breeze, smell the pine needles, and feel the ground beneath your feet. Once you can conjure this space, add details. Explore your way around so that every time you return, you have something new to look forward to visualizing. After a few sessions, change the location to a beach, a romantic city, a favorite vacation spot, or anywhere that elicits happy memories.

IMPROVING MOOD AND MEMORY WITH MUSIC

On some level, we all have experienced the power of music. If you've attended a rock concert or a classical performance, or even spent hours

Make New Connections

Nurturing your spiritual side through prayer, meditation, conversation, or even communing with nature is an effective way to deepen your worldview and become smarter. Spirituality forces you to look outside your own existence and open your mind to "the big picture" as you ponder your place in the universe. You don't have to be a deeply religious person to obtain the benefits. Just thinking outside the box for a few minutes every day lets your brain relax so that you can open up to a world full of possibilities.

Like spirituality, nurturing relationships allows your brain to relax. Relationships fraught with stress and antagonism eventually wear down your brain chemistry. On the other hand, a pattern of healthy, rewarding relationships—with associates, friends, or loved ones—can have lifelong advantages. Surround yourself with people who love and appreciate you and make you feel good about yourself. Develop honest relationships in which you can ask for exactly what you want, without hiding behind formalities or insecurities. And stretch yourself to make friends with people who are not "just like you." A balanced brain needs to make room for new ideas that come from other cultural and philosophical norms.

listening to the radio, you may have noticed a change in your behavior or mood based on the music you've heard. Music can motivate us to exercise, or wind us down from a particularly stressful day. Now, researchers are finding that listening to music actually makes long-term changes to the brain and may stimulate neurogenesis. One study published in the *New England Journal of Medicine* found that among leisure activities, playing musical instruments and dancing were among the best for reducing the risk of dementia.

The songs or melodies that we have running through our heads make the memories associated with them more vibrant. That's because listening to and understanding music stimulates both sides of the brain and synchronizes the left and right hemispheres. Memory and emotion go hand in hand, and songs can trigger an emotional response.

There is healthy debate as to whether music actually makes us smarter. Researchers recently tested the benefits of music on dementia patients by asking them questions about themselves that would force them to concentrate deeply. At the same time, they played different background noises ranging from silence to cafeteria clatter, familiar music, and novel music. The scientists found that music playing in the background significantly improved the patients' recall ability. Music can also enhance memory consolidation during sleep. Studies have shown that listening to specific sounds during sleep may help you remember during the daytime. Another recent study showed that a 6-week intensive music therapy program improved thinking skills, increasing the production of both acetylcholine and serotonin. Studies on the "Mozart effect" showed increased understanding of spatial relationships when participants were exposed to classical music before performing their tasks. However, most research is now indicating that it's not the specific type of music, nor the act of listening to music, that makes us smarter. Instead, it's the change that music brings about in our personality that allows us to cognitively grow. According to Dr. Glenn Schellenberg, while music listening does lead to enhanced performance on a variety of cognitive tests, such effects are short term and stem from the impact of music on arousal level and mood, which, in turn, affect cognitive performance.

The latest research demonstrates what many of us have always known: People who are deeply connected to their favorite music are less agitated and maintain a better mood. And as we've learned, we can remember more and concentrate better when we maintain a positive disposition. Listening to familiar songs and singing them are similarly effective in enhancing creativity—so it doesn't matter whether you are listening to the best performer in the world or singing in your own shower.

You can create your own music therapy program for retraining your brain to lessen your stress and improve your mood. It's as easy as creating a playlist. All you'll need is a computer or MP3 player (like an iPod). Your goal is to put together 30 minutes of music that you are familiar with and that is upbeat. The prescription: Listen to this soundtrack to improve your mood whenever you are feeling blue or anxious.

TECHNOLOGY STIMULATES THE BRAIN

The environment, meaning the expectations of our culture, can increase your neuronal output. For example, from what I've been seeing, I'm convinced that learning how to use electronic devices such as smartphones and computers is increasing our intelligence. I notice this every day just by walking down the street: There are plenty of men and women with average or lower-than-average IQs who know exactly how to work a BlackBerry.

Studies have also shown that mastering video games increases our attention by providing a distraction-free environment for prolonged periods of time. While I'm not in favor of some of the violent or sexual content in some of these video games, you can pick and choose the ones that are good at increasing both attention and memory skills while not offending your morals. Some of my favorite resources for brain-enhancing games are:

- **Lumosity.** Lumos Labs has used cutting-edge science to create a set of Web-based software tools that empower people to exercise their brains and achieve maximum performance. The assessments, games, and training courses on the Lumosity Web site (www.lumosity .com) are based on real science and are presented in an appealing, engaging form that makes it fun to exercise the brain.

- **Posit Science.** This Web site offers a vast array of software that has been scientifically proven to sharpen focus and improve memory.

- **Brain Age and Big Brain.** These games for the Nintendo DS and Wii systems are fast and fun. Inspired by the work of Japanese neuroscientist Dr. Ryuta Kawashima, the games feature activities designed to help stimulate your brain with solving math problems, counting currency, drawing pictures, and unscrambling letters.

- **Merriam-Webster.** This Web site (www.merriam-webster.com) has a fantastic app for your smartphone or tablet computer. These dictionary folks will deliver a new word to you every day, along with a quiz to test your memory of previously learned words. It's a great way to expand your vocabulary and train your brain to learn something new at the same time.

ON CELL PHONES, TEXTING IS BETTER THAN TALKING

Cell phone use is distracting and oftentimes stressful, and it might also be dangerous to your brain cells. A 2011 study published in the *Journal of the American Medical Association* indicated that cell phone use could alter brain activity due to the emission of electromagnetic radiation. Today's cell phones and smartphones emit more radiation than ever before as they transmit complex data. While the report said it was unclear whether the increase in glucose metabolism after using the phone for less than an hour had any negative health or behavioral effects, my colleague Dr. Nora Volkow, who headed the study for the National Institutes of Health, recommends that we keep cell phones at a distance by putting them on speaker mode or using a wired headset whenever possible. The next-best option is a wireless Bluetooth headset or earpiece, which emits radiation but at a far lower level. Just holding your phone slightly away from your ear can make a big difference; the intensity of radiation diminishes sharply with distance. That's why I think texting is better than talking on a phone, because you have to hold the phone completely away from your brain.

Cell phones emit the most radiation when they initially establish contact with the cell towers. To reduce exposure, wait a few seconds until after your call has been connected to put your phone next to your ear. Then tilt the phone away from your ear when you are talking and bring it in close to your ear only when you are listening. This works because the emission of radiation is "significantly less when a cell phone is receiving signals than when it is transmitting," said Lin Zhong, assistant professor of electrical and computer engineering at Rice University in Houston.

Your cell phone also emits less radiation when you are standing still. When you are moving, your signal moves with you from tower to tower and must generate little bursts of radiation to make each digital connection. And any situation where your cell phone has a weak signal indicates that it has to work harder and will emit more radiation. Fewer bars means more radiation, so bad calling locations are inside buildings and elevators and in rural areas.

MANAGE STRESS WITH A HEART RATE MONITOR

Using a heart rate monitor that you can buy from a local pharmacy or sporting equipment store can help you visually see what stress is doing to your body. A normal resting heart rate is 60 to 80 beats per minute. Wearing a monitor throughout the day—especially when you aren't exercising—will alert you to an increase in your heart rate, which means that you are stressed. As soon as you see the increase, you can start making changes to lower your stress earlier in the cycle.

Heart rate monitors are worn like watches. They have a transmitter that you attach to your skin, which then continually sends signals back to the monitor. Some monitors allow you to store readings and use the data to track changes over time. This is helpful in seeing how efforts to reduce stress are working.

TREATING MOOD AND MEMORY WITH CRANIAL ELECTRICAL STIMULATION

Cranial electrical stimulation, or CES, is a therapeutic tool that uses mild electrical pulses generated from a battery-powered stimulator that is roughly the size of a cell phone. It has been successfully used and FDA approved for the treatment of anxiety, depression, addiction, insomnia, and cognitive dysfunction. There have been more than 100 completed studies that highlight this therapy's effectiveness and ease of use.

CES was originally developed in the 1940s by Soviet scientists who were researching sleep disorders. However, its treatment of insomnia was soon overshadowed by its successful application for treating depression and anxiety. It works by altering the abnormal electrical connections and normalizing dysfunctional brain patterns that are caused by environmental toxins, electromagnetic frequency (such as too much cell phone exposure), or brain chemistry imbalances. It helps balance brain waves by increasing the uptake of amino acids and their conversion to brain chemicals. CES has been shown to raise the level of conversion of amino acids into dopamine. It promotes the conversion of choline to produce acetylcholine and can improve GABA and serotonin levels by making the user feel less overwhelmed and improving mood. CES therapy also stimulates neurogenesis by helping the brain replenish damaged brain cells with fresh ones.

The CES device might be best known for improving sleep without the side effects of tranquilizers or other sleep medications. In the first 2 to 3 days, you can experience a normalization of sleep patterns and fall asleep faster upon going to bed. What's more, you will feel rested upon waking in the morning, and wake up during the night for fewer and shorter periods. Many users also report that they experience the most vivid, most colorful dreams immediately after use. I attribute this to the fact that for many, they are first experiencing the deep REM sleep that had eluded them prior to treatment.

CES can be an important component during addiction withdrawal programs. It has been successfully used by abusers of marijuana, cocaine, alcohol, heroin, and nicotine, but I believe that it can be used to treat any type of addiction, including behavioral addictions. Studies suggest that when CES is used to reduce anxiety, cognition also tends to improve. As we discussed earlier, when anxiety diminishes and sleep is enhanced, you will regain your mental quickness and attention.

Obtaining a CES device requires a prescription from a physician. I have been prescribing the CES device to my patients for many years and have seen hundreds of positive responses. The CES device is particularly effective for men who are prone to tension or who have had issues with substance abuse. Positive results may be experienced immediately, though for some it can take up to 3 to 4 weeks.

CES Therapy
Stimulates Neurogenesis

- Accelerated learning
- Diminished mental confusion
- Heightened ability to focus
- Heightened clarity and alertness
- Improved information recall
- Increased mental energy

- Improved task concentration
- Reduced anxiety
- Reduced depression
- Reduced insomnia
- Reduced withdrawal symptoms

Patient Profile: Toxins Were Affecting Naomi's Thinking

In March 2010, I was introduced to Naomi, who came to see me when she turned 40. Her main concern was her anxiety. She just wasn't happy with where she was in her life on the whole. Her weight had been an issue since she was young, but now she felt more out of control than ever. Although she was overweight, she didn't complain of any other physical symptoms except recurring indigestion. Her bigger issues were that she was having frequent migraine headaches and experiencing brain fog. We decided to do a full workup to see what was going on with her brain health.

One part of my early testing protocol is to run blood work for various toxins. In Naomi's case, that blood work provided a major clue to her brain health problems: Naomi's body was full of many of the typical toxins I find in people who live or work in and around New York City, including arsenic, lead, and aluminum. What surprised me even more was that she had very high levels of wood residue in her blood.

I asked Naomi if she burned fires in her home frequently, or if she spent a lot of time on a wood deck. She told me that she supplements her home heating system with a wood-burning fireplace in the winter,

A typical prescription for CES is to wear the unit for 45 minutes every evening while relaxing, reading, or watching TV for a period of 3 weeks, or until maximum improvement has occurred. Many times my patients report that they did not need to follow the therapy for the full 3 weeks. The stimulation is applied using tiny clips attached to the ears. The experience feels like a gentle tingling sensation. Its most immediate impact is the reduction of anxiety—initially, just during the treatment, and with repetitive use, lasting hours or as long as several days after the treatment. Immediately afterward, you will feel both alert and relaxed. My patients have reported that they feel that their bodies are lighter and more relaxed and their minds more alert and clear. The results are cumulative and lasting.

which she and her family frequently enjoy sitting by. I told Naomi that this combination of toxins was probably one major cause of her constant weight battle, so we began a chelation program to rid her of them. I also started her on a dairy-free diet and prescribed several supplements that would aid the chelation.

By the summer, Naomi came back to my office after several chelation sessions. Now that the winter was over, she was using her wood-burning fireplace less, and all her toxin levels were down. She told me that she'd stopped cooking with aluminum foil and disposable roasting pans. She'd also started eating more leafy greens, which are filled with chlorophyll, a very efficient detoxifier. Naomi also told me that her thinking was much clearer and that her anxiety levels had dropped significantly. She shared that her life felt more orderly. She was also beginning to lose weight for the first time in her life.

A year later, Naomi was happy to report that she had lost a total of 35 pounds and had been able to keep it off. Better still, without dairy in her diet, her thinking improved. She had very few migraines, and her digestion improved. She also told me that the minute she made a mistake and ate something with dairy, her body instantly responded with an unsettling feeling. But when she went back to her regimen, she felt and thought much better.

The Positive Responses to CES

I get thank-you calls all the time from my patients who absolutely love CES therapy and find it to be life changing. Mostly, they are excited because they no longer need to rely on antidepressants, anxiety medications, or sleep aids. With the CES device, I'm often able to reduce the dosages of these medications, or get my patients off over-the-counter sleep remedies like diphenhydramine, which is the active ingredient in Benadryl, Nytol, and Unisom. Many of my patients find that they no longer need nutrients such as melatonin and tryptophan to fall asleep. Patients who previously relied on alcohol or marijuana to relax tell me that they feel better using their CES devices instead, especially because those addictive behaviors are so destructive. Others use the device whenever they have a panic attack or high anxiety.

After 2 to 3 weeks of use, many of my patients tell me that their mental confusion has diminished and that they have a heightened clarity and alertness, with improvements in task concentration. Many tell me that they have been about to regain their previous information recall, and some tell me that their recall is now better than it ever was before. They also report an increase in mental energy and are able to learn new tasks and information faster than before. In all, they feel younger and smarter.

TALK TO YOUR DOCTOR
ABOUT CHELATION CLEANSING

We are surrounded by filth in our overpolluted world. Every day we put our lives at risk just by inhaling harmful heavy metals such as lead and mercury that are found in the air we breathe. And the fish that is so healthy for our diet is filled with mercury. These toxic metals not only harm the body but also affect its powerhouse: the brain. Yet there is no number of showers that can remove these metals. The only way to rid us of these chemicals is through an internal cleansing. Yet cleansing in the 21st century has to take on a new level. I believe that chelation is the best way to completely rid the body of environmental toxins.

Chelation therapy is an IV medical treatment that improves metabolic and circulatory function by removing toxic metals and abnormally located nutritional metallic ions. It works by literally flushing out the toxins in our bodies, fully cleansing out the harmful chemicals that are affecting our thinking. Chelation therapy includes a series of measurements and calculations, and administration of chelating agents. A 3-hour chelation is performed, during which time the necessary supplements and chelating agents are administered through an IV bag while you sit back comfortably in a lounge chair, free to chat, read, nap, or watch television. In as little as 10 treatments, you can rid your body of the harmful toxins that may be affecting your thinking.

A chelation challenge is a central part of becoming younger and smarter. If you can't find a doctor who can do this for you, there are certain nutrients that you can take that will chelate you naturally. These include zinc, selenium, and l-acetylcysteine nutrient supplements. They will help to rid your body of mercury, aluminum, cadmium, and lead.

These techniques are important first steps to balancing your brain. The next chapter will teach you how making several small but lasting changes to your diet can transform your thinking without making you feel hungry, or adding to your anxiety. You'll actually learn that you need to eat more as you get older to feed your brain exactly what it needs for maximum functioning.

Chapter 9

Step Three: Diet and Nutrition for a Younger, Smarter You

A healthy brain contains a large amount of body fat, which is necessary for you to achieve optimal mental alertness. Fat insulates nerve fibers and facilitates transmission of chemical signals between brain cells. When you gain weight, you add body fat everywhere, including your brain. But being overweight is not the right way to speed thinking. Excess fat in the brain makes it work harder, which can damage cell membranes and eventually slow down your thinking.

In order to be younger and smarter, you need to be thinner as well. Being overweight puts you at greater risk of having decreased cognitive abilities and suffering steeper cognitive decline later in life. My PATH Foundation is currently working on a study that links dementia and obesity to similar hormonal imbalances, while scientists at the University of Pittsburgh have already found that obese people have smaller brains than their age-matched, normal-weight peers. Other recent studies show that obesity is associated with accelerated brain atrophy. In a study from the University of Turku in Finland, researchers found that white matter volumes in the brain were decreased in obese subjects. However, this white matter loss was partially reversed once the participants lost weight. While gray matter comprises the collection of neurons where mental computation takes place and memories are stored, underneath is a bedrock of white matter that fills nearly half of the brain. White matter is composed of millions of myelin-coated axons that connect neurons in one region of the brain with those in other regions. Although gray matter does the brain's thinking and calculating, white matter controls the signals that neurons share, coordinating how well brain regions work together.

If you are overweight, losing those extra pounds will help you look younger and feel smarter. One way you can determine whether you need to lose weight is by identifying your leptin levels. Leptin, whose name is derived from the Greek word *leptos,* meaning "thin," is a hormone secreted by the body's fat cells. Its receptor is found in the hypothalamus, the part of the brain that controls hunger and body weight. The recent discovery of this hormone has led doctors to have a better understanding of how fat cells are formed and how we respond to hunger. These cells are no longer viewed as a part of tissue that merely stores excess calories. Instead, we now know that they are dynamic cells that work with the endocrine system to produce hormones that regulate appetite and metabolism.

Each fat cell has an internal sensor that demands food. As more fat enters the fat cell, that cell secretes leptin in response, which signals the brain that you've achieved satiety: the feeling you get when you've eaten enough. The more leptin present, the stronger the signal to the brain, and the less hungry you feel. However, if there is a leptin overload, which often occurs when you are overweight, or if the signal doesn't get received, your brain won't transmit the message to stop eating, so you will continue to eat past the point of satiety, which leads to the accumulation of body fat, and subsequently more fat cells whose food requirements need to be met.

As you age, your body can become resistant to the leptin message, much like a person with type 2 diabetes has become resistant to insulin. This happens because the heavier you get, the more resistant you become to the leptin you produce, resulting in a weaker signal to the brain. A low leptin signal sets off a cascade of brain chemical reactions, particularly in relation to metabolism. For example, when leptin is released, dopamine production also increases, and you'll be able to burn off the foods you eat instead of storing them as fat cells. However, without the leptin message, metabolism falls as well.

Your leptin level, which can be determined by a simple blood test, can be used to manage obesity as well as brain health in much the same way that cholesterol is managed for avoiding heart disease. High leptin levels are correlated with obesity, while moderate to low levels are associated with better fitness. However, extremely low leptin levels may be associated with other hormonal loss. For example, increased levels of the hormone cortisol also lead to increased leptin resistance, which contributes to even more weight gain. Cortisol is linked to stress, and high levels can cause increased belly fat, general inflammation, restlessness, and an increase in appetite. Low leptin levels also lead to lower levels of estrogen and progesterone, which signal menopause, and for men, testosterone, which signal male menopause. Because of this hormonal connection, low leptin is also associated with dementia.

My research team has found a correlation between low levels of leptin and dementia because of its relationship with the hypothalamus. This is the same area of the brain that's integral for maintaining your cognitive abilities. When the hypothalamus misses the leptin signal, the receptors it stores subsequently die off, and at the same time dementia begins. In one of my more recent studies, we used PET scans to determine the metabolic rate of the brain under different leptin levels. We found that in the temporal region, lower leptin signals correlated again with low dopamine, meaning lower brain processing speed and lower voltage.

A weak leptin signal can alter your ability to learn new tasks and retain and recall memories, and can affect attention. Lower circulating leptin is correlated with the development of cognitive impairment, while higher circulated leptin is correlated with reduced incidence of dementia. Leptin also reduces the amount of amyloid B, which is responsible for the plaques in Alzheimer's disease.

Therefore, it would be beneficial to maintain high leptin levels so that you can stay thin and feel fuller as you enhance your brain chemistry. This is one of the many reasons why I do not promote a calorie-restricted diet. As you get older, you need to eat more food, not less, to produce leptin. However, you want to be careful to choose the right foods—those that will be fully digested and can increase your metabolism—so that you do not increase your total number of fat cells.

Nutrients That Positively Affect Leptin

- Acetyl-L-carnitine
- Carnitine (easily found as a powder)
- Conjugated linoleic acid
- Integra-Lean irvingia
- Melatonin
- Omega-3 fatty acids
- Resveratrol
- Vitamin D

Another way to manage your leptin is to decrease stress by following the lifestyle suggestions in Chapter 8 and to increase physical activity as we'll discuss in Chapter 10. For example, consistently getting 7 hours of sleep is one of the best ways to de-stress the brain, increase serotonin, and make sure your hypothalamus can continue to receive the leptin message.

DIET FOR A YOUNGER, SMARTER YOU

Losing weight is hard enough, so when you are successful, you don't want the pounds to come rolling back. That's why it's important to lose weight the right way. I advocate a slow and steady approach to weight loss that maximizes your chances of keeping the weight you lost off for good. When you reduce your caloric intake too much or too quickly, your body will not respond with weight loss for the long term. If you cut down your intake by more than 15 percent from what you are currently eating, your body begins to think that it is starving, and instead of shedding body fat, it holds on to it for later use. Worse, very low-calorie meals decrease brain speed and voltage, affecting memory and concentration even more.

The key is to choose the right foods that will counteract your brain chemical deficiencies while keeping you feeling full and satisfied. My earlier book, *The Younger (Thinner) You Diet,* uses nutrient-rich foods in combination with other tools in order to achieve lasting weight loss. This same diet is perfect for upgrading your thinking, as well as preventing or reversing mild cognitive impairment (MCI). The diet I've devised is high in proteins that create dopamine, which controls both metabolism and brain power; the same foods that will speed your metabolism will reignite your ability to stay focused throughout the day. Acetylcholine-producing foods will increase brain speed as well as improve thinking so that you can make better decisions about the foods you eat. GABA foods improve memory and recall and keep you calm so that you won't fall into the trap of emotional eating. Lastly, serotonin foods allow your brain to reboot so that you can get a good night's rest and think better in the morning.

This diet will also give you the best chance to maintain proper leptin levels without gaining excess weight. The following foods should be incorporated into your meal plan every day because they stimulate leptin production. But if you were going to choose only one, go for broccoli: Not only does it contain leptin enhancers, it's high in fiber. Whether you steam the broccoli in the microwave, roast it, or serve it raw, eat as much as you can.

- Apples
- Berries
- Broccoli
- Carrots
- Coconut oil
- Cruciferous vegetables
- Eggs
- Flaxseed oil
- Leafy greens
- Lean meats
- Low-fat yogurt
- Olive oil
- Oranges
- Pears
- Plums
- Poultry
- Salmon and other fatty fish
- Spinach
- Unsalted almonds

The diet allows you to choose from a wide variety of fresh foods, herbs, spices, and teas that will help you lose weight and keep those pounds from coming back. They are also made from the amino acids, vitamins, and minerals your brain needs for optimal thinking.

These foods have been specially chosen to create long-lasting satiety so you won't feel hungry. Eating foods that are nutrient dense, rather than calorie dense, is the key to maintaining weight loss. You want every square inch of your food to be packed with nutrients, not calories. Low-volume, high-calorie foods can delay the brain's and stomach's activation of the feeling of fullness, so you eat more of these poor food choices. Eating nutrient-dense foods is a much better way of dieting than traditional calorie restriction, which causes decreased mental output.

Many people complain that changes achieved through diet and nutrition are very slow to come. But over the course of your life, I can guarantee that they will have the longest, biggest impact on making you smarter. The key is to find foods that you love that fit the parameters for better brain health. Hopefully, these suggestions will make those choices easier for you to determine.

FOODS THAT IMPROVE YOUR MOOD

We all know that "white" foods—such as breads, pastas, rice, pastries, and potatoes—are not good for us because they are simple carbohydrates that immediately convert to sugars, then to body fat if eaten in excess. Complex carbohydrates are better choices because they take longer to digest. But, more important, they supply the body and brain with glutamine, the amino acid that is the precursor to GABA. This allows the body's natural processes to function and keeps your mood stable so that you can think clearly.

Complex carbohydrates include fruits and vegetables as well as whole grains such as millet, brown rice, barley, corn, oats, quinoa, and buckwheat. These foods are absorbed slowly by the body, thus keeping glucose and insulin low and providing long-lasting energy. They provide the unique ability to prevent the steep declines in blood sugar levels that give rise to fatigue, mood swings, and food cravings.

You'll also want to choose foods that are high in inositol. This is a vitamin in the B-complex family, which is also related to GABA. People suffering from MCI often do not have enough of the B vitamins in their diets. Concentrate on the Bs—bananas, broccoli, and brown rice—because they are all packed with inositol.

Foods that are high in both glutamine and inositol are the best choices:

- Bananas
- Beef liver and other organ meats
- Broccoli
- Brown rice
- Citrus fruits
- Halibut
- Lentils
- Spinach
- Tree nuts
- Whole grain products

CHOOSE THESE FOODS WHEN YOU'RE FEELING BLUE

Another category of foods that boost brain power are those that have high concentrations of omega-3 fatty acids, such as walnuts or salmon. One Finnish study found that people who frequently eat these foods are 31 percent less likely to suffer from depression. Oily fish, such as salmon, is a direct source of omega-3 fatty acids, shown to be essential for cognitive development and enhancing brain functioning. Fish consumption has long been associated with lowering the risk of dementia. Recent studies have suggested that consumption of one omega-3 fatty acid in particular, docosahexaenoic acid (DHA), is important for memory performance. Besides salmon, other fish that can improve your mood are trout, herring, sardines, and mackerel.

Aside from fish, other good choices for boosting mood are foods packed with the nutrient biotin, including egg yolks, soybeans, and whole grains; or foods high in purine, such as calf's liver and mushrooms. High-purine foods should be avoided if you have gout. For a mood-boosting snack, go for a handful of nuts. Brazil nuts are a good source of the mineral selenium, which helps prevent depression.

Tryptophan is an amino acid that stimulates the production of serotonin but cannot make it on its own. Tryptophan is so effective in creating more serotonin that you might see instant results after eating foods that contain lots of it. For example, if you feel sad, eating foods rich in tryptophan can quickly improve your mood.

If you are depressed or having trouble sleeping, you need to have at least 2 grams of tryptophan every day. Choose from these foods:

FOOD	AMOUNT OF TRYPTOPHAN (GRAMS PER 6- TO 8-OUNCE SERVING)
Avocado	0.40
Chicken	0.28
Chocolate	0.11
Cottage cheese	0.40
Duck	0.40
Egg	0.40
Pork	1.0
Turkey	37.0
Wheat germ	40.0

FEED YOURSELF FOR BETTER MEMORY

The most effective way to boost your brain speed is to start by changing your diet to include foods that create more acetylcholine. When your brain speed slows down, you may crave foods high in fat because fat is a main source of choline, a building block of this brain chemical.

Choline is the key building block needed for creating myelin. Essentially, choline is a good fat that protects the body from the dangerous electricity that courses through it every day. Every single wire in the human body is insulated with choline derivatives. In order for your brain speed to remain high, there needs to be enough insulation around the neurons so that information to and from the brain does not get lost. Without choline, you would literally burn up. Choline is so important to brain function that food manufacturers are now adding it to a wide variety of products. The US government has established a 55-milligram-per-portion requirement—which is just 10 percent of the recommended daily allowance—for manufacturers to claim that their food is "a good source of choline."

However, poor choices of choline are foods high in bad types of fat as listed in the next section, which will literally clog your brain and circumvent its natural mechanism for the production of acetylcholine. When the brain can't produce acetylcholine on its own, and the fats you are feeding it aren't helping, the brain will further deplete its stores, creating an even larger deficiency.

Healthy, high-choline foods also have plenty of B vitamins. Experts agree that an adequate amount of choline per day would be 425 milligrams for women and 550 milligrams for men. Healthy foods naturally high in choline include these choices:

FOOD	AMOUNT OF CHOLINE (MILLIGRAMS PER 6- TO 8-OUNCE SERVING)
Almonds	100
Beef	170
Broccoli	80
Broccoli rabe	60
Cabbage	80
Egg (including the yolk)	500
Fish	160
Hazelnuts	90
Liver, beef	840
Liver, chicken	600
Peanuts and peanut butter	130
Tofu	160
Wheat germ	300

Choosing Healthy Fats

Choosing the best sources of choline means being picky about the types of fats you eat. Diets that are high in saturated fat and cholesterol are significantly linked to an increased risk of dementia, while diets high in healthier fat choices, such as omega-3 fatty acids and olive oil, are linked to a significantly reduced risk of dementia. Yet a small amount of saturated fat is not unhealthy as long as it is combined with the other types of fats. I tell my patients to choose low-fat (1 percent or 2 percent) milk instead of fat-free and to choose low-fat yogurt instead of fat-free.

Fish Oil Supplements
Keep Your Brain Flexible

Fish oil supplementation has long been known to be beneficial for the entire body. Now we know that it is also good for the brain. Docosahexaenoic acid (DHA), found in fish oils, is necessary for preserving flexible cell membranes, especially for the brain and the eyes. This is thought to help maintain cognition throughout life. Fish oil also appears to have mood-stabilizing properties. You'll need to take at least 1,000 to 4,000 milligrams a day to get the amount of DHA you'll need to improve mood and memory.

Monounsaturated fatty acids are liquid or soft at room temperature and are the best fats to choose from. They are found in foods such as olive oil, avocado, nuts, seeds, and egg yolks. Polyunsaturated fatty acids are slightly more complicated. They are also a good source of fat and are found in many plant and animal foods. There are two types of polyunsaturated fats, the omega-3s and the omega-6s. Omega-3 fats play a pivotal role in maintaining good health: They have the ability to increase bloodflow so that fats are more easily delivered to the sites of metabolism, where they then stimulate metabolism. They are also thought to combat depression and improve cognition.

Omega-3 and omega-6 fats are called "essential" because the human body is not capable of manufacturing them, so we need to get them from food. Unfortunately, omega-3 fats are found naturally in only a few plants, such as flax; a few fish, such as salmon and shrimp; and specially raised eggs. Fish oil is rich in two omega-3 polyunsaturated fatty acids called eicosapentaenoic acid (EPA) and docosahexaenoic acid (DHA) and is the best source of omega-3 essential fatty acids.

The omega-6 polyunsaturated fatty acids are found in highest quantities in vegetable oils like corn, soybean, and safflower oil. The omega-6s are also the polyunsaturated fat found in land-based animals such as chicken, beef, and pork. Because omega-6s are found in so many of the foods we normally eat, we usually get enough of these fats to meet

Lecithin Builds Memory

You also need to ensure that you have enough lecithin, a nutrient that can synthesize choline. When your diet is healthy and balanced, your liver produces enough lecithin on its own. But if your brain is unbalanced, it's a sign in and of itself that your diet is less than optimal. Only a limited number of foods contain sufficient amounts of lecithin, so work these into your diet at least once a week:

- Cauliflower
- Egg yolks
- Liver
- Milk
- Peanuts
- Soybeans
- Wheat germ

our dietary needs. Getting more omega-3 fats through food and possibly supplements requires more effort, because they are not abundantly found in many food sources.

Choosing the Best Dairy Products

Foods that are high in calcium are some of the best food choices to boost acetylcholine. Calcium is easily found in dairy products such as milk, cheese, and yogurt. Our need for calcium increases as we age, yet at the same time our ability to digest dairy decreases. Worse, dairy products are typically high in calories and saturated fats.

In order to boost your acetylcholine without the calories or bloating problems associated with dairy, a better strategy is to choose foods that are high in calcium and contain the healthiest fats, yet are not dairy products, such as:

- Almonds
- Blueberries
- Brazil nuts
- Collard greens
- Molasses
- Sardines
- Soy milk
- Soy nuts
- Spinach
- Tofu

FOODS THAT ALLOW YOU TO FOCUS

Intuitive parents have long suspected that poor school performance was linked to poor nutrition. New scientific studies are beginning to confirm these suspicions. Many doctors believe as I do that a dopamine imbalance can be exacerbated by poor nutrition. However, the good news is that it can also be corrected through diet.

Waning attention may be a sign that the foods you choose do not include the building blocks needed to support and create dopamine. Focus on foods containing the amino acids that are the building blocks of dopamine: those rich in tyrosine and phenylalanine. You'll need to include protein in every meal. A high-protein diet, particularly at breakfast, sets you up for successful thinking throughout the day.

FOOD	TYROSINE AND PHENYLALANINE (GRAMS PER 6- TO 8-OUNCE SERVING)
Beef, lean	1.10
Chicken	2.00
Chocolate, dark	0.80
Cottage cheese	3.40
Duck	2.20
Eggs (1 egg)	0.60
Granola	1.05
Oat flakes	0.85
Pork	2.50
Ricotta cheese	1.85
Soy	1.20
Turkey	2.30
Walnuts	1.40
Wheat germ	2.35
Wild game	4.10
Yogurt (especially Greek-style)	0.80

Besides being in the foods in the table on page 147, phenylalanine can be found in the sugar substitute aspartame, which is sold as either NutraSweet or Equal. These artificial sweeteners are safe and nutritious. Aspartame has been the subject of more than 200 research studies for more than 30 years in which its safety has continued to be demonstrated.

AVOID THESE FOODS TO INCREASE ATTENTION

Many researchers have connected attention deficit disorder (ADD) to foods that are high in artificial coloring, flavorings, or preservatives, like monosodium glutamate (MSG). These are found in most convenience foods: store-bought, mass-produced baked or packaged foods. You'll need to become a detective label-reader and avoid products that have these ingredients. In general, these foods are typically low in nutrient value, so you should avoid them whenever possible. But if you don't have the time or inclination to make your own versions, and you must have them to celebrate a special occasion, choose organic options of packaged foods: These will typically have fewer bad ingredients.

If you have found that loss of attention is your issue, avoid fruits and vegetables that contain salicylate, a naturally occurring chemical found in plants. Even though these are considered otherwise "healthy options," they do not work for you. Salicylate is also found in aspirin and other pain-relieving medications. See if you notice a difference in your thinking after taking these medications, and if so, find an alternative treatment.

The salicylate foods to avoid:

- Almonds
- Apples
- Apricots
- Berries, all kinds
- Cherries
- Cucumbers
- Currants
- Oranges
- Peaches
- Peppers
- Plums
- Prunes
- Tomatoes

10 RULES FOR A YOUNGER, SMARTER YOU

The food suggestions we've discussed will help you reverse MCI, increase attention, and improve mood. They are the means by which you can personalize your diet to address your particular brain chemical deficiencies. However, they are only one part of the eating plan. The following 10 rules will help you use these superfoods in the right combination with other important nutrients to maximize your results.

Keep these rules in mind as you create your own eating plan.

1. Add spices to every meal.

2. The right caffeine improves cognition.

3. Eat yogurt every day to enhance brain speed.

4. Lean proteins create the most brain power.

5. Kick the sugar habit.

6. Choose fiber-filled foods to cleanse your body.

7. Drink water.

8. Eat colorful fruits and vegetables to slow cognitive decline.

9. Choose high-quality produce.

10. Include all three basic food groups (carbs, protein, and fats) at every meal.

Rule #1: Add Spices to Every Meal

One of the greatest brain defenses is the addition of spices to your meals. Spices function like little brain medications. They are nutrient dense: Each can provide between 20 and 80 different nutrients. By using them often, you are benefiting by getting more important vitamins, minerals, and even antioxidants. They allow your foods to be better metabolized, because calories are burned more easily when they are accompanied by nutrients.

Herbs and spices maximize nutrient density because they contain antioxidants, minerals, and multivitamins without one additional calorie—so every time you add spice, you're adding nutrients and upgrading your meal. They are just as important as fruits and vegetables for their antioxidant content and healing power. I tell all my patients to spice up every meal by adding at least three spices to each dish. Choose ones that taste great together and that also help your particular brain chemical deficiency. By doing so, you can create superfoods that are abundantly healthy.

Some spices and herbs also increase your overall feeling of fullness and satiety, so you'll eat less. One study conducted at Maastricht University in the Netherlands showed that when healthy subjects consumed an appetizer with half a teaspoon of red pepper flakes before each meal, it decreased their calorie intake by 10 to 16 percent. And when you flavor your foods with spices instead of salt, you'll immediately see the difference in your body. With less salt in your diet, you won't retain as much water, so you won't feel as bloated. Plus, your overall health will improve, especially if you have high blood pressure.

The following spices are known to have specific medicinal properties that improve cognitive performance, decrease inflammation of the brain, or reduce anxiety. Adding any and all of these to your meals will help you enhance neurogenesis. You can also focus on the ones that are particularly well suited to your results on the Braverman Brain Advantage Test by matching the descriptions to your particular needs. And don't be afraid to use them liberally—they are completely calorie-free, and you'll get the best results from the highest doses.

- **Allspice** helps reduce blood pressure and protects against neurodegenerative conditions.

- **Anise** appears to sharpen brain power and can help alleviate depression.

- **Basil** improves circulation to the brain and reduces nervous headaches.

- **Black pepper** may increase alertness and attention.

- **Cayenne pepper (chile pepper)** reduces fatigue and may stimulate the release of endorphins, which can block pain. Its primary nutrient is capsaicin, which raises your body's heat index and causes a boost in both brain and body metabolism, thereby increasing your brain power.

- **Clove** may be beneficial for pain relief.

- **Coriander** has been proven to chelate toxic metals from our bodies.

- **Cumin** contains zinc, which cleanses the body and brain, because it is a natural chelating agent.

- **Dill** can help alleviate depression.

- **Fennel** improves brain metabolism.

- **Garlic** improves blood circulation to the brain.

- **Ginger** improves blood circulation to the brain and alleviates anxiety.

- **Lemon balm,** an herb used commonly in tea, is a possible treatment for Alzheimer's disease. It is an antioxidant that stimulates acetylcholine receptors and works as a mild sedative.

- **Lemongrass** may sedate the central nervous system.

- **Marjoram** alleviates insomnia and may stimulate the central nervous system. It can help alleviate depression.

- **Mustard seed** increases metabolism.

- **Nutmeg** can help alleviate depression.

- **Peppermint** can help alleviate depression.

- **Rosemary** improves blood circulation to the brain, stimulates the central nervous system, alleviates headaches, and may improve memory.

- **Saffron** can help alleviate depression and may inhibit the ability of alcohol to impair long-term memory.

- **Sage** may increase alertness and concentration and may inhibit the further progression of Alzheimer's disease.

Fresh Herb Facts

- One teaspoon of dried herbs equals 3 teaspoons of fresh herbs.
- Add fresh herbs near the end of your cooking time for the most flavor and benefits.
- Refrigerate herbs except for basil, which is best stored at room temperature.

- **Sesame seeds** contain folic acid, an important B vitamin that aids with attention.

- **Spearmint** can help alleviate depression.

- **Turmeric** can help alleviate depression, stimulates the production of acetylcholine, and has been proven to help unclog amyloid, the garbage that mucks up the pathways of the brain.

Rule #2: The Right Caffeine Improves Cognition

Caffeine is the most consumed compound in the world that directly affects the mind. It is well documented that caffeine temporarily increases attention span because it stimulates the central nervous system and gets blood pumping to the brain. Regular caffeine consumption has a positive effect on memory storage and retrieval performance, as well as delayed recall, both over the short term and the long term. However, caffeine consumption is detrimental to those who consume it on an irregular basis, or in too high (or too low) a dose. And high doses of caffeine have also been shown to have negative effects on long-term memory.

To get the most out of caffeine consumption, it should be daily, in moderate doses, and at around the same time. The most pronounced effect of caffeine on memory appears to be on people between the ages of 26 and 64. Consumption with caffeine, generally aids cognitive performance for people of this age group, as long as they do not exceed the recommended dose of 300 milligrams per day.

Most people choose coffee or caffeinated sodas for the daily energy hit. However, a more nutritious caffeine option is tea. I like to think of tea as the Tree of Life that saves your health. It is a much healthier option compared with coffee, because it is also high in nutrients and antioxidants, yet does not contain a single calorie. The darker teas offer the highest antioxidant values.

A cup of hot tea is the perfect antidote for calming an anxious mind. Both black tea and white tea are derived from the same plant as green tea, *Camellia sinensis,* but each has a different taste and appearance. White tea is growing in popularity because it has a higher antioxidant value than green and black tea. It is made from the unfermented young, delicate tea leaves that are covered in fine, white hairs. Green tea is made from the same leaves that have been left on the plant to mature. Black tea is also made from mature leaves, which are then fermented.

All these types of teas contain the nutrient L-theanine. Research has shown that L-theanine stimulates alpha brain waves, associated with a relaxed but alert mental state, which may increase attention span. Theanine appears to work quickly and is most effective when someone is stressed. It may also help enhance your attention and focus. Because theanine helps the mind stop racing, it also seems to help promote a more restful, sound sleep, which will not be interrupted by random thoughts.

The most scientific research has been recorded for green teas. Green tea can increase metabolism, decrease appetite, and provide more energy for exercise. It is also linked to preventing a host of diseases that are associated with cognitive decline, from heart disease to cancer to allergies and diabetes. Green tea may also reduce the absorption of all dietary fats by approximately 40 percent by blocking the production of digestive enzymes that facilitate the absorption of dietary fats. It can also help reduce fat by inhibiting the effects of insulin so that sugars are sent directly to the muscles for instant use, instead of being stored as body fat.

Results of a 2004 study from the University of Newcastle upon Tyne in England found that both green and black teas inhibit the activity of the enzyme acetylcholinesterase, which breaks down acetylcholine, the loss of which is associated with memory loss. The findings suggested tea could boost the memory of everyday drinkers. The study found that both green and black teas inhibited the activity of enzymes associated with the development of Alzheimer's, but coffee had no significant effect.

Green tea and black tea also hinder the activity of the enzyme butyrylcholinesterase, which has been discovered in protein deposits that are found on the brains of patients with Alzheimer's. Green tea is even more effective because it obstructs the activity of beta-secretase, which plays a role in the production of protein deposits in the brain that are associated with Alzheimer's disease. Scientists also found that it continued to have its inhibitive effect for a week, whereas black tea's enzyme-inhibiting properties lasted for only 1 day.

All three of these teas have distinctive tastes, and while some yield better results, the differences are modest. Choose the type of tea that you will enjoy drinking most often. Fresh brewed tea from loose tea leaves has far more nutrients than tea found in tea bags, because it is less processed and more likely to be fresh. Bottled tea beverages may also be diluted or sweetened, adding unnecessary calories. Worse, their antioxidant levels are 10 to 100 times lower than those in brewed tea. Instead of drinking any bottled tea, I brew it myself and often combine two or three teas to get the most color and, therefore, the most benefit. For example, I brew a pot that makes 3 to 4 cups, and I combine red rooibos, blueberry, and green tea.

If you are choosing a tea to relax, pick either a decaffeinated version of regular tea, or any herbal variety. Decaffeinated teas still have plenty of theanine. However, herbal teas are not really teas at all: They are tisanes, or infusions made from the bark, leaves, and flowers of other plants. While they do not contain theanine, they have plenty of other nutrients and health benefits.

The following herbal teas have specific brain-enhancing properties:

Chamomile, a mild, relaxing tea with a delicate flavor, alleviates pain and lessens anxiety.

Lemon balm reduces anxiety and restlessness, taming tension and nervousness.

Passionflower is recommended when sleep is disturbed by anxiety.

Rooibos is a red South African herbal tea that is packed with vitamin C and 50 percent more antioxidants than green tea. For an added nutrient bonus, try a rooibos tea brewed with cinnamon.

Rule #3: Eat Yogurt Every Day to Enhance Brain Speed

Eating a single 8-ounce cup of low-fat unflavored yogurt every day offers a high dose of protein and healthy fat, which increases your brain speed. Best of all, yogurt may help burn fat and promote weight loss because it is high in both calcium and protein. A University of Tennessee study in 2005 showed that dieters who ate three servings of yogurt a day lost 22 percent more weight and 61 percent more body fat than those who simply cut calories and didn't add calcium to their eating plan.

Choose low-fat over fat-free, because you do need some fat in your diet every day. I'm partial to the new Greek varieties, because they are higher in protein and less processed than traditional yogurts, even the organic versions. And stay clear of the flavored varieties—they typically

Top 5 Brain-Boosting Snacks

- 1 handful of raw, unsalted nuts
- 1 to 2 hard-cooked eggs
- ½ cup hummus and raw carrots
- 8 ounces of unflavored low-fat Greek yogurt with fresh fruit
- 8-ounce yogurt smoothie made with fresh fruit, ice, and whey protein

contain unnecessary sugars. Instead, feel free to cut up some fresh fruit to add to your cup of yogurt, or blend into a smoothie with fruit and a little ice for a satisfying drink.

Rule #4: Lean Proteins Create the Most Brain Power

Several key factors influence your thinking, including glucose and its relationship to producing insulin. Although glucose and insulin are not brain chemicals, they are essential for normal brain function. Glucose is the principal fuel of brain cells, and insulin regulates glucose levels. The foods you eat influence levels of both glucose and insulin, and their levels affect your ability to think clearly. People function at their best when their blood sugar is within a fairly narrow range of glucose levels. In general, a healthy range for fasting blood sugar is between 75 and 85 milligrams per deciliter (mg/dl), and less than 140 mg/dl after eating.

Foods rich in protein (fish, chicken, beans, and lean meats) or fiber produce only modest increases in glucose and insulin, keeping both within a fairly tight normal range. This is also why higher-protein, lower-carb diets help people lose weight—they curb hunger by stabilizing glucose. Another reason why a high-protein diet is important is that it is rich in the amino acid precursors of dopamine and serotonin, which modify behavior and can help improve mood.

Fish and chicken can be eaten every day, and so can eggs. You can also choose from other proteins in moderation, including lamb, pork, lean red meats, veal, turkey, Cornish hen, soy, and low-fat dairy products such as skim or low-fat milk and, of course, yogurt.

Eggs are critical when you want to get smarter, because they naturally increase levels of acetylcholine and are related to all the other brain chemical families. Eggs are referred to as a perfect protein, because they are rich in amino acids and contain very little fat. Back in the 1980s and 1990s, eggs were categorized as off-limits because of their high cholesterol content. However, research has shown that foods such as eggs, which are high in dietary cholesterol, do not raise blood cholesterol levels by more than 2 percent.

Choose eggs that are enhanced with omega-3s—they contain five times the omega-3s found in ordinary eggs. Then sprinkle your eggs with your favorite spices and create a brain-boosting superfood!

Rule #5: Kick the Sugar Habit

New research confirms what I have thought for some time: Sugar is an addictive substance, just like cigarettes. Once you start to eat foods that are high in any type of sugar, you find yourself craving more of them because they seem to restore energy and improve your mood.

However, they also contribute to the breakdown of your body's metabolic machinery, which drains the brain of energy. Sugar and its many hidden forms—high fructose corn syrup, fructose, dextrose, sucralose, molasses, and honey—all deplete dopamine. You may be addicted to sugar if you are constantly craving something sweet—like a small bite of chocolate—after every meal, or if you think about dessert all day. With the adult obesity rates climbing as high as 56 percent, lots of us are sugar addicts.

When you are addicted to sugar, you feel moody when you don't eat sugar. The smell, sight, or touch of sugary foods can give you an instant high or rush and spark a craving. And when you are not eating sugar, you're thinking about it. You literally cannot go 1 day without it. What's more, when you do eat sugar, you tend to indulge, or eat too much.

The first step in breaking free from a diet high in sugar is to switch to sugar substitutes. While this won't end the cravings for something sweet, it will drastically lower your calorie intake. Then slowly decrease the amount you are using by half each time. Once you're off sugar, replace the taste with something highly spiced, so that you are beginning to increase your nutrients. For example, instead of sprinkling sugar on your oatmeal, try a sprinkle of cinnamon. Instead of sweetening your tea, try adding lemon.

Last, you can balance your brain's chemistry to beat the sugar withdrawal. Drink lots of green tea to flush out the sugar stored in your body. You'll also be helping your body get rid of other harmful toxins and gain nutrients.

Rule #6: Choose Fiber-Filled Foods to Cleanse Your Body

Fiber is like a scrub brush for your digestion, scouring your system until it is sparkling clean. It cleans out your colon, helps to control your blood sugar, pulls fat from your arteries, raises your HDL ("good") cholesterol, and detoxifies your body, making your skin sparkle. What's more, it's bulky: Fiber fills you up so that you aren't hungry, and you will eat less and feel full faster.

There are two types of fiber: soluble and insoluble. Soluble fiber is acted upon by the normal bacteria in your intestines. Good sources of

Foods That Eliminate Environmental Toxins

Certain foods are important to add to your diet if you know you have been exposed to the following environmental toxins:

Lead. Several foods contain nutrients that act as powerful chelating agents. Yogurt and milk products are high in calcium; clams and bananas are high in iron and potassium; oysters are high in vitamin B_{12}; citrus fruits, broccoli, and red peppers are high in vitamin C; and soy, pumpkin seeds, and salmon contain zinc and magnesium.

Aluminum. Coffee, cheese, meat, black and green teas, cabbage, cucumbers, tomatoes, turnips, spinach, and radishes will combat this toxin. (Also, do not cook with aluminum foil, stainless steel, or iron cookware.)

Mercury. Coriander, green tea, fresh oranges, and almonds are good to add to your diet.

soluble fiber include oats, beans, dried peas, fruits, vegetables, and legumes. Insoluble fiber, which is not digested by the body, increases intestinal transit. It also promotes regularity and softens stools. Wheat bran, whole grain products, and vegetables are good sources of insoluble fiber.

The American Dietetic Association recommends that a healthy diet deliver 25 to 35 grams of fiber a day, including both soluble and insoluble fiber. However, Americans consume only about half that amount. Check labels for fiber content in baked goods, and always choose breads, cereals, and pastas made from whole grains instead of the "white" variety. Leafy greens, root vegetables, beans, and lentils are all good sources. Other fiber-abundant foods I recommend are quinoa, millet, bulgur, buckwheat, seeds, and nuts. They are absorbed slowly by the body, thus keeping glucose and insulin low and providing long-lasting energy. They provide the unique ability to prevent the steep declines in blood sugar levels that give rise to fatigue, mood swings, and food cravings.

Rule #7: Drink Water

Drinking plenty of water will increase your attention. Your brain is much more effective when it is well hydrated. It makes dopamine more abundant and more easily received by its receptors. It also enhances neurogenesis, because new cells need water to survive. Water also continually flushes your digestive system, moving food particles along at a rapid rate, which leads to weight loss. And if you're drinking water all day, you won't need to drink higher-calorie beverages like sodas or juices. If you drink water 30 minutes before a meal, it will actually fill you up so you will eat less. This is especially true for older individuals who are typically borderline dehydrated because they forget to drink water throughout the day. Drinking coffee and tea counts, especially teas with deep colors for a greater nutritional punch.

Rule #8: Eat Colorful Fruits and Vegetables to Slow Cognitive Decline

Brightly colored fruits and vegetables are probably the most advantageous foods that we can choose. These colors are actually an indication of phytonutrients, plant-derived compounds that help us maintain health. Fruits and vegetables also provide extra fiber, vitamins, and powerful antioxidants that boost our immune system.

A 2007 study from France showed that abundant intake of dietary flavonoids helps protect against cognitive decline. Flavonoids are the nutrients that give fruits and vegetables their bright colors. They are also natural antioxidants. In the study, researchers tracked 1,600 men and women who were initially dementia free over the course of 10 years.

The participants who ate the most fruits and vegetables had the highest cognitive performance, and the ones with the lowest flavonoid intake experienced nearly twice the rate of cognitive decline of the ones in the highest-intake group. Other tests conducted in Switzerland over a 20-year period showed that people who followed a diet high in antioxidants had significantly higher memory scores than those who didn't.

To ensure a healthy diet, I tell my patients to eat every color of the rainbow every day.

Red fruits, such as tomatoes, watermelon, and pomegranate, contain lycopene, which supports the cardiovascular system to keep blood pumping to all your organs, including your brain, which allows you to think faster.

Orange and yellow fruits and vegetables, including carrots, oranges, and mangoes, contain carotenoids that can protect vision, which is necessary for improving memory.

Green foods, such as celery, brussels sprouts, and all types of lettuces and salad greens, have lutein, which may decrease your risk of cancers and helps maintain strong muscles and bones—vital for remaining young and vibrant.

Blue, violet, and purple plants, including blueberries and grapes, contain resveratrol, which can improve memory.

Rule #9: Choose High-Quality Produce

When you are shopping for fresh fruits and vegetables, the healthiest choice is both local and organic. Locally grown fruits and vegetables are healthier than conventionally farmed, out-of-season products. They contain more vitamins and minerals because they are left to ripen on the plant instead of ripening during shipping. Organic choices are free from

Feeling Ravenous Just an Hour after Eating?

This phenomenon happens if you choose meals consisting mainly of simple carbohydrates, such as white bread or pasta. While they suppress your hunger quickly, they don't really do the job. Chemically, high-carb meals rapidly suppress the hunger hormone ghrelin, causing you to feel satisfied just after eating. But ghrelin rises within a few hours to above-normal levels, causing you to feel even hungrier than before.

That's why I recommend that you create meals rich in protein—featuring eggs, chicken, fish, lentils, nuts, or cottage cheese—which won't suppress ghrelin as quickly and will help you feel full and satisfied for longer. For example, eating a breakfast containing a protein and a complex carbohydrate will set you up better than a bowl of cereal or some toast. Studies show that people who eat a breakfast containing two eggs tend to eat fewer calories throughout the day than those who eat a high-carb/low-protein breakfast.

harmful pesticides, and some studies have shown that they contain higher levels of nutrients.

Raw fruits and vegetables contain higher amounts of fiber than when they are cooked. And many of the important nutrients, vitamins, and enzymes (which may help with digestion) are destroyed or inactivated during cooking, i.e., thrown out with the boiling water. For example, steaming broccoli on a stovetop can deplete its vitamin C content by as much as 34 percent, reports the *Journal of Food Science*. Microwaving is a better alternative—the broccoli retains as much as 90 percent of its nutrients.

Rule #10: Include All Three Basic Food Groups (Carbs, Protein, and Fats) at Every Meal

For the best weight-loss results, plan your meals ahead of time. At every meal, fill your plate with one protein and two different fruits or vegetables with bright colors. Use healthy fats for cooking, and limit complex carbohydrates to no more than one meal and one snack a day.

Each meal should be at least 70 percent plant based and no more than 30 percent animal based to maximize your fiber and minimize calories. This can look like a lunch- or dinner-size salad with grilled chicken breast strips, or two eggs served with a half grapefruit and banana slices for breakfast.

The old USDA Food Pyramid has finally been replaced by something that is easy to follow and makes sense for both dieters and doctors. I'm even more pleased because its recommendations are very close to my eating plan. Visit www.choosemyplate.gov to learn more.

REGIONAL SPECIALTIES ARE ALSO BRAIN-BOOSTING AGENTS

The only way a diet truly works is if you can stick with it for the long term. It has to be flexible to meet your daily demands, and interesting enough to keep you motivated. You also need to be able to replicate the tastes that you already love, or find healthier varieties that offer the same food memories.

I've scoured the globe to find the healthiest options for increasing brain capacity. No matter where you're from, or what culinary regions you favor most, the following chart can help you choose the best options that fit into the 10 Rules or directly affect brain chemistry. This way you'll be able to re-create the tastes you love with foods that are better for you.

Dining in Africa . . .

GUINEA	
Cayenne	The heat produced by cayenne is caused by its high concentration of a substance called capsaicin, which has been widely studied for its pain-reducing effects, its cardiovascular benefits, and its ability to help improve brain and body metabolism.
Other staple superfoods include:	
Cassava (yellow food)	
Cinnamon (phytonutrients)	
Coffee (caffeine)	
Vanilla (antioxidants)	

(continued on next page)

GUINEA	
Watermelon	Watermelon is an excellent source of vitamin C and a very good source of vitamin A, notably through its concentration of beta-carotene and lycopene, both of which improve bloodflow to the brain.
Other staple superfoods include: Bison (tyrosine) Okra (green food) Sweet potatoes (high in fiber)	

Dining in Asia . . .

CHINA	
Sea vegetables	Many brown-colored sea vegetables, such as hijiki, contain fucoidan, which is a nutrient that has anti-inflammatory benefits.
Other staple superfoods include: Bamboo shoots (high in fiber) Ginger (antioxidant) Oolong tea (a form of black tea) Rice (choose brown) (high in fiber)	

JAPAN	
Miso, tofu, tempeh (fermented soy)	Soy is an important protein that contains the building blocks of both dopamine and acetylcholine. Increasing your soy consumption can also help combat the symptoms of menopause. Studies have shown that Asian women experience far fewer menopausal symptoms compared with American women of European origin. In one study that compared postmenopausal American women to postmenopausal Japanese women, more than 30 to 35 percent of American women complained of hot flashes, lack of energy, and depression compared with only 6 to 10 percent of Japanese women. I believe that this is most likely due to the composition of their diets.
Other staple superfoods include: Coconut (potassium) Coriander (phytonutrients) Papaya (yellow food) Pineapple (yellow food)	

THAILAND	
Shiitake mushrooms	A symbol of longevity in Asia because of their health-promoting properties, shiitake mushrooms contain eritadenine, which is thought to lower cholesterol by blocking the absorption of cholesterol into the bloodstream.
Other staple superfoods include: Chiles (increase metabolism) Lemongrass (phytonutrients) Lime (green food)	

INDIA	
Turmeric	Turmeric is a powerful spice that contains curcumin and has long been used in the Chinese and Indian systems of medicine. It is currently thought to prevent and slow the progression of Alzheimer's disease by removing amyloid plaque buildup in the brain.
Other staple superfoods include: Cardamom (antioxidants) Mango (yellow food) Mustard seed (B vitamins) Saffron (riboflavin)	

Dining in Central and South America . . .

MEXICO	
Avocado	Avocado is a powerful anti-inflammatory that is high in monounsaturated fat—the "good" kind that actually lowers cholesterol levels. Avocados are rich in beta-sitosterol, which can significantly lower blood cholesterol levels and increase bloodflow to the brain.
Other staple superfoods include: Black beans (high in protein and fiber) Cilantro (phytonutrients) Onions (yellow food)	

PERU	
Tomato	Tomatoes (and everything made from them) contain lycopene, which has been extensively studied for its antioxidant and cancer-preventing properties. They are also a very good source of fiber, which has been shown to lower high cholesterol levels, keep blood sugar levels from getting too high, reduce the risk of heart disease, and increase bloodflow to the brain.
Other staple superfoods include: Banana (potassium) Corn (yellow food) Duck (tyrosine)	

(continued on next page)

Dining in Europe . . .

GERMANY	
Rye	Rye is a good source of fiber. Rye fiber has an exceptionally high water-binding capacity, which quickly provides a feeling of fullness and satiety, making rye bread a good choice for anyone trying to lose weight.
Other staple superfoods include:	
Beets (red/yellow food)	
Kale (green food)	
Sauerkraut (green food)	

NORWAY	
Lingonberries	The lingonberry is a close relative of the cranberry. Lingonberries provide powerful brain-boosting antioxidants, including provitamin A; the B vitamins thiamin, riboflavin, and niacin; vitamin C; resveratrol; phosphorus; calcium; magnesium; and potassium. In addition, the seeds are rich in omega-3 fatty acids.
Other staple superfoods include:	
Barley (high fiber)	
Buckwheat (high fiber)	
Fatty fish (omega-3s)	
Wild game (tyrosine)	

SWEDEN	
Blueberries	Packed with antioxidant phytonutrients called anthocyanidins, blueberries are also high in resveratrol.
Other staple superfoods include:	
Blackberries (purple foods)	
Oats (high fiber)	
Raspberries (red foods)	
Turnips (red foods)	

FRANCE	
Eggs	Choline is found in the yolk of the egg and is a key component of many fat-containing structures in brain cell membranes, whose flexibility and integrity depend on adequate supplies of choline. Two fatlike molecules in the brain, phosphatidylcholine and sphingomyelin, account for an unusually high percentage of the brain's total mass, so choline is particularly important for brain function and health.
Other staple superfoods include:	
Bay leaf (phytonutrients)	
Dark chocolate (resveratrol)	
Grapes (resveratrol)	
Tarragon (phytonutrients)	

ITALY	
Basil	The huge number of flavonoids found in basil provides protection to the brain and body at the cellular level. Basil's volatile oils have also been shown to provide protection against unwanted bacterial growth.
Other staple superfoods include:	
Oregano (phytonutrients)	
Parsley (phytonutrients)	
Thyme (phytonutrients)	

SPAIN	
Olives	Olives are concentrated in monounsaturated fats and are a good source of vitamin E. Because monounsaturated fats are less easily damaged than polyunsaturated fats, they are essential for protecting the brain cells' outer membranes and other cellular structures. The stability of monounsaturated fats translates into a protective effect on brain cells that, especially when combined with the antioxidant protection offered by vitamin E, can lower the risk of damage and inflammation. Olives also contain a variety of beneficial active phytonutrient compounds, including polyphenols and flavonoids, which have anti-inflammatory properties.
Other staple superfoods include:	
Almonds (calcium)	
Lentils (fiber)	
Olive oil (healthy fats)	
Paprika (phytonutrients)	
Sardines (calcium)	

GREECE	
Garlic	The cardioprotective benefits of garlic may partly rest on the production of hydrogen sulfide (H_2S) gas. Our red blood cells can take sulfur-containing molecules in garlic (called polysulfides) and use them to produce H_2S. This H_2S, in turn, can help our blood vessels expand, facilitating good bloodflow to the brain and keeping our blood pressure in check.
Other staple superfoods include:	
Grape leaves (phytonutrients)	
Greek yogurt (protein and calcium)	
Walnuts (healthy fats)	

(continued on next page)

TURKEY	
Yogurt and kefir	*Lactobacillus casei,* a strain of friendly bacteria found in cultured foods such
Other staple superfoods include:	as yogurt and kefir, may help you live
Dates (antioxidants)	longer, fortify your immune system, and increase brain metabolism. As noted
Figs (antioxidants)	earlier, yogurt boosts both acetylcho-
Lamb (tyrosine)	line and dopamine, and therefore
Mentha/mint (phytonutrients)	increases brain speed and power.

PUTTING IT ALL TOGETHER: ORDERING A BRAIN-BALANCING MEAL

One change you will have to make when you balance your brain is to become more assertive. You'll feel that life is less stressful when you have the confidence to ask for what you really want. And you'll feel a whole lot smarter once you begin to fulfill your desires.

The best place to start is with your food. Next time you are out for dinner, order your meal with all these recommendations in mind. And don't hesitate to make sure your server is perfectly clear so that you can stay on track. When you eat out, make sure you know or ask:

Which selections are stir-fried, sautéed, baked, or steamed? Best options: baked or steamed. While stir-fried and sautéed options are good for home cooking, restaurants will typically use much more oil in their preparation than you would at home. And avoid all deep-fried and battered choices.

Which items are made from whole grains? Best options: brown rice, bulgur, quinoa, and whole wheat breads and pastas. Better yet, ask for the bread basket to be removed from the table.

Which items are organic and locally grown? Best options: locally grown organic fruits and vegetables. They trump those that are just organic, because locally grown produce travels less and can ripen "on the vine."

Can salad dressings be served on the side? Restaurants will use more dressing than you would at home. Also, avoid any that contain high fructose corn syrup, or sugar in general. Best options: pesto, olive oil, mustard, salsa, or a simple balsamic vinaigrette.

Can my meal be prepared without salt? Even for those who don't have high blood pressure, restaurants use an alarming amount of salt, which isn't good for anyone. Best option: Ask for your meal to be prepared with other spices instead.

NUTRIENTS THAT MAKE YOU SMARTER

Even when you follow my eating plan, the fruits, vegetables, and proteins you eat can't supply enough of the essential nutrients we need to enhance thinking and cognition. What's more, the digestive system is inefficient and can't absorb all the nutrients available from food before it passes from the body. For these reasons, I believe that nutritional supplementation is an essential part of a proper diet to balance the brain. Readily available vitamins and nutrient supplements are an excellent way to make sure you have a full complement of nutrients that support brain health and grow new brain cells while you follow this eating plan.

Nutrients directly impact mood and memory. The following chart shows just how easily poor nutrition affects the way you think:

NUTRIENT DEPLETION	EFFECT ON THINKING
Amino acids (proteins)	Mood changes, slower thinking
Choline	Memory loss
Chromium	Depression
Essential fatty acids	Lethargy, irritability, depression, and memory loss
Folic acid	Irritability and depression
Iron	Confusion, lethargy, difficulty learning
Magnesium	Depression, confusion
Potassium	Apathy and confusion
Riboflavin (vitamin B$_2$)	Memory loss, confusion, and senility
Selenium	Anxiety and depression
Sodium	Confusion and poor memory

(continued on next page)

NUTRIENT DEPLETION	EFFECT ON THINKING
Thiamin (vitamin B₁)	Mental confusion, personality change, memory loss, mood swings, shortened attention span, irritability, depression, and fatigue
Vitamin E	Lethargy and depression
Zinc	Mood changes

Choose from upcoming lists based on your results from the Braverman Brain Advantage Test starting on page 95. You don't have to take all of those listed in each section. I've given you lots of choices because you may find that some supplements work better for you than others. It's also important to follow the dosage and time directions for each type of supplement for best results. When choosing dietary supplements, avoid heavily coated or sustained-release products, which can be difficult to break down. Instead, whenever possible, choose liquids, powders, or sublingual (under-the-tongue dissolvable) forms.

Lastly, don't be afraid of high dosages or multiple nutrient prescriptions. I know it sounds like a lot of pills, but if you put them in a glass, it would barely fill a quarter of a cup. And of course, talk with your physician before starting a supplement program like the ones listed here.

I Call Resveratrol "Reverse-It-All"

Whatever your deficiency, one supplement that I highly recommend to become smarter is the antioxidant resveratrol. This compound is naturally found in red wine and grape skins. Alcohol in general increases GABA levels, which makes you feel more relaxed. We've known since a well-documented French study from 1991 that consumption of red wine is linked to decreased heart disease. A few years later, it was found that red wine contains many polyphenols. These are the most abundant antioxidants in our food chain, and the ones responsible for giving fruits and vegetables their vibrant colors—specifically quercetin and catechins, which are linked to the prevention of heart attacks, cancer, and strokes. Red wine was also found to be a great source of the polyphenol resveratrol.

Resveratrol is considered to be in a class of polyphenols called sirtuin gene activators. These have been found to help directly repair genes and make them more resistant to damage, thereby increasing human longevity by decreasing cellular death. These "super repair genes" are thought to slow down the aging process because they trick the body into a natural response similar to what occurs during calorie restriction. When you restrict your calories, the body learns to modify its processes and becomes more efficient because it doesn't have any resources to waste. A new chemical pathway called the sirtuin pathway is activated, which instructs the body to use less energy in all its functions. The result is that on the cellular level, the body produces less toxicity, and individual cells actually live longer. However, a vibrant brain needs more energy, not less. Resveratrol is able to turn on the sirtuin pathway without calorie restriction, so that the brain and body can continue to operate at a rate that is best suited for optimal brain health. Better still,

Choose Treats Wisely

It's normal to take a small detour from dieting every once in a while, so you might as well choose a treat that's still good for you. Resveratrol is found in many of the "cheats" we crave most. But don't rely on these foods for your resveratrol fix; you'd need to eat copious amounts in order to match the resveratrol amounts in supplements. Because many of these foods are high in fat or sugar, though, you don't want to eat too much of any of them, so this is not a license to indulge.

- Blueberries
- Cranberry juice
- Dark chocolate
- Grapes
- Hops (found in beer)
- Peanuts
- Pistachios
- Pomegranate juice
- Port and sherry
- Red grape juice
- Red wine
- White grape juice
- White wine

because they literally slow down aging, they reduce obesity and increase muscle mass; help protect the body from infection, inflammation, and cancer; and protect the heart and brain.

In a landmark study, Harvard University researchers tested individuals on their memory and reaction time after consuming resveratrol. Using the most up-to-date computerized testing, researchers found a marked improvement in visual and verbal memory and in reaction time. Resveratrol has also been found to influence and block the free radicals that lead to brain cell death. It is also thought to protect the brain from Alzheimer's disease by removing the toxic beta-amyloid plaques that form in the brain. In addition, resveratrol has been found to open the arteries by enhancing the production of nitric oxide. Nitric oxide lets the blood vessels expand, allowing for better thinking as more blood flows to the brain.

However, the amount of resveratrol found in red wine is relatively small. Wine regions that produce the highest concentrations per grape include Argentina, Sardinia, and Russia. If you drank two glasses a day of the highest-resveratrol wine, you would be receiving only 1.5 milligrams. I can't recommend more than two glasses, and frankly, the recommended dosage of resveratrol for the highest health benefits is more in the 100- to 500-milligrams-per-day range.

The good news is that there are resveratrol supplements so that you can have the benefits of red wine without the alcohol, or the calories. The supplements made from the highest-quality raw materials include those manufactured by Resveratrol Partners, Biotivia, and RevGenetics.

Nutrients That Lower Stress and Fight Depression

GABA and serotonin nutrients are best taken from the late afternoon through the early evening—these supplements will help you relax and unwind. These nutrients will relax the brain so that you feel less anxious and more confident, so you can stop worrying about losing your mind.

Nutrients That Encourage Faster Thinking

Bloodflow enhancers like quercetin (also found in red wine) and D-phenylalanine, and herbs such as huperzine, *Rhodiola rosea*, and

NATURAL TREATMENT	SUGGESTED DAILY DOSAGE	HOW IT AFFECTS THINKING
GABA	500–3,000 mg	Controls anxiety
Melatonin	1–10 mg	Improves sleep
SAMe	400–1,600 mg	May alleviate depression and improves activation of key brain chemicals and hormones

ginkgo biloba are thought to improve memory and focus. In one 2010 study from Korea, researchers were able to monitor cerebral bloodflow using brain imaging. After 4 months of treatment to increase bloodflow, researchers noted significant increases in bloodflow in the areas of the brain typically associated with damage caused by Alzheimer's. More important, the study volunteers revealed increased cognitive function and decreased levels of dementia.

Supplements such as Cognitex, ProCog, and my Brain Youth and Brain Memory formulas are as vital to memory and cognitive functions. These supplements and the ones listed below are best taken in the early morning through the afternoon to keep you sharp during the day, at least a half hour before eating.

NATURAL TREATMENT	SUGGESTED DAILY DOSAGE	HOW IT AFFECTS THINKING
Acetyl-L-carnitine	500–5,000 mg	May increase attention span; may also reduce leptin resistance
Alpha-lipoic acid	50–500 mg	A small molecule that easily enters the brain to protect it from free radical damage, it prevents breakdown of all membranes and preserves acetylcholine.
Boron	1–5 mg	Improves memory function
Choline	200–3,000 mg	A precursor to acetylcholine

(continued on next page)

NATURAL TREATMENT	SUGGESTED DAILY DOSAGE	HOW IT AFFECTS THINKING
Dimethylamino-ethanol (DMAE)	100–3,000 mg	Opens neuronal pathways in the brain; once DMAE crosses the blood-brain barrier, it converts to choline
Dimethylglycine (DMG)	100–200 mg	Helps to maintain mental acuity
GPC (glycerol phosphorylcholine choline)	200–1,000 mg	May improve memory as it imitates acetylcholine
Huperzine A	50–100 mg twice daily	Prevents breakdown of all membranes and blocks the enzyme that breaks down acetylcholine
Lecithin (source of choline and inositol)	1–2 Tbsp	Protects brain cell function
L-methionine	500–3,000 mg	Part of the lipotropic group of amino acids and helps to remove heavy metals from the body, which are thought to cause cognitive decline
Manganese	2–10 mg	Helps synthesize acetyl-L-carnitine
NAC (N-acetyl-L-cysteine)	600–1,200 mg	Protects acetylcholine depletion triggered by pesticides and other toxins
Omega-3 fatty acids (fish oil, flaxseed oil)	500–3,000 mg	Used for treating attention disorders
Phosphatidylcho-line	500–2,000 mg	May improve memory as it imitates acetylcholine
Vinpocetine	10–40 mg	Increases blood supply to the brain; may improve memory

NATURAL TREATMENT	SUGGESTED DAILY DOSAGE	HOW IT AFFECTS THINKING
Vitamin B$_{12}$	100–5,000 mcg	May improve some aspects of intelligence
Vitamin C	1,000–5,000 mg	May increase intelligence

Attention-Boosting Nutrients

Because the supplements that boost dopamine are energy related, they are best taken on a full stomach after you've eaten breakfast or lunch.

NATURAL TREATMENT	SUGGESTED DAILY DOSAGE	HOW IT AFFECTS THINKING
B-50 complex	1–2 caps	Improves attention
Boron	1–5 mg	A deficiency is thought to reduce attention.
Calcium (citrate)	500–1,000 mg	Improves attention
Dimethylglycine (DMG)	100–200 mg	Helps to maintain mental acuity
Ginkgo biloba	50–300 mg	Improves attention and intelligence by improving cerebral circulation and destroying free radicals that harm brain cells
Ginseng (Panax, Asian, or American)	500–2,000 mg	May increase attention span and enhance memory; may improve accuracy in tasks that require attention
GLA (omega-6 from borage oil)	100–500 mg	Improves attention
L-phenylalanine	500–4,000 mg	Converted to L-tyrosine, and then to dopamine and norepinephrine; promotes alertness and improves learning and memory

(continued on next page)

NATURAL TREATMENT	SUGGESTED DAILY DOSAGE	HOW IT AFFECTS THINKING
Magnesium	300–1,000 mg	Decreased attention span is one of the symptoms of severe magnesium deficiency.
NADH (nicotinamide adenine dinucleotide)	5–20 mg	A form of niacin that is essential for production of energy
Theanine	100–500 mg	May increase alpha brain wave activity, indicating that theanine may improve attention span
Trimethylglycine (TMG)	500–5,000 mg	Assists the body in utilizing B vitamins, rids the body of toxins, and increases naturally occurring mood elevators
Vitamin C	1,000–5,000 mg in divided doses	Improves cerebral circulation
Vitamin E	100–400 IU	Improves cerebral circulation
Yohimbe	200–400 mg	Has dopamine and acetyl-choline effects on the brain
Zinc	15–50 mg	Improves attention and aids in heavy metal detoxification

SUPPLEMENTS FOR ENHANCING EXERCISE PERFORMANCE

The next chapter outlines a brain and body exercise program that will help create new brain cells and enhance brain chemistry. Here are some supplements you can consider while following that program. You'll see some overlap between this list and the previous ones in this chapter. If the duplicates address your particular brain chemical imbalance, start with those to maximize your nutrition.

Coenzyme Q10. Leads to the production of a high-energy molecule (ATP) that may increase endurance in any kind of physical activity. CoQ10 is also an excellent fat-soluble antioxidant.

Creatine. A high-energy molecule that may be of benefit during short periods of strenuous exercise.

Glucosamine and/or chondroitin. Provide joint support by reducing inflammation and promoting the rebuilding of worn-out joints.

Glutamine. Helps restore glutamine lost during intense exercise in order to build muscles. Glutamine also supports the immune system and reduces infections.

L-carnitine. A vitamin-like molecule that helps to burn long-chain fatty acids (fat). It is particularly good for the heart, since the heart gets most of its fuel from fat.

Whey protein. The highest-quality protein that is also easily and quickly absorbed. Although it is not as good as real protein, it contains high amounts of the branched chain amino acids (BCAA) that muscles use as an energy source, although not enough for your brain to absorb. Whey protein also contains compounds that support the immune system.

Not All Supplement Brands Are Equal

Many people are wary of supplement products, and for good reason. Supplements are manufactured by a wide variety of sources with little or no government regulation. Some manufacturers have been known to deliver fewer nutrients than are promised on the label. Others bulk up their products with fillers, like sugars.

I tell my patients to buy their supplements from reliable resources, and unfortunately, this often means the higher-priced vendors. In order to keep pricing in line with quality and feel secure in what I prescribe, I've developed my own line of supplements, called Total Health Nutrients, or THN. These products were developed to contain the right proportions of vitamins, minerals, and essential fatty acids without danger of toxic buildup and without dangerous side effects. Each ingredient is selected for its absorbability, competitive relationship with other nutrients, allergic potential, and long-term safety. They are manufactured in a cGMP (current good manufacturing practices) facility that meets the highest industry standards, ensuring you a pure product that meets label potency. Look for these products wherever you buy your vitamins, or on my Web site, www.pathmed.com.

Patient Profile: Justine Got Smarter When She Got Thinner

Justine first came to see me 2 years ago, when she was 54. She came into my office completely out of breath and told me in no uncertain terms that she was done feeling like an old woman. She always felt tired and cranky. She had no patience for her family and was irritable all the time. She knew that she was going through menopause, and she was becoming increasingly annoyed at her inability to finish tasks that she used to master easily. At the end of the day, she felt as if she hadn't accomplished anything in her busy real estate office. She almost cried when she told me that years ago she was "top of her class and sharp as a tack," but with each passing year, she was becoming increasingly confused and was beginning to be depressed.

I assured Justine that aging didn't have to be this way. First, we did a thorough checkup, and Justine completed the Braverman Brain Advantage Test. While Justine knew that she was going through menopause, she didn't realize that the excess weight she had gained over the past 10 years was just one sign of dopamine imbalance. Not only was her metabolism slower, her brain power was waning, which is why she was having so much trouble at work and at home.

The first step to balancing Justine's brain would be to make her look and feel younger. I started her on the Braverman Protocol and had her follow the Younger (Thinner) You Diet. She learned to add more spices to her food and stop using salt completely. She also started to take my Brain Energy and Brain Calm vitamin formulas, which increased her metabolism and lowered her anxiety.

Four months later, Justine came back to my office 40 pounds lighter. She was proud to tell me that she was both feeling good and looking better. Her high level of energy had returned, and even her sex life had improved. She confided that her husband commented on how much calmer and nicer she had become. But best of all, her brain fog cleared up, and for the first time in years she was able to stay focused all day long.

Two years later, Justine looks as great as she did when she initially lost the weight. Her business is once again successful, and her brain can keep up with the younger men and women in the office. She even told me that her memory now is fantastic, better than it ever was.

Justine is just one of many of my patients who have started eating better, looking better, and feeling smarter. By following the diet program outlined in this chapter and supplementing these foods with the right vitamins for your particular issues, you will quickly see improvements in your overall health as well as your thinking. Yet eating right is just one part of the Braverman Protocol. In the next chapter, you'll learn how to integrate both mind and body exercises into your lifestyle every day for maximum positive results.

Chapter 10

Step Four: Exercises That Boost Your Brain

The health benefits of physical exercise have been well documented and range from helping you lose weight—and keep it off—to improving sexual function, cardiovascular health, and bone density. In fact, there is no area of the body that doesn't benefit from regular exercise, and that includes the brain. In this instance, exercise helps to develop what scientists call cognitive reserve. This concept suggests that ongoing physical, educational, and social life experiences may help develop your prefrontal cortex and allow you to avoid or reverse mild cognitive impairment (MCI). Evidence from functional imaging studies has shown that cognitive reserve is a type of neuroplasticity, helping you strengthen and grow neuronal connections and develop more efficient cognitive networks. In the Rush Religious Orders Study of 2004, it was found that those participants who had done more to activate their neurons were about half as likely to develop Alzheimer's. In short, cognitive reserve is the buffer against an aging brain. And these brain reserves can be built at any time in our lives.

If you constantly engage in mental and physical activities, particularly those that get more difficult as you progress, you can increase your cognitive reserve. This chapter will review two distinct programs. The first one is a comprehensive brain workout that teaches you how to strengthen and improve your memory and attention through a variety of exercises. The second is a physical fitness regimen that increases endurance, muscle mass, and bloodflow, or angiogenesis, as well as participates in neurogenesis.

THE BRAVERMAN BRAIN WORKOUT

Increasing brain speed—without sacrificing accuracy—is possibly the most effective means of reversing cognitive decline and increasing cognitive reserve. Stimulating brain activities are those that you can do by yourself in which seeking or processing information is central. But not all brain games are equally effective. And our cognition is only as strong as our weakest point. Before you begin, you need to determine which cognitive domain you need to enhance: memory, attention, or both. Then think which of the four domains of IQ needs work: abstract, creative, emotional, or common sense. Study your Braverman Brain Advantage Test in detail and look for your lowest scores. Those are the areas that you need to work on first.

Then follow the protocol as outlined on subsequent pages for the domain you want to improve. For example, if you need to work on your emotional IQ, solving crossword puzzles will not help. A better choice would be playing chess or Scrabble with a friend (not a computer), because these are games that can improve abstract IQ while you socialize, which improves your emotional IQ.

Memorizing new words is important if you want great abstract IQ, but it isn't going to help your brain become more resilient. This program is not about memorizing phone book entries just for the sake of doing it. In fact, that's the last thing I want you to do, because it is not a skill you need to master any longer. The Internet has taken away the need to memorize anything—the information is there for the taking 24/7. So while we used to be in awe of memory prodigies, such as the famous Russian mnemonists (memory artists), idiot savants, and others who were able to demonstrate perfect photographic memory, or mathematicians who can do lightning calculations, or others who have incredible auditory memory for music and speeches and have the ability to memorize and recite classical poetry, it no longer impresses me. While these genius powers are intriguing, there is not much use for this type of memory in our daily living. These traits do not necessarily enhance attention, or even prove intelligence. It is more important to have a well-rounded memory that meets the needs of your daily life.

You can enhance your memory and attention capabilities by following the lessons in this chapter, in conjunction with boosting your brain chemistry. These exercises require little more than a journal to keep track of your progress, a deck of playing cards, and a timer. They are the first line of defense against memory loss, and it's never too early to apply them. The key is repetition. In order to achieve stronger cognitive capacities, one must exercise those parts of the brain over and over. Only by repeating these exercises will you gain progress in strengthening your memory—and even small bits of a brain workout count. I suggest you start with 10 minutes of brain exercises every day, working up to a goal of 1 hour before bedtime. You'll find this type of workout both stimulating and relaxing, and it will help you separate the business of the day from your bedtime ritual. You can think of this as your daily Sabbath for the brain.

Lastly, remember that brain exercise is just like physical exercise. If your mental capacities are burnt to a crisp, then a whole hour of mind-numbing puzzling is not going to make a difference. So start slowly and build up your brain stamina so that you can really enjoy the mental stretch.

Skip the Scrabble

I know that lots of books and doctors recommend word games and crossword puzzles as a way to boost your brain, but they are not my first choice. Mostly, they offer an opportunity to fill your head with inane knowledge without building your capacity for memory. For example, I have one patient who is an enormous Scrabble player who proudly tells me that her scores are around 540 a game. But she has no common sense. The trivia of information she is carrying isn't helping her out of her brain fog, either. It's as if she is wallowing in 10,000 e-mails because she can't locate the important ones.

If you like games, a better choice is math puzzles such as Sudoku or KenKen. They will increase your attention span, as well as your attention to detail, and build abstract IQ.

BRAVERMAN BRAIN GAMES FOR ENHANCING MEMORY

Improve Your Visual Memory

1. Draw a map from your home to the nearest grocery store. Label each street and landmark that you pass. Each time you do this exercise, go to the next most frequently visited destination in your town. Use a different piece of paper each time you do this test so that you can start from the beginning.

2. Take five playing cards from a deck. Look at them one at a time. Memorize the card number and suit. Turn the cards over and write down what you saw in the correct order. Each time you do this, add one more card to your list.

3. Take out a photo album or go to Facebook or your favorite social networking site. First, pull up your photos and select one. Write down as many details as you can about your memories from that day.

Improve Your Verbal Memory

1. Listen to the news on your favorite radio station for 2 minutes. Then turn off the radio and write down everything that you heard about the first two stories. Progressively add more minutes of news time and write more stories.

2. Think of songs that contain the word *blue* in the title or in the lyrics. The first day, write down five, and each subsequent day, add one to three more. After 4 days, move on to another word.

3. Memorize a haiku, put the book down, and repeat from memory. Move on to more complex poems as you go.

Improve Your Immediate Memory

1. Before you go to bed, make a list of everything that you ate that day.

2. Close your eyes and describe what you are wearing right now. Then, to make this more challenging, write down what your spouse/partner, child, or a friend wore when you saw them last.

3. List five people you spoke to today. Each day add one more.

Improve Your Working Memory

1. Go through your address book or e-mail contact list. Remind yourself of how you know each of the people listed, what they look like, and when you saw them last.

2. Write down how much money you spent at every transaction during the day.

3. Chunking is a way of sorting a large amount of information into subgroups based on common characteristics. By looking at information and seeing patterns of associations, you can make large lists more manageable. The way we remember a phone number or a Social Security number is a form of chunking. Your Social Security number is a three-two-four combination; your phone number is a three-three-four combination. A grocery list broken up by aisle, or where the items will be placed in your kitchen (refrigerator, pantry, etc.), is another example of chunking. A good exercise is to look around your home, taking one room at a time, and see how many different categories of items you have in that room. For example, a living room might simply have furnishings and entertainment media; your kitchen has appliances, furniture, and food. If you can do this with every room you walk into, you'll begin to notice more details, and it's very likely that you'll be able to set up new systems to find the things you are looking for—because you'll put them with like items.

Focus on Pattern Recognition

The brain registers patterns subconsciously, well before you will realize that you have learned something new. By learning how to classify—or chunk—information, you can build your own intuition quickly. For example, in one experiment noted in a 2011 article in the *New York Times*, researchers from Brown University found that people were better able to distinguish the painting styles of 12 distinct yet unfamiliar artists after viewing mixed collections of their works rather than after viewing one artist's work at a time. The research showed that with practice, the neurons in the visual cortex can identify patterns, and finding them frees up other mental resources.

BRAVERMAN BRAIN GAMES
FOR ENHANCING ATTENTION

1. See how many times you can tap the edge of a table hard enough to make a noise. Set a timer and tap as fast as you can for 30 seconds. Write down the result in your journal. Each day add another 15 seconds until you get to 2 minutes; then concentrate on tapping faster each time.

2. Can you read while there is music playing in the background? Practice this kind of reading every day, either with a book, the newspaper, a magazine, or your favorite Web site for news. It doesn't matter what you read or what you listen to. The goal is to see if you can continue and comprehend what you are reading. Other types of dual-activity multitasking, such as watching TV or listening to music while you work out, are also good options. See if you can increase your time for these activities by 5 minutes each time. Then tell someone or write down what you've learned from your reading to make sure you're really getting the facts correct.

3. Play the Game of Five Differences. There are many versions of this game in books and on the Internet. There are even apps for a smartphone that use the same principle. You are looking for a game that will show you two images that seem identical, but five small details have been changed. Your goal is to find all five differences. For a greater challenge, limit your time. Use a timer or stopwatch and set it for 2 minutes, then decrease your time in increments of 15 seconds each time you play.

4. Take a walk. You can work on enhancing your reaction time by monitoring your walking speed. I find that my patients who walk fast can think fast as well. To do this, you'll need a pedometer or step counter. This is a portable electronic device that counts each step you take by detecting your hip motion, even though it's worn on the wrist. If you wear this while you walk for a specific amount of time, you'll see how many steps you've taken. Instead of increasing the time you'll walk each day, see if you can increase your speed, which will show in the number of steps you'll add.

BRAVERMAN BRAIN GAMES FOR ENHANCING IQ

Improving abstract IQ: One factor in developing a cognitive reserve is lifelong education. The best way to increase your bandwidth is to read a national or local newspaper, cover to cover.

Improving creative IQ: The goal is to develop flexibility of thought so that you can see the perspectives of others and learn from them. With an open mind, you can then piece together different types of information. As you go about your day, you think in terms of possibilities. The best and most effective way to do this is by repeatedly asking one simple question: "What if . . . ?" The challenge is to see if you can approach problems differently to find real solutions, or even look at the things that are working about your life and see what you can do to make them even better.

Improving emotional IQ: Socialization is also hugely beneficial to the brain. Getting out of the house and going to lectures, listening to sermons, and joining a book group are all good ways to meet new people with similar interests. Talking to others with different points of view is another way to stretch your brain and make new neuronal connections.

Improving perceptive IQ: Strive to be a good role model and teacher. By earnestly discerning the needs of those who know less than you, you will become more perceptive, flexible, and patient and, thus, both a better leader and a better follower.

Left Brain/Right Brain Exercises

Everyone can benefit from left brain/right brain exercises, because they will teach the less dominant side of your brain to become more nimble and effective. There are two ways to improve the relationship between your right and left brains. The first is to tackle the physical, because developing better right and left brain balance can improve brain speed. The goal is to train your brain to use the less dominant side more effectively. For example, if you are right-handed, a great brain challenge is to learn to use utensils or write with your left hand.

A second way you can train your brain is by bending your personality. Depending on the results of Test Eight: Left Brain/Right Brain Test in Chapter 7, you need to work on the opposite side of your personality. So if you are left-brained, you need to be more intuitive and empathetic. If you are right-brained, then you need to develop your rational side.

Exercises to Become More Sensitive and Intuitive

1. **Sharing.** Share a private thought with someone who is not a close friend.

2. **Variety.** Try two or three new recreational activities each month.

3. **Going beyond the present.** Think of 20 different solutions to a problem (for example, how to plan for retirement).

4. **Spontaneity.** Start a day without any set plans. Choose an activity that you have never done, and do it.

5. **Cultivating intimacy.** Compliment your spouse/partner, a friend, or a relative on his or her personality or appearance, not an accomplishment.

6. **Build empathy.** Quietly observe your spouse or partner for 20 minutes while he or she is going about the day. Focus on the verbal and body cues to identify what he or she may be feeling. Later, ask if your hypotheses were accurate.

Exercises to Become More Rational

1. **Listening.** Listen to what others are saying, staying attentive to them rather than formulating a response in your own mind. Let people talk without interruption.

2. **Calmness.** When you experience an emotion surfacing that you do not want to share with others, remove yourself from the triggering environment. Once you are calm, return and explain why you were so emotionally charged, and then work together to achieve a positive result.

3. **Structure.** Examine your home. Look at the work space, kitchen, bathroom, and bedroom. Are these spaces organized in a way that really works best? Do they meet your comfort, efficiency, and aesthetic needs?

4. **Planning/scheduling.** Plan out your day in advance, even the weekends. List the activities you want to do and where you want to go. Construct a plan that allows you to do all of them. Revise your list if there are too many or too few.

Break Bad Habits

- Become aware when a habit of yours creates pain for you or someone else.

- Recognize that change happens slowly: Give change time to occur.

- Enlist the support of your family and friends.

- Remove yourself from any environment that reinforces your bad habits.

- Create new activities to replace old habits.

5. **Using logic and precision.** Create an "if then" statement for a single goal: *I want X. If I get X, then I will Y. If Y, then I will Z.* For example, you can start with the statement "I want to be more relaxed at work. If I'm relaxed at work, I will be able to focus on my tasks. If I can focus on my tasks, then I will be more productive."

6. **Determining the consequences.** Reexamine your goals and think through to where you would be if you were to achieve them.

A WEEKLY BRAIN EXERCISE WORKOUT

Think of this like cross-training: While you are focusing on your area that needs the most work, do one extra exercise from each category every day so that your brain gets its maximum workout and the greatest opportunity to reverse cognitive impairment. For example, if you need to develop your visual memory, on Monday do one visual memory exercise, plus one IQ-enhancing exercise. On Tuesday, try another visual memory exercise and one attention exercise, and continue in that way throughout the week.

Monday: IQ enhancing

Tuesday: Attention

Wednesday: Visual memory

Thursday: Verbal memory

Friday: Immediate memory

Saturday: Working memory

Sunday: Left brain/right brain exercise

GET MOVING AND BEAT MCI

Physical exercise and mental sharpening are linked: By exercising your body, you are also working out your brain. Adults who exercise at least three times a week have a 30 to 40 percent lower risk of developing dementia later in life than those who do not exercise. Even moderate exercise, such as taking a brisk walk for 30 minutes or more, increases bloodflow to the brain, thus keeping brain cells strong and resilient. That's exactly why exercise is often referred to as recreation—by doing it regularly, you are re-creating your brain and body.

Exercise enhances all of your brain chemicals. Aerobic exercise increases dopamine and acetylcholine, which affect your memory and attention. Yoga and Pilates are great for balancing GABA levels and relieving anxiety. Both resistance training and exercises that involve lots of physical movement, like swimming, are great ways to increase your serotonin, which improves sleep and subsequently affects neurogenesis. What's more, there is a large collection of ongoing clinical trials that are beginning to show a correlation between a substantial reduction of Alzheimer's disease in populations that take part in regular exercise.

Try Something New Every Day

The world is full of endless possibilities, and just by exploring them, you will increase your brain functioning. By trying a new game, task, book, television show, food, or activity, you are expanding your brain to create new neuronal connections. You don't have to master the activity, or even like it, for it to change your brain. The point is to get out of your comfort zone for as little as 15 minutes to see what sparks your interest. Surf the web for new ideas, or think about the things that you really like and the ways you can expand the experience. For example, if you love to take walks, choose a different route than usual. Even small changes count!

Exercise also increases production of brain-derived neurotrophic factor (BDNF), a protein that supports neurogenesis and has been associated with enhanced cognitive function and brain plasticity.

Exercise is also a great way to deal with anxiety and depression, which may be affecting your thinking. According to Dr. John Ratey, the author of *Spark: The Revolutionary New Science of Exercise and the Brain,* exercise provides the distraction the brain needs to stop worrying. His studies have shown that anxious people respond well to directed distractions—like exercise—both in the moment and in the long term. Exercise also relieves muscle tension, which reduces the feeling of anxiety. It also increases serotonin and GABA, which lowers anxiety and increases your memory capacity. Lastly, exercise releases endorphins, hormones produced in the brain and body that are known to elevate mood.

I know it's hard to fit exercise into an already busy schedule, but it *is* doable, and it should be a mandatory part of every day. You need 7 hours of exercise a week for maximum effect. That means you should start slowly, but work toward a goal of 1 hour of exercise a day, either all together or broken into two or three intervals. And for the maximum results, you need both types of exercise—aerobic as well as resistance training.

Aerobics Increases Bloodflow

The most recent science has focused on the role of aerobic exercise in improving our brain functioning. Aerobic exercise, which includes any type of exercise that increases your heart rate, like running, jogging, swimming, or cycling, causes a steep spike in blood movement to the brain, an action that is necessary for neurogenesis. Running and other forms of aerobic exercise have been shown to create new brain cells in those portions of the brain associated with memory and thinking. Aerobic activity will also improve your reaction time and overall attention.

In an experiment published in the *Journal of the American College of Sports Medicine,* 21 students at the University of Illinois were asked to memorize a string of letters and then pick them out from a list flashed at them. Then they were asked to do one of three things for 30 minutes—sit quietly, run on a treadmill, or lift weights—before performing the letter test again. After an additional 30-minute cooldown, they were tested once more. The students were noticeably quicker and more accurate after they ran compared with the other two options, and they continued to perform better when tested after the cooldown. In another study by scientists at the University of Illinois, elderly people were assigned a 6-month program of either stretching exercises or brisk walking. The stretchers increased their flexibility but did not improve on tests of cognition. However, those who took the brisk walks showed noticeable improvements on their mental test scores.

You Need Muscle Mass for Better Thinking

Just how resistance training initiates changes in cognition remains somewhat mysterious. We know that resistance training has significant benefits for cardiovascular health. Some researchers speculate that when the heart is strengthened, blood flow to the brain improves, which is associated with better cognitive function. A 2009 study from the University of Groningen in the Netherlands showed that building muscle mass leads to both neurogenesis, the creation of new brain cells, and angiogenesis, the increase in the amount of blood that flows to the brain. Another study from the Brain Research Center at the University of British Columbia showed that older women who lifted weights performed significantly better on various tests of cognitive functioning than women who completed toning or stretching classes.

Competitive Sports Make You Think Faster

Certain sports can develop your ability to think faster. And you don't have to be a professional athlete to get the most out of them in terms of your brain. Choose any physical activity that involves movements you're not able to anticipate and quick changes in direction. Tennis, soccer, basketball, or even Ping-Pong can provide a mental challenge greater than activities like golf, which has long lags during the game. Even the video game versions work to improve brain speed: Wii Tennis is better for the brain than Wii Golf. And to get the most out of the activity, do it with a friend. The social component increases your competitive nature, making you work harder. What's more, just being out with someone can help you increase your emotional IQ.

Are You Ready to Exercise?

While exercise should involve pushing yourself to new physical and mental limits, consistent pain should not be a part of the program. Make sure to discuss any new exercise program with your doctor. In my office, all patients are screened by a chiropractor to assess for the correct level of entry or reentry into an exercise regimen. Consult your physician and have a complete medical health checkup, including an assessment for underlying injuries. And before engaging in physical activity, answer the following questions:

- Have you been told that you have a heart condition and that physical activity is in any way restricted?
- Do you feel pain in your chest or are you short of breath when you perform physical activity?
- In the past month, have you had chest pain or shortness of breath when you were not engaging in physical activity?
- Do you lose your balance because of dizziness?
- Do you ever lose consciousness?
- Have you been told that you have a bone or joint problem that could be made worse by a change in physical activity?
- Are you taking blood pressure medications for a heart condition?
- Are you pregnant?
- Do you suffer from lower-back problems or chronic numbness in your hands or feet?

If you have answered yes to one or more of these questions, talk to your physician about those particular questions. Your physician might

Mix It Up

Keeping the element of surprise in your exercise routine helps keep your brain flexible. Choose different exercise classes each week, or find one in which the instructor varies the activity during the hour. Dance classes, yoga, and martial arts are good choices for this reason.

be able to tailor the following program based on your particular health requirements.

THE PATH TO EXERCISE

My PATH medical office has created a five-phase program to introduce exercise into a previously sedentary lifestyle. Each phase features a different classification of exercise, and you can focus on what you like to do within each phase that best suits your schedule and temperament. When you believe that you've mastered the phase, move on to the next. Each consecutive phase becomes more physically vigorous and challenging.

Some people find that they are more successful working out at the gym, either alone or with a friend, or even with a personal trainer. Others like to exercise in the privacy of their own homes. Whatever will work for you and your schedule is the best choice, as long as you keep the commitment to exercise.

When my patients ask me how much they should exercise, I ask them how much better they want to feel. With exercise, I strongly believe that more is better. However, I don't want you to hurt yourself so that you can't continue an exercise program. Most of the studies on exercise and brain enhancement have been done with walking. In a 2011 study published in the *Proceedings of the National Academy of Sciences,* a year of *modest* aerobic exercise reversed normal brain shrinkage by 1 to 2 years. So the key is that you need to be able to exercise for the long haul instead of burning out or getting frustrated or hurt. So do as much as you can whenever you can, working toward your goal of 7 hours a week for maximum results.

Phase 1. This preliminary phase of basic stretching and warmup shouldn't last longer than a week. Start by doing basic stretches that will help unlock tight muscles and joints. Work up to walking for 15 continuous minutes every day. Make sure that all your stretching is completely pain free. If you do feel pain, stop immediately, then start again using less pressure.

Phase 2. Move into dynamic combinations of stretches that induce bloodflow and get your heart pumping. Yoga, Pilates, and low-intensity aerobic movements offer complex sequences of individual positions to transition you toward more vigorous exercise.

Patient Profile: Carlos Exercised His Way Back to Better Thinking

Carlos came to see me a few years ago in a complete state of depression. He was 45 and considered himself to be quite an athlete. He had played soccer in high school as well as for a Division I college, and he was still playing in a weekly league until his accident. One day during practice, Carlos collided with another team member and had a serious concussion along with multiple bruises. He told me that ever since, he wasn't feeling or thinking like he used to, and he was in constant pain. What's more, he was afraid to get back to soccer because he thought it would exacerbate his condition.

I assured Carlos that with the right treatment, he would be able to get back in the game. We did a full battery of testing and found that his brain speed was definitely slower than it should be for someone so young. Otherwise, he was in relatively good health. I decided to focus on lifestyle changes, including the CES device, so that he could sleep better and lessen his anxiety and depression. I also developed an exercise program for him that would get his brain and body back in shape without incurring further damage.

Phase 3. This phase involves aerobic/cardiovascular training that requires rhythm and synchrony of the whole body in various actions. Running, speedwalking, swimming, tennis, and basketball are all good choices, as is any other activity you like to participate in. Dancing is a great Phase 3 activity, especially if you do not like traditional exercise.

Phase 4. Next is weight lifting/resistance training to strengthen muscles and bones. Resistance training also offers the opportunity to break bad habits like poor posture that have persisted for decades and that may cause injury. Specific guidelines that promote injury-free exercise designed for human ergonomics can be found in a variety of resources, including specialized books and Web sites.

Phase 5. Cross-training combines Phase 3 cardio and Phase 4 resistance to enhance hormone balance, break down scar tissue, and strengthen connective muscular tissue. It is the highest level of exercise for peak

Carlos spent an hour each day working on short brain games to rebuild his confidence and attention without putting too much pressure on his cognition. His physical exercise program included low-stress activities that he could do at his local gym. He found that a weekly regimen of doing aquatic exercise, using an elliptical machine, and strength training with low weights made him feel better mentally and physically. At first he could not do anything for more than 15 minutes. Gradually, he worked up to a total of 3 hours a week of these combined activities, and within a few months he was able to shake his brain fog completely and get back on the soccer field.

When Carlos finally returned to playing, he was tentative for a long time. I assured him that his behavior was completely natural, especially after experiencing the kind of trauma he had. I reminded him that the nature of most sports injuries is their unpredictability. However, if he remained alert and attentive, which he could do now that he had retrained his brain, he would be able to watch the field carefully and avoid injuries to the best of his ability.

performance. Cross-training programs that combine the two regimens help you achieve this goal while keeping your brain and body sharp.

Sample Schedule of a Five-Phase Program

Phase 1. Work with a basic stretching video at home, then walk for 15 minutes a day. Complete Phase 1 in 1 week.

Phase 2. Work with a vinyasa yoga or Pilates video at home, or join a class at your local Y, gym, or studio. Complete Phase 2 in 2 to 4 weeks, exercising at least three times a week. You can go back to Phase 1 on the days you are not doing Phase 2 activities.

Phase 3. Start with a 20-minute cardio workout that you can do on your own, work with a video, or complete at the gym. Work your way up to a solid 60-minute workout. Choose jogging, running, speedwalking, swimming, cycling, or dancing. Complete Phase 3 in 8 to 16 weeks, exercising at least three or four times a week. You can go back to Phase 2 on the days you are not doing Phase 3 activities.

Phase 4. Start with a 20-minute resistance training workout that you can do on your own, work with a video, or complete at the gym with the help of a personal trainer. Work your way up to a solid 40-minute workout. Complete Phase 4 in 8 to 16 weeks, exercising at least three or four times a week. You can go back to Phase 3 on the days you are not doing Phase 4 activities.

Phase 5. Daily, perform a half-hour cardio workout followed by a full strength-training workout, alternating focus on the upper and lower body each day. Once you have mastered your Phase 5 fitness program, it becomes important to continue increasing the difficulty level of exercise in order to keep improving your health.

Chapter 11

Step Five: Natural Hormones Jump-Start Quick Thinking

Natural hormones are produced by glands throughout the body and in the brain. In fact, there are more than 100 types of hormones that act as brain chemicals, sending messages to specific organs to complete specific tasks. The brain also regulates, translates, and interprets its electrical code as hormonal output. When hormone output is high, you feel healthy, smart, and young. Yet as you get older, your organs slow down their particular hormone production. Without maintaining the right hormone levels, your organs will slowly begin to stop functioning and will literally age faster than the rest of you, leading to various diseases—such as hypothyroidism and heart disease—and menopause. The brain tries desperately to resurrect these aging parts by sending tons of electrical signals to the hypothalamus, the area of the brain that releases its own hormones to the pituitary gland in order to stimulate the aging organs in an attempt to save them. But no such luck. Instead, the stress hormone cortisol increases, and you end up feeling lots of anxiety, falling into a deep and debilitating brain fog, and collecting belly fat. Worse, as each organ begins to fail, it affects every part of your health, including your cognition.

This correlation is particularly important because your hormones control different aspects of cognition at each of the developmental stages of life. You reach your highest levels of memory and attention just after puberty, a time of dramatic increase in hormone production. You'll also find that your memory and attention begin to wane at the start of hormonal decline, known as menopause for women and andropause for men. Many of the same hormones associated with increases in processing speed are also associated with neurogenesis, which can continue to occur under the right conditions throughout your life. These conditions are particularly dependent on your hormone levels.

A decline in your hormone levels is the most likely reason for your performance gap, or why your brain fog seems to get worse every year. Without the right levels, you will become increasingly tired and anxious, so you won't be able to keep up with the younger men and women in your office. This chapter will cover all the hormones that are necessary for maintaining excellent brain health and mental clarity. The good news is that it is very easy to bring back optimal levels of these hormones and resurrect old body parts, including your brain. The goal will be to restore your natural hormones to the levels you had when you were at your peak intelligence, in order to have peak physical health and peak brain performance.

I have been using more than 20 bioidentical hormone supplementations with my patients for more than 2 decades: I find it to be one of the most effective preventive treatments against the development of dementia, as well as a successful course of action to reverse mild cognitive impairment (MCI). This is true for both men and women. If you follow a program like mine that boosts these hormones, it is possible to get smarter as you grow older.

Bioidentical hormone supplements work as nutrients that feed an aging brain. They not only restore health, they make your brain more resilient to failure. Hormone replacement enhances brain speed, the most important function of the brain in terms of your thinking. What's more, it won't bulk you up, or cause cancer, or any of the other misguided rumors you might have heard. In fact, many of the supplements I prescribe are so gentle that they are sold over the counter.

By providing your body and brain with the same hormones it already produces in their most natural forms, you can continue to enhance the production of the brain chemicals we've been referring to throughout this book: dopamine, acetylcholine, GABA, and serotonin. The hormone

Hormonal Decline Predicts
the Performance Gap

This chart represents the typical ages that the following hormone levels begin to change. By the age of 50, the typical person is already deficient in seven important hormones that help maintain cognition and overall health. Without supplementation, there's nowhere to run from the performance gap, because your aging brain and body are competing against others that are younger, brighter, and healthier.

Age 30	HGH, IGF-1, IGF-3
Age 40	Estrogen
Age 50	Testosterone, DHEA, thyroid
Age 60	Progesterone, parathyroid
Age 70	Calcitonin, erythropoietin

therapies for enhancing dopamine, which lead to increased attention, include testosterone, DHEA, and human growth hormone (HGH). The most effective hormone for increasing acetylcholine for faster processing speed and greater memory is estrogen. The hormone that balances GABA to lessen anxiety is progesterone, while melatonin will help you win your battle with depression and help you sleep by increasing serotonin.

STARTING A BIOIDENTICAL HORMONE PROGRAM

I strongly believe in the benefits of bioidentical hormone therapies, and I often use them as the first line of treatment for my patients who have not been able to achieve the results they were looking for from diet, exercise, and lifestyle changes. However, I believe a hormone program works best in concert with all the therapies in the Braverman Protocol. Talk with your physician to see if you are ready to add this type of therapy to the changes in lifestyle you've already made. You'll need to have various blood, urine, or saliva tests run to see if you are truly deficient.

Maintaining the correct hormone balance is critical to every aspect of your health as you age. Many of my patients are reluctant at first to start hormone therapy, and I understand their concerns. But once I explain the differences between natural hormones and traditional hormone therapies, they can make a more informed decision. Read through the following descriptions of the 19 hormone supplements available that can help reverse or treat MCI. Talk to your doctor about the ones that most accurately match the symptoms or conditions you may be experiencing. Then make it perfectly clear that you are only interested in bioidentical versions.

Bioidentical hormones are created at compounding pharmacies, not by the big pharmaceutical industrial complex. They are often made from plant sources, as opposed to the compounds made from human cadavers or horse urine that have been directly implicated in cancers and disease. The recent medical attacks on estrogen therapies target traditional synthetic hormones. Plants do not make human hormones, but some plants contain compounds that have a similar hormonal effect. These, in their natural form, are called phytohormones (meaning "plant-based" hormones) and are the basis for natural hormone therapies.

The molecular structures of natural hormones are identical to those of the actual hormones produced in your body. This is the most important difference between the two types of hormone therapies. In reality, both types are "synthetic," meaning that they are produced artificially and not found in nature. But while the "hormone" Provera is a pharmaceutical made from the same substances that progesterone is made from, the molecular configuration has been changed in the laboratory so that it is not identical to anything found in nature. The molecular structure of natural progesterone made in the compounding pharmacy, on the other hand, is identical—which is why we refer to these therapies as bioidentical—to the molecular structure of the progesterone that is made in your body. In other words, what makes a substance "synthetic" or "natural" is not whether it can be found in nature, but whether it identically matches the one made in the body.

Another example is the pharmaceutical Premarin. This compound is made from two types of estrogen, which taken separately are natural (found in nature) and not synthetic. But not all of the estrogen in Premarin is natural to humans. About half of it is human estrogen, and about

Avoid These Nonbioidentical Hormones

- Methyltestosterone (such as Android, Testred, Virilon)
- Conjugated estrogens (Prempro, Premarin)
- Medroxyprogesterone (Provera)
- Cadaver growth hormones (cadaver-GH)
- Birth control pills

half is horse estrogen derived from urine—a molecule clearly not available or produced in the human body. On the other hand, natural estrogens extracted from wild yams or soybeans that are identical to those made by the human body are easily available by prescription in the form of creams, tablets, and patches. These are estrone, estradiol, and estriol, so there is no need to take horse-based estrogen.

You and your doctor will be able to create a program that suits your particular health needs. Any hormone replacement program requires constant contact with your physician, who will work with you to determine whether you are at the right levels and how long you will have to follow your regimen. Make sure you are working with a physician who understands the importance of both short- and long-term monitoring, not just prescription writing: Balancing hormones to optimal levels is a delicate process but worth the effort so that you will not experience negative side effects.

19 HORMONES YOU NEED TO KNOW

The following are the 19 hormones your brain needs to be smarter:

Aldosterone. Regulates sodium and potassium levels as well as maintains appropriate blood volumes, and may have a protective effect on hearing and verbal memory. Fluids and proper levels of sodium and potassium are essential for inner ear nerve signaling to the brain—a process critical for normal hearing. Researchers discovered that people with age-related hearing loss may have only half the aldosterone they need. This is available with a doctor's prescription.

Dehydroepiandrosterone (DHEA). Produced by the adrenal glands, testicles, and brain, DHEA plays an important role for both men and women. DHEA is the precursor of all sex hormones. DHEA levels peak in your fifties and then begin to decline. Most individuals in their seventies have levels as low as 20 percent of original production. These lowered levels are associated with memory loss and decreased cognitive function, because low DHEA increases cortisol levels, leading to weight gain, then vascular problems, and ultimately MCI. When DHEA is used in conjunction with testosterone therapy, it enhances the benefits of testosterone and reduces the negative side effects. Supplementing can help to mediate adult neurogenesis as well as increase dopamine production. It is also used to treat chronic fatigue syndrome, depression, menopause, and osteoporosis, and to protect the brain from Alzheimer's disease. DHEA can be purchased over the counter as a supplement. Watch for labels marked as 7-keto-DHEA: This variety should be avoided. 7-keto-DHEA is a by-product of DHEA. But unlike DHEA, 7-keto-DHEA is not converted to androgen or estrogen.

DHEA-Sulfate (DHEA-S). Higher DHEA-S levels have been shown to be associated with better cognitive function, primarily related to better executive function, concentration, and working memory. This can be purchased over the counter as a supplement.

Erythropoietin (EPO). Produced by the kidneys, this hormone regulates red blood cell production in the bone marrow. A 2008 study from Göttingen, Germany, reported that EPO improves hippocampus-oriented memory by controlling plasticity, synaptic connectivity, and activity of memory-related neuronal networks. The memory-enhancing effects of EPO are not related to its effects on blood production but are due to direct influences on neurons in the brain. This bioidentical hormone can be obtained with a doctor's prescription.

Estrogen. This hormone is produced by follicles in the ovaries and the brain. Some estrogens are also produced in smaller amounts by other tissues, such as the liver, adrenal glands, breasts, and testes. Estrogen levels are higher in women than in men. Estrogen keeps the brain young by stimulating acetylcholine production. Bioidentical estrogen replacement therapy in menopausal women has led to a significant improvement in information processing as indexed by a significant increase in P300 speed. Other studies have shown that treating younger women with estrogen therapies leads to higher scores on attention tests.

Estradiol. A natural form of estrogen, estradiol is reliable for preventing neurodegenerative disease. However, estradiol is a poor agent for treatment of existing MCI. This hormone can be obtained with a doctor's prescription.

Estriol. This hormone is one of the three main estrogens produced in the body. Studies suggest that estriol reduces symptoms of menopause, such as hot flashes and vaginal dryness, but with a better safety profile compared with more potent estrogens. It is usually applied topically in the form of a cream and is available with a doctor's prescription.

Estrone. The weakest type of estrogen is estrone. It is produced by the conversion of cholesterol and found in fatty tissue. Often sold as a cream (like Ogen), this can be obtained with a doctor's prescription.

Human growth hormone (HGH). This hormone is produced by the pituitary gland. Despite its misleading name, it is first and foremost a repair hormone that is present in the body during all stages of life. Growth hormone stimulates the production of insulin-like growth factor-1 (IGF-1), a hormone that aids in forming new brain and muscle cells, new blood components, and better metabolism, giving you a tremendous mental advantage. Growth hormone levels decrease so significantly with aging that raising them only slightly promotes an improvement in total-body functioning, including many areas of cognitive development. Its supplementation increases all aspects of brain electrical function, including brain speed and processing. It has also been shown to affect cognition, emotion, and mood and to boost cellular metabolism, leading to increased energy. In patients with suboptimal growth hormone (GH) levels, GH replacement therapy has been shown to decrease the symptoms of MCI and increase processing speed after just 6 months of use. GH replacement enhances neurogenesis throughout the brain, including the hippocampus, a likely target for dementia treatment. GH deficiency is also associated with memory impairments, while its replacement can enhance memory and increases in IQ. HGH can be obtained with a doctor's prescription.

Increlex, or insulin-like growth factor (IGF). Increlex is a pure form of IGF-1. This hormone is given to women to increase muscle mass, which increases bloodflow throughout the body, including the brain. This increased bloodflow may enhance neurogenesis. Increlex is available only by prescription.

Melatonin. Melatonin deficiency deprives people of antioxidant protection and also results in loss of sleep or poor sleep quality, which hinders your cognitive abilities the next day. I've also found that supplementing with melatonin may improve some cognitive impairments. This can be purchased over the counter as a supplement.

Parathyroid hormone (PTH). Levels of this hormone naturally increase with age, and when this increase becomes excessive, it is linked to cognitive decline. My foundation has studied this correlation and found that hyperparathyroidism (excessive production of parathyroid hormone) that occurs with osteoporosis can lead to calcifications throughout the body, and also in the brain, reducing processing speed. This is why I believe that surgical removal of one or more parathyroid glands may be an important treatment for protecting the brain against MCI. Parathyroid hormone is also an important treatment for osteoporosis and for healing bone fractures in older adults.

Pregnenolone. A naturally occurring hormone, pregnenolone is produced in the body from cholesterol. It is often referred to as the "grandmother of hormones," because the body uses it to create many other hormones, including testosterone, cortisone, progesterone, estrogen, DHEA, and others. Taking pregnenolone supplements allows you to keep all your hormones at more youthful levels. Pregnenolone also has a very calming effect: It appears to block cortisol release, preventing stress. My patients often find that pregnenolone improves their energy, vision, memory, clarity of thinking, and well-being. This is because pregnenolone, working as an anti-inflammatory, protects the brain from shrinkage.

Progesterone. This hormone is produced by the corpus luteum after ovulation, and in smaller quantities by the adrenal gland. It is synthesized from cholesterol and turned first into pregnenolone, and later converted into progesterone. Progesterone is then the precursor of corticosteroids and testosterone. Once converted, progesterone has multiple roles in your body. It affects every tissue, including the uterus, cervix, and vagina; the endocrine (hormonal) system; brain cells; fat metabolism; thyroid hormone function; water balance; peripheral nerve myelin sheath synthesis; bone cells; energy production; and the immune system.

The fall of progesterone levels at menopause is proportionately much greater than the fall of estrogen levels. While estrogen falls only 40 to

60 percent from the average baseline levels, progesterone can decline to nearly zero. Supplementing with progesterone has been shown to help with sleep, anxiety, and physical pain, and when these problems are alleviated, it can positively affect cognition.

Testosterone. Declining testosterone has been linked to amyloid deposition, leading to chronic fatigue, depression, MCI, and ultimately dementia. Maintaining youthful testosterone levels for men and women compared to the levels typical for their age positively correlates with brain speed and has been shown to enhance neurogenesis and, specifically, visual memory and IQ. I strongly believe that this type of therapy must be used to prevent Alzheimer's, dementia, and other forms of MCI.

Synthetically produced testosterone was first introduced as methyl testosterone, but this was pulled from the market long ago because of its link to liver cancer. Instead, natural testosterone that is produced from plant sources is safe and widely available through a prescription.

Thyroid–T3 and T4. Low levels of thyroid hormone, a condition known as hypothyroidism, lower brain metabolism and are associated with poor concentration, memory disturbances, depression, decreased cognitive function, and dementia. Recently, the diagnosis of hypothyroidism has changed, and now doctors can begin treatment at a much earlier stage. As of 2003, the American Association of Clinical Endocrinologists is recommending that the normal range run

Optimal Hormone Levels Are Needed to Manage Leptin

Your hormone levels help you maintain every aspect of good health, including weight loss as monitored by leptin. If brain fog and weight gain are two issues for you, balancing your hormones might be the answer. To reverse them, you'll need:

- Increased testosterone levels
- Increased DHEA levels
- Increased estrogen levels (for women only)

Patient Profile: Tammy Talked to Her Friends about Bioidentical Hormones

Tammy is one of my favorite patients because as a nurse, she really gets how her body has changed as she has gotten older, and she isn't afraid to take her health care seriously. Her story is sadly typical of the women I've worked with who have made decisions based on poor information and who have let their health suffer. Her story is so powerful that I'm compelled to share it with you in her own words.

"As a 50-year-old nurse, I worked with women all day long who have become forgetful and moody as they have gotten older. I didn't want to become like them, and my menopausal symptoms were unbearable. So about 5 years ago, I took charge of my health and researched everything I could get my hands on, and decided to take bioidentical hormone replacement therapy.

"I felt a difference right away. First I noticed that my sleep was better than it had been in years. All of a sudden my brain was much clearer, and I could think better; it felt like a veil had lifted, and suddenly I knew exactly where my car keys were all the time. I felt like a new person.

"I stopped the program after 3 years. I had a sister who had breast cancer and then died, and frankly, I was scared. I talked about it with my gynecologist, who took me off them, and I went back to my old, sick self: hot flashes, night sweats, and no sleep. Without sleep, my brain turned to mush. So I asked my doctor to put me back on, and she refused. As a nurse, I know you have to be your own health advocate. So when I didn't like what I heard, I found another doctor: I've been working with Dr. Braverman for 2 years, and I feel wonderful.

from 0.3 to 3.0, versus the older range of 0.5 to 5.5. According to the new standards, levels above 3.0 are evidence of hypothyroidism, and levels below 0.3 are evidence of hyperthyroidism. T4 and T3 are two distinct thyroid hormones that when supplemented can help relieve depression, brain fog, and general fatigue. They can be obtained with a doctor's prescription.

"Now that I'm back to my smarter self, my co-workers can see the difference in my demeanor, and they ask me what I do to stay so sharp. When I tell my nursing friends that I'm back on hormones, they completely shut down and tell me, 'Oh, it's the worst thing for you. You shouldn't be on it.' But for the most part, they are the ones that are complaining about their health all the time. And I'm older than they are, and they say, 'You know, you're so sharp and you remember everything.' And I say, 'Well, I'm on bioidentical hormones. I choose to be on it, and I've done a lot of research, and it's very good for you. And, you know, maybe if you did a little bit more reading, maybe it's something you would want to try.' Meanwhile, they're fanning themselves all day long with the hot flashes, and I'm 5 to 6 years older than they are.

"I know without a doubt that without the hormones, I don't think I would be sleeping. And without the sleep, I would not be as sharp as I am. If you don't sleep, you don't have a rested brain, and then you can't expect to function the next day. I've taken sleep medications before, and they do not work as well for me. Yes, they did help me sleep. But I still was waking up because I had hot flashes. When you wake up and you have the hot flashes, you have to change your clothes and your sheets, or you spend the night throwing the covers on and off, and you can't achieve restful sleep. Once we got my hormones properly balanced, I no longer had night sweats and hot flashes, and I slept through the night. Best, I was able to stop taking the other medication that was helping me to sleep, because I don't need it. Now, I get on the pillow and within 20 minutes, I'm sound asleep, and I sleep straight through the night. I don't get up to go to the bathroom. I don't get up until that alarm goes off in the morning. And I jump out of bed and I'm ready to face whatever the day will bring."

Vasopressin. Also known as an antidiuretic hormone, vasopressin is secreted by the posterior pituitary gland and is regulated by the hypothalamus. Vasopressin is transported in the blood to its primary target organ, the kidney, where it stimulates the cells to reabsorb water from urine. This causes a decrease in urine output and a rise in blood volume and, consequently, blood pressure. Vasopressin is also important for regulating cortisol secretion and body temperature. It also acts as a chemical messenger in the brain and controls multiple processes, including memory, sleep, behavior and thought. It is obtained with a doctor's prescription.

Vitamin D. Vitamin D was actually misnamed. Since 2009 we have known that it is a hormone produced by the skin that works as a total-body steroid, anti-inflammatory, and brain chemical augmenter. Without it, the body is susceptible to a host of diseases ranging from cancer to chronic fatigue. While our skin can manufacture some vitamin D from sunlight, most people do not get enough sun every day. For example, many women use moisturizers or sunscreens that filter out vitamin D. However, this hormone is invaluable in strengthening overall health and combating aging, particularly in menopausal women. Vitamin D can be obtained with a doctor's prescription and is also available as an over-the-counter supplement.

NATURAL HORMONES ARE ONE CHOICE FOR MENOPAUSAL WOMEN

Hormonal factors explain why women have increased rates of cognitive decline and dementia. We now know that MCI and menopause are dynamically related. This may be the reason why women generally develop dementia more frequently than men: Their earlier hormone loss, particularly with declining estrogen, combined with longer life expectancy, is a significant risk factor for Alzheimer's disease. It might also explain the disparity between men and women at the top of their fields. Hormone loss increases the performance gap exponentially, so much so that many menopausal women believe that they cannot mentally keep up with their same-age male counterparts in the workplace.

Without estrogen, the brain becomes less effective in sending messages to the other organs to produce hormones. This forces the organs to age, and a vicious cycle appears: The more we age, the more hormones we lose. The number one thing that you can do to enhance brain chemistry and rejuvenate an aging brain is to treat menopause.

For women ages 22 to 40, there are two hormones that relate to menopause and MCI the most dramatically: luteinizing hormone (LH) and follicle-stimulating hormone (FSH). These hormones start to rise from a baseline level of 1. As these levels rise, they reflect declining hormones, which are damaging to your brain. Menopause is measured by an increase in the production of FSH.

Studies have shown that there is a correlation of elevated FSH and LH levels with the prevalence of Alzheimer's disease. Research has shown that women who have had their ovaries removed (known as an oophorectomy) typically lose 10 milliseconds of processing speed. This is due to the fact that an oophorectomy results in a rapid rise in both FSH and LH.

While oophorectomy is a one-time surgical procedure, the process of menopause is fundamentally the same thing—your ovaries are rendered useless as they stop producing estrogen. Research at my PATH Foundation has shown that this loss of estrogen produces a snowball effect. The decline in processing speed sets off a cascade of loss of cognitive function, which begins with memory decline. These memory impairments, in turn, lead to declines in attention.

However, even though estrogen is produced primarily in the ovaries, it is also produced in the uterus, skin, brain, bones, vascular system, liver, adrenal glands, and breasts. After the ovaries stop producing estrogen, the other sites continue, but in smaller quantities. The key is to increase these areas of production so that you can modify the severity of menopause. Specifically, estrogen that continues to be produced in both brain and bone tissues can positively affect cognitive function.

Natural estrogen therapies have also been shown to positively interact with the cholinergic system and influence cognition as it reactivates acetylcholine receptors in the hippocampus, temporal lobes, and frontal lobes. When activated, these receptors activate processes that are beneficial to thinking.

Yet estrogen is not the only culprit. One study conducted in my PATH Foundation has found that menopausal women develop many different hormonal deficiencies, including progesterone, testosterone, DHEA, and declines in thyroid-stimulating hormone (TSH) and leptin. Each of these hormones has individual and interrelated functions in the human body, as we discussed earlier in the chapter. This is why it is so important to have all your hormone levels checked and supplemented as you enter menopause. By doing so, you can close the performance gap at work and live a happier, less anxious life at home.

What Menopause Looks Like

Menopause is often referred to as "the change," but this term is misleading. It implies that the changes associated with menopause are a one-time occurrence. Unfortunately, this is not the case. The seemingly abrupt changes of menopause actually continue for many years even after ovulation ends.

The signs and symptoms of menopause are clear. For many women, menopause can look and feel like a march into "shrinkhood": Women lose height, get weaker, notice drying and wrinkled skin as well as decreased sensitivity to touch, and start to believe that they are going crazy because their memory and attention disappear. Symptoms and their severity vary from woman to woman. Some experience almost none, while others may experience any combination of the following:

- Aching joints
- Attention deficiencies
- Backache
- Bladder infection
- Breast tenderness
- Cold sweats
- Confusion
- Constipation
- Decreased bone density
- Depression
- Diarrhea
- Dizzy spells
- Dry eyes
- Dry nose and mouth
- Dry skin
- Facial hair growth
- Fatigue
- Fine lines around mouth and eyes
- Headaches
- Hot flashes
- Increased gas
- Increased incidence of cysts
- Insomnia
- Irritability
- Irritable bowel syndrome
- Loss of appetite
- Memory loss
- Mood swings
- Nervous tension
- Night sweats
- Rapid heartbeat
- Shortness of breath
- Skin rash/irritation
- Sore throat
- Swelling
- Thinning hair or hair loss
- Tingling in hands and feet

- Urinary incontinence, discomfort, or changes in frequency
- Vaginal discharge
- Vaginal dryness
- Vaginal numbness
- Weakness
- Weight gain

Fortunately, women have the ability to diminish cognitive declines as well as these other symptoms if they are recognized early on. The best prescription for dealing with menopausal symptoms is to naturally replace all the hormones that your body is no longer making, or is making at less-than-optimal levels. By doing so, you are virtually turning your brain into that of a 30-year-old, because many hormones are precursors to, or act just like, the specific brain chemicals you rely on to keep your thinking sharp.

Perimenopause Precedes Menopause

Women will start to lose their hormones almost as soon as they appear, at the beginning of adulthood. Perimenopause, which is defined as the time during which a woman's body makes a natural shift from regular cycles of ovulation and menstruation toward menopause, can begin as early as age 22. By the time you reach your forties, you may start noticing changes that go beyond your menstrual cycle.

There are many factors that contribute to when you begin perimenopause. Aside from family genetics, most of them are in your control:

- Depression
- Exposure to environmental toxins, including smoking, chemotherapy, and irradiation
- Obesity
- Prior oral contraceptive use
- Stress

During the transition from perimenopause to menopause, your menstrual flow can change erratically:

- Heavy periods accompanied by blood clots
- Periods that last several days longer than usual

- Spotting between periods
- Spotting after sex
- Periods that occur closer together
- Light periods
- Skipped periods

The most important lesson you can learn from this book is that it is never too late to take care of yourself. Whether you are in perimenopause or just experiencing menopausal symptoms for the first time, or menopause has been 10 years past, you can regain your health, your vitality, and your cognitive function.

MEN MENOPAUSE TOO

As men age, our brain chemistry dwindles as we begin to lose testosterone and other important hormones. Andropause, the male equivalent of menopause, is marked by this hormonal decline. Testosterone therapies have been positively linked with preventing MCI and dementia. It's therefore equally important for men to replace low levels of hormones.

Andropause can begin as early as age 40, or even earlier if you are under enormous stress or have episodes of depression, excessive athleticism, or frequent drug use. However, most men find that just by taking better care of their health through lifestyle and diet changes, they are able to get their testosterone levels to increase naturally. An exercise program, like the one I outlined in Chapter 10, plays a major role in increasing both testosterone and growth hormone.

What's more, if you are losing testosterone simply because you are getting older, then you can replace this hormone, and others, and reverse your health. Aside from waning sexual desire and function, low testosterone levels affect your overall health, your mood, and your mental quickness. Here are a few warning signs that your testosterone level is lagging:

- Anxiety
- Decreased beard growth
- Decreased hair and nail growth
- Depressed mood
- Excessive sweating
- Fatigue

The Stages of Menopause

Stage 1. Premenopause/late reproductive stage begins while you are still fertile, so there is a healthy quality and quantity of egg cells in the ovaries. At this point there is a minimal increase in FSH.

Stage 2. During perimenopause, FSH levels increase. This is accompanied by a decline in the quantity and quality of egg cells, and your ability to become pregnant diminishes.

Stage 3. Late perimenopause is the stage when FSH levels increase significantly and the menstrual cycle occurs infrequently.

Stage 4. At menopause, the complete cessation of the menstrual cycle, high FSH levels plateau.

- Irritability
- Joint pain and muscle achiness
- Loss of skin elasticity
- Loss of vitality
- Sleep disturbances

MAKE YOUR DOCTOR YOUR PARTNER

For many of my patients, natural, bioidentical hormone therapies make all the difference in their ability to reverse MCI and bridge the performance gap. By following the diet and losing weight, taking the right supplements, and exercising regularly, you may be able to increase your hormone levels naturally. Talk to your doctor about these therapies if you are not achieving results from the other parts of the protocol. Bring this book with you to show that you understand the difference between synthetic hormones and natural ones. You can show your doctor the References section of this book, where I've clearly outlined the hundreds of studies available that demonstrate the efficacy of these treatments. And if your doctor is not open to these types of treatments, it might be time to find another doctor who is more current with the medical literature on aging and cognitive decline.

You might also want to keep a log, or journal, after you've started these types of therapies, so that you can monitor for yourself the progress

(continued on page 214)

Patient Profile: Lucy Feels Better—And Thinks Faster—With Bioidentical Hormones

My patient Lucy was 52 and living in Vancouver, Canada, when she first came all the way to New York City to see me. Frankly, Lucy was in terrible shape. When I took her patient history, I was shocked to find out that her health complaints went back to an incident that had happened 23 years earlier. At the time, she was a sales trainer and a single mom, working hard at supporting her family. And in 1 day, all her hard work had come to an end.

Lucy explained to me that she took one last promotion but was forced to work such long hours that she ended up with pneumonia, and since then had never been able to go back to work. She was constantly fatigued during the day and couldn't sleep at night. Lucy told me that she couldn't keep her thoughts straight and could never remember what day of the week she was in. Worst of all, she had terrible balance: She was falling all the time. After lying on the living room couch for a year, Lucy started looking for a solution.

The first doctor she saw was convinced that she had AIDS. Others recommended that she change her lifestyle for one that was less stressful, but it didn't help. She saw a holistic therapist who suggested that she remove her mercury dental fillings, which did seem to help. Lucy told me that after that procedure, she was able to get out of bed, but for only a limited amount of time. Six years went by before she was diagnosed with chronic fatigue. She then trained as an energy healer in order to heal herself, but this course didn't change her health. Finally, she convinced herself to see a psychologist, who recommended that she read one of Suzanne Somers's books about natural hormone replacement therapies. Lucy learned about my practice from Somers's book and made an appointment to see me.

I have to admit that I was equally perplexed, but started her on the Braverman Protocol, beginning with thorough and comprehensive brain testing and blood work. Her score on the Braverman Memory Test was the lowest I had ever seen for a woman her age. She had absolutely no data retrieval ability. In fact, it took her 3 minutes just to tell me what season it was. I was afraid to tell her my deepest fear: She was on the borderline for dementia at just 52.

When all the results were in, we discovered that her problems did not come from a single bout of pneumonia; instead, she was suffering from otherwise undiagnosed recurring seizures from head injuries that went back to a car accident that occurred when she was just 5 years old. The seizures were affecting her brain chemistry to the point that she was strongly deficient in all brain chemicals. She also had tumors and cysts throughout her body and was significantly overweight.

Lucy's condition was severe enough that we started immediately with nutrients, medications, and a natural hormone program to renew her brain and her body. A week later she called me from Canada, and I could hardly recognize her voice. She told me that she had slept for the first time in years and was beginning to feel much better, although her memory was still very foggy. I told her to give the protocol a few more weeks and to come and see me in a month.

When Lucy came back to my office, I literally didn't recognize her: At first I thought she was her daughter. Lucy had lost 35 pounds and seemed to have boundless energy. She told me that it took a full 3 weeks of living in a zombie state until the protocol medications, hormones, and nutrients began to work together synergistically. Once that happened, she began to get better cognitively. She reported that she still couldn't take on too much, but was beginning to return to her type A self.

A year later, Lucy is still following my program. She is off most of her medications but continues to take her natural bioidentical hormones and is following the Younger (Thinner) You Diet to maintain her weight loss. She practices her brain-boosting exercises every day and reports that her thinking is now better than ever, and she has gone back to work. After 23 years of sickness, she feels as though she is living for the first time.

Testosterone Treatments for Men

Discuss with your doctor these bioidentical testosterone therapy options:

- AndroGel
- Compounded gel
- Injectable

you are making. Many doctors who provide these therapies will want to see you often to make sure your dosage is correct. This is a very important part of the treatment program, because subtle changes in your prescription might be needed depending on your results.

The next chapter concludes the Braverman Protocol with a discussion of the medications that you can take to lessen anxiety and improve cognition. These may be right for you if you have not had success with other areas of the program. But I find that each part of the protocol works in conjunction with the others, which is another important reason to keep your doctor in the loop while you are following this program.

Chapter 12

Step Six: Brain-Balancing Medications

Traditional medications are often prescribed for a brain chemical deficiency in conjunction with other therapies, or when other treatments have not been effective. These medications can safely help return the brain's chemistry to a more normal, or even enhanced, level. Some work because they imitate a particular brain chemical, triggering the brain to respond as if it were producing the particular brain chemical itself. Others block the chemical from being absorbed by other receptors, making the chemical more available to the brain and the rest of the body.

The following are medications that I commonly prescribe to my patients, depending on their symptoms and brain chemical deficiencies. Many of them have a cumulative effect: The ones that increase dopamine will help you regain or enhance your attention, because they give your brain more power. The ones that enhance acetylcholine production will improve your memory. The GABA medications will relieve anxiety, and you may find that without the worry, your memory issues resolve themselves. Lastly, the serotonin medications treat depression and sleep issues, both of which negatively affect your thinking. At the same time, you might find that the physical symptoms you are experiencing will also resolve once you rebalance your brain chemistry. This is because most physical issues are directly related to your brain chemical status. In the next chapter we will discuss this relationship more thoroughly, but in terms of medications, you may find that overall, you will feel better—and even younger—once you balance your brain.

Just as with nutrients and hormone therapies, discuss all options with your doctor in order to determine which of these suggestions is best for your current health status and existing prescription load.

GABA MEDICATIONS LESSEN ANXIETY AND INCREASE CONFIDENCE

Anticonvulsants. These drugs are typically used to prevent or treat convulsions or seizures. I find that in low doses they are also effective

GENERIC NAME	BRAND NAME
Carbamazepine	Carbatrol, Epitol, Equetro, Tegretol
Ethosuximide	Zarontin
Ethotoin	Peganone
Felbamate	Felbatol
Fosphenytoin	Cerebyx, Prodilantin
Gabapentin	Neurontin
Lamotrigine	Lamictal
Levetiracetam	Keppra
Mephenytoin	Mesantoin
Methsuximide	Celontin
Oxcarbazepine	Trileptal
Phensuximide	Milontin
Phenytoin	Dilantin
Primidone	Mysoline
Topiramate	Topamax
Trimethadione	Tridione
Valproic acid	Depakote
Zonisamide	Zonegran

ways to treat chronic pain, nerve pain, and fibromyalgia, as well as mood. Experts do not know exactly how anticonvulsants work to reduce chronic pain and improve mood. It is thought that they may block the flow of pain signals from the central nervous system.

Benzodiazepines. These medications are tranquilizers and slow down the nervous system. Some are used to relieve anxiety; others treat insomnia. The benzodiazepine family produces a sedative effect, inducing sleep at night and relieving anxiety and muscle spasms during the day. In general, benzodiazepines are considered as hypnotics, or sleep medications, in high doses; anxiolytics, or anxiety reducers, in moderate doses; and sedatives, or calming medications, in low doses.

GENERIC NAME	BRAND NAME
Alprazolam	Xanax
Chlordiazepoxide	Librium
Clonazepam	Klonopin
Clorazepate	Tranxene, Tranxene-SD
Diazepam	Valium
Estazolam	ProSom
Flurazepam	Dalmane
Halazepam	Paxipam
Lorazepam	Ativan
Midazolam	Versed
Oxazepam	Serax
Prazepam	Centrax
Quazepam	Doral
Temazepam	Restoril
Triazolam	Halcion

Sodium oxybate (Xyrem). This is used to treat narcolepsy and daytime sleepiness.

SEROTONIN-ENHANCING MEDICATIONS

Antidepressants are the most common type of serotonin-enhancing medications. They are known stimulants of neurogenesis, as they help grow new brain cells. Antidepressants also preserve brain chemicals and allow us to upregulate, or increase, the response, due to an increase in the number of receptors on the cell surface. Because of this, antidepressants are known to improve brain processing speed.

Antidepressants fall into different categories, although most share a common property: They increase the amount of serotonin.

Monoamine oxidase (MAO) inhibitors. These drugs act on a mitochondrial enzyme that breaks down both dopamine and serotonin. By inhibiting the enzyme in serotonin-releasing neurons, the drugs cause more serotonin to be deposited in the synapses. MAO inhibitors are not frequently prescribed because of adverse side effects, as well as the improved efficacy of other antidepressants.

GENERIC NAME	BRAND NAME
Isocarboxazid	Marplan
Phenelzine	Nardil
Tranylcypromine	Parnate

Tricyclics. These drugs block the reuptake of dopamine and serotonin, causing an increase in the level of these brain chemicals in the synapses. Today, tricyclics are most commonly prescribed for chronic physical pain relief. Tricyclics are not frequently prescribed because of adverse side effects, as well as the improved efficacy of other, newer antidepressants.

GENERIC NAME	BRAND NAME
Amitriptyline	Elavil
Clomipramine	Anafranil
Doxepin	Sinequan
Imipramine	Tofranil
Nortriptyline	Pamelor

Selective serotonin reuptake inhibitors (SSRIs). These drugs quickly increase the amount of serotonin in the brain, resolving depression and allowing you to think more clearly. However, this type of antidepressant can take 2 to 4 weeks to build up its effect to work fully. A normal course of antidepressants lasts at least 6 months after symptoms have eased. Side effects may occur but are often minor. At the end of the course of treatment, gradually reduce the dose as directed by your doctor before stopping completely.

Examples:

GENERIC NAME	BRAND NAME
Citalopram	Celexa
Escitalopram	Lexapro
Fluoxetine	Prozac
Paroxetine	Paxil
Sertraline	Zoloft

Serotonin and norepinephrine reuptake inhibitors (SNRIs). Increasing both serotonin and dopamine's cousin, norepinephrine, this category of antidepressants is also known as dual reuptake inhibitors. This type of medication will improve mood and focus.

GENERIC NAME	BRAND NAME
Duloxetine	Cymbalta
Milnacipran	Savella
Venlafaxine	Effexor

Bupropion (Wellbutrin). This medication blocks the reuptake of dopamine. Although it does not interfere with the uptake of serotonin, it is an effective antidepressant. A 2007 study from the North Carolina Neuropsychiatry Clinics showed that depressed patients treated with bupropion performed as well as patients without depression on a battery of neurocognitive tests, while other types of antidepressants were not able to improve cognition.

Aspirin May Be Good for Your Thinking

Over-the-counter nonsteroidal anti-inflammatory drugs (NSAIDs), including aspirin and ibuprofen, may reduce your risk for Alzheimer's disease if taken daily at low doses. One study that followed participants for more than 2 years found that low-dose aspirin taken regularly reduced the beta-amyloid plaques that accumulate in the brain. Aspirin also keeps platelets from sticking together, which prevents blood clotting and allows for blood to be dispersed through the brain and body more easily. Both of these traits may help delay the onset of mild cognitive impairment (MCI).

Buspirone (BuSpar). This drug is used for the management of symptoms of mild sleep disorders and anxiety by affecting dopamine and serotonin levels. It is not an effective treatment for those suffering from severe anxiety, panic disorders, or obsessive-compulsive disorders. It may also help improve symptoms of depression along with generalized anxiety disorder.

MEDICINES THAT RESTORE MEMORY

There are many drugs already on the market that can slow down dementia or stop further memory loss. Some of these medications include blood pressure medications like atenolol (sold as Tenormin), because they improve the vascular system and increase bloodflow to the brain. For 6 years, scientists observed a group of 3,300 people over the age of 65 who were on various medications to reduce blood pressure. It was found that by taking any kind of blood pressure medicine, these study participants decreased their chances of getting Alzheimer's by 36 percent. Subjects on diuretics showed the greatest reduction, up to a 74 percent decrease. Surprisingly, these strong results were achieved whether or not the medicine had any effect on blood pressure.

Acetylcholine medications do not treat blood pressure, but they do boost the strength of existing brain signals. While these drugs can reverse symptoms, they do not cure mild cognitive impairment (MCI). And keep in mind that an improvement in cognition may last only as long as you stay on the medication.

Memantine (Namenda) is in another class of medication, which does not increase acetylcholine but does help with memory.

I have found some success with the following acetylcholine-enhancing medications that can temporarily alleviate symptoms of MCI:

GENERIC NAME	BRAND NAME
Donepezil	Aricept
Galantamine	Reminyl, Razadyne
Rivastigmine	Exelon
Tacrine	Cognex

DOPAMINE MEDICATIONS HELP INCREASE ATTENTION

The improvement of attention through medication is very successful, especially with dopamine-friendly prescriptions. If you tested positively

Treating Alzheimer's Disease

While Alzheimer's disease cannot be completely reversed, there are a number of treatments that can reduce symptoms if prescribed at the earliest stages. The enzyme acetylcholinesterase rapidly breaks down acetylcholine but may be blocked with new medications. These are called cholinesterase inhibitors. They may help improve cognitive and neuropsychiatric symptoms, and they might affect the long-term course of the disease.

As Alzheimer's progresses, a common behavior symptom includes increasing agitation, making the sufferer feel confused and restless toward the end of the day. This symptom is referred to as sundowning. Patients with Alzheimer's may also awaken or even wander at night. If these problems cannot be managed through adjusting living environments, these individuals may benefit from sedative medications such as the ones listed earlier.

to inconsistent attention in the Braverman Brain Advantage Test, you may respond well to the dopamine-boosting therapies listed below. However, if you are more prone to making omission errors, you would be better served by the acetylcholine medications previously listed that restore memory. The following is a list of dopamine-boosting medications that are commonly prescribed for individuals coping with attention deficit disorder (ADD).

GENERIC NAME	BRAND NAME
Atomoxetine HCl	Strattera
Bupropion	Aplenzin, Wellbutrin
Dexmethylphenidate	Focalin
Dextroamphetamine	Dexedrine, DextroStat
Dextroamphetamine + amphetamine (Barr)	Adderall, Adderall XR
Guanfacine	Intuniv, Intuniv ER, Tenex
Lisdexamfetamine dimesylate	Vyvanse
Methamphetamine	Desoxyn
Methylphenidate	Concerta, Daytrana, Daytrana TD, Metadate, Methylin, Ritalin, Ritalin LA, Ritalin SR

Levitra and Cialis Raise Dopamine and Brain Metabolism

Erectile dysfunction medications such as Viagra, Levitra, and Cialis are dopamine enhancers because they are meant to increase blood-flow. If you or your spouse is taking these medications, you might also find that attention has improved along with other low dopamine–related symptoms, including weight loss.

LEPTIN-ENHANCING MEDICATIONS

Once you balance your brain chemistry, your leptin will self-regulate. While it is best to regulate your leptin naturally, there are a few medications that may be beneficial to maintaining leptin balance. These medications are important to recognize, because you may be taking them for other health concerns. Or, if you have similar health concerns but your

TYPICALLY PRESCRIBED FOR...	GENERIC NAME	BRAND NAME
Weight loss	Leptin analog	Metreleptin
Acne	Tretinoin	Retin-A
Depression, attention	Bupropion	Wellbutrin
Seizures, anxiety	Topiramate	Topamax
Seizures, anxiety	Zonisamide	Zonegran
Cardiac	Omega-3 polyunsaturated fatty acids	Omacor
Cardiac	Valsartan	Diovan
Cardiac	Candesartan	Atacand
Cardiac	Pindolol	Visken
Cardiac	Ramipril	Altace
Cardiac	Amlodipine	Norvasc
Cardiac	Efonidipine	Landel
Cardiac	Atorvastatin	Lipitor
Antidiabetic	Exenatide	Byetta
Antidiabetic	Rosiglitazone	Avandia
Antidiabetic	Metformin	Glucophage
Antidiabetic	Pramlintide	Symlin
Antidiabetic	Liraglutide	Victoza
Neurological	Bromocriptine	Parlodel

Patient Profile: John Thinks Better at 63 Than He Did at 40

John came to see me almost 2 years ago because he was having problems with his memory and concentration. He was particularly agitated because even though his health was fine, he felt like he could no longer mentally keep up with the other men in his accounting office. John told me that he used to have a "head for details" but was now afraid that he was going to lose his job of more than 20 years because he couldn't remember even his oldest clients' information.

I understood just what John meant when he told me that he felt like a walking dead man. I've met many men over the years who were close to retirement age but still identified heavily with their careers and weren't ready to give them up. The economic times weren't making it any easier, either. John told me that his goal was to bring back what he called his "inner Einstein," the mental fire he once possessed that had made him so successful at his job in the past.

The most upsetting part of John's story was the fact that he had already seen a number of doctors, each of whom had told him that there was nothing wrong with his health. They were right: He was trim, his heart was healthy, and he had no physical issues. He presented himself as intelligent and didn't complain about depression or even trouble sleeping. But what the other doctors never took into consideration was his brain health. Luckily, John was desperate to find a solution to his sluggish thinking, and finally came to see me.

We started John on the Braverman Protocol, beginning with comprehensive testing. His scores on the Braverman Memory Test showed major deficiencies in all his brain chemicals. In fact, I was surprised to find that the rest of his health was relatively good, considering how badly damaged his brain was. Following the results on the tests, he started the program with the mental and physical workout. The goal here would be to get his brain and body back into shape as quickly as possible. I switched his diet to include more healthy fats and foods with omega-3 fatty acids to boost his acetylcholine without weight gain. I also prescribed the use of the CES device so that at night he could give his brain the rest it needed. Lastly, I prescribed medications that would boost all areas of brain health. I suggested Depakote in order to rebalance his GABA and lower his anxiety, Adderall to improve his dopamine and attention, Namenda to improve his memory, Cymbalta to balance his serotonin, and testosterone to give him more mental and physical energy and treat his declining hormone levels.

In just 3 weeks, John stopped by my office without an appointment just to tell me personally how much better he felt. He was more than relieved that once again he could remember details, and his concentration at work quickly became a lot better.

Two years later, at 63, John now thinks and feels like a 20-year-old. Because the medications and exercise programs were so effective, I ept him on them for almost a year, then gently weaned him off the medications and replaced them with nutrient supplements, including resveratrol and carnitine. The last time I saw him, he thanked me again for giving him his life back, then had to rush back to his office to meet with another new client.

John is one of my favorite patients, because his story shows exactly how every aspect of the Braverman Protocol comes together to best results. Other doctors would have dismissed his complaints as part of aging. But John knew, as I do, that you don't have to get worse as you get older: You can get better. John wasn't afraid to take charge of his health, and he wasn't willing to take no for an answer when others told him that there was nothing wrong with him. And in a very short period of time, John's hopes were answered, and he was able to get back on track with his career.

Medical Marijuana Won't
Help Your Thinking

Medical marijuana is a hot topic right now, and I'm not referring to the kind you smoke. Most responsible doctors who treat patients with a cannabis-based therapy prescribe Marinol pills—not in any sort of tobacco form. I've prescribed Marinol for a small set of my patients suffering from cataracts or cancer. But in the long run, medical marijuana is still dope and is neurotoxic, meaning that it destroys the brain. Worse, it's often unclear when, or whether, it might work better than traditional drugs, which come with established dosing regimens.

doctor has prescribed a different medication, use this chart to discuss other options that might also work for managing your leptin levels. These medications affect either hormones or brain chemistry, particularly enhancing serotonin, dopamine, and GABA. Some of these chemicals work in the same regions of the brain as leptin.

The next chapter explores other health problems you may be faced with and shows how they can negatively affect your thinking. The fix for these issues is the same as here: By following the Braverman Protocol and rebalancing your brain with the right lifestyle changes, exercise regimen, nutrition, hormones, and even medications, you may find that these health issues will resolve as well, and your memory and attention will return. Or, even better, you might find that with your health restored, you'll be smarter than ever before.

Part III

Your Brain, Your Body

Chapter 13

Reversing Disease Makes You Smarter

I know it seems obvious, but many people forget that their heads are attached to their bodies. So it makes perfect sense that just as your brain controls your bodily functions, your body's health influences just how smart you actually are.

The truth is that almost every illness of the body wears down the brain. The brain burns up when metabolism is out of control; it swells in an inflammatory response to an immune system issue; it dries out as it calcifies from bone density loss; it rusts from exposure to metals and toxins; and it gets choked to death from a diminished or polluted blood supply. All these scenarios lead to cellular death, declining brain speed, and diminished brain chemical activity. And as we know, when that goes, so do your cognitive capabilities.

Fortunately, we can prevent these brain calamities by addressing health concerns early on, and by maintaining control of brain and body health throughout your lifetime. The good news is that one way your brain can be healed so that you can get smarter is by reversing the body's diseases that affect its functioning. When you follow the Braverman Protocol, beginning with proper screening, illnesses can be detected and treated before they progress to affect other areas of your health, or further weaken your thinking. Best of all, you'll be able to see real improvement in your mild cognitive impairment (MCI) when you reverse illness throughout your body.

Medical conditions do not happen overnight: They can often begin as long as 10 to 20 years before you may experience the first signs or symptoms. The fact is that disease occurs as just one part of general aging. I explain to my patients all the time that I believe that each disease influences your entire health like a game of dominoes. When one part of your body becomes prematurely old, you'll experience illness. For example, if your heart wears down, it is aging faster than the rest of your body, and that's when you develop heart disease. When this "older" part of your body begins to fail, it tips the first domino in the line, and you'll quickly see that the rest of your health will begin to cascade, pulling everything down in its path. This is why I say that you're only as young as your oldest part. Even if you are 45 and in great physical shape, if your heart health is declining and your heart is working like the heart of a 60-year-old, then you are living like a 60-year-old.

One reason why you may not have noticed that your internal systems are aging is that they get older just as imperceptibly as your brain. Let's think back to the train analogy we used at the beginning of the book. Since all internal activity is occurring at the same pace, there is no external reference to evaluate against. Therefore, you might think that you are healthy in your forties or fifties, but in reality, inside your skin are deteriorating organs and systems that are aging too slowly to be recognized by your own declining judgment. For example, your once-powerful muscles are no longer pushing the same amount of blood up to your brain, which is why cerebral bloodflow decreases dramatically with age.

The majority of people over 40 years of age have a minimum of five hidden illnesses, all of which are linked to brain chemistry and, subsequently, cognition. By the time you reach your midfifties, age-related diseases are noticeable. You will probably recognize your MCI symptoms much earlier than you will experience the first signs of disease. This is why the cascade of poor health is so often experienced in the following order of events:

- Loss of brain power and speed
- Loss of visual, verbal, and working memory
- Loss of complex attention

- Loss of cognition, abstract thinking ability, inductive reasoning, and spatial orientation
- Glands and organs of the body begin to fail

THE BODY AGES WHEN BRAIN SPEED DECLINES

Conversely, when your memory begins to deteriorate, it's just as if another domino pushed down your health. For example, when the brain loses acetylcholine, it sends a death code to the organs and hormone-producing glands of the body that it is losing the necessary moisture to keep your brain and body well lubricated. This loss directly affects other parts of your body that need to be moist, such as your bones and joints. Because of this, a loss of acetylcholine not only affects your memory, it affects your bone health and predicts a likely development of arthritis. Bone loss has also been shown to predict cognitive decline in older, osteoporotic women, a decline that may be caused by calcifications in the brain. And this is also why we know that a weak frame equals a weak brain, and why doctors like me can correlate osteoporosis based on levels of anxiety and/or depression and even cognitive decline.

All the diseases of the body can be traced in one way or another to brain chemical imbalances. A dopamine deficiency will manifest as lack of attention because your brain is losing the power to stay focused. This loss of power will also affect your body, particularly in areas that are affected by metabolism, leading to weight gain or loss of muscular control, as in Parkinson's disease. GABA deficiencies linked to mental anxiety manifest as chronic physical pain, inflammation, or digestive upsets, such as irritable bowel syndrome, as your brain's balance is disturbed. Serotonin deficiencies are linked to mood changes because your brain cannot rest and reset. When the body cannot rest and reset, this can turn into high blood pressure.

The following chart shows which illnesses and conditions are directly linked to specific brain chemical deficiencies. If you've already identified a particular brain chemical imbalance, use this chart to see if you are experiencing any of the earliest signs and symptoms of these related diseases. Keep in mind that all these conditions are preventable and treatable if you catch them at their earliest stages and continue to rebalance your brain.

Brain Chemical Deficiencies Leading to Physical Health Breakdowns

Confusion/Loss of Attention—Dopamine Deficiency Physical Symptoms

- Addiction
- Anemia
- Bone density loss
- Constipation
- Diabetes
- Difficulty achieving orgasm
- Digestion problems
- Excessive sleep
- High blood pressure
- Hypoglycemia
- Impotence
- Inability to lose weight
- Involuntary movements
- Joint pain
- Kidney problems
- Lack of quickness
- Low sex drive
- Narcolepsy
- Obesity
- Parkinson's disease
- Poor blood sugar stability
- Poor physical strength
- Poor walking
- Shuffling gait
- Slow metabolism
- Slow or rigid movements
- Thyroid disorders
- Wide-based gait

Loss of Memory—Acetylcholine Deficiency Physical Symptoms

- Arthritis
- Cholesterol elevation
- Diabetes
- Difficulty urinating
- Dry cough
- Dry mouth
- Eye disorders
- Glaucoma
- Inflammatory disorders (sinusitis, allergies, hay fever, colitis, atherosclerosis, rheumatoid arthritis, and even some cancers)
- Multiple sclerosis
- Myasthenia gravis (an autoimmune disease that causes fatigue and muscle weakness)
- Osteoporosis
- Sexual dysfunction
- Speech problems

Depression—Serotonin Deficiency Physical Symptoms

- Allergies
- Carbohydrate craving
- Hallucinations
- Hypersensitivity
- Hypertension
- Nausea
- Night sweats
- PMS
- Premature ejaculation
- Vomiting
- Weight gain

Anxiety/Panic—GABA Deficiency Physical Symptoms

- Abnormal sense of smell
- Backache
- Blurred vision
- Butterflies in stomach
- Cardiac arrhythmias
- Chest pain or discomfort
- Choking sensation
- Chronic pain
- Cold/clammy hands
- Cough/choking
- Diarrhea
- Difficulty swallowing
- Dizziness
- Dribbling
- Dry mouth (xerostomia)
- Excessive menstrual bleeding
- Flushing or pallor
- Headache
- High blood pressure
- High startle responses
- Hyperactivity
- Hypersomnia/insomnia
- Hyperventilation
- Hypervigilance
- Irritable bowel syndrome
- Muscle loss
- Muscle tension/aches
- Nausea
- Night sweats
- Palpitations
- Paresthesia (numbness or tingling of the skin)
- Seizures
- Sexual dysfunction
- Shortness of breath
- Sweating
- Tachycardia
- Tinnitus (ringing in ears)
- TMJ
- Trembling
- Twitching
- Urinary frequency
- Vomiting

The Pauses

As they age, the body's organs and internal systems can be viewed as going through their own *pauses*: time markers that identify the wear and tear of every part of the body. Like menopause, all the pauses occur along with diminishing hormone production. During these pauses, the failing organ becomes older than the rest of your body and slowly, or in some cases rapidly, starts to die. When this occurs, its associated hormone levels drop, sending a signal to the rest of the body: Its purpose is to broadcast that the system is failing. This signal also begins the process whereby the whole body will begin to shut down.

In my book *Younger You,* I review many of these pauses in much greater detail. The book includes a simple test called the AgePrint, which you can take to identify which pauses you may be experiencing. This test is also available on my website, www.pathmed.com.

Many of these symptoms and conditions can be reversed by following the Braverman Protocol, including simple lifestyle changes, proper diet and exercise, nutritional supplementation, bioidentical hormone therapies, and medications, when necessary. By taking care of the pauses, not only will you feel better, you can increase your vitality and physical strength, and reduce the likelihood of cognitive decline.

The chart on the following page shows each of the pauses, and how they affect your thinking as you age.

DISEASES THAT AFFECT COGNITION

The following diseases directly affect memory and cognition in ways that have not been previously described. Many are related to diminished bloodflow to the brain, which can lead to memory loss and slower thinking, as well as structural damage. Vascular disease is the second-most-common cause of dementia in the United States. Without the proper bloodflow, the brain becomes deficient in many key nutrients, particularly the B vitamins. The brain is surrounded by a protective casing known as the blood-brain barrier, which allows only certain substances to pass from the bloodstream into the brain. If blood becomes too thick with sugars, cholesterol, or plaque, the amount of blood that can pass through the barrier decreases. Over time, this can

PAUSE	DECLINE IN . . .	ASSOCIATED DISEASES/CONDITIONS THAT AFFECT COGNITION
Adipause	Leptin, ghrelin	Obesity, metabolic syndrome
Adrenopause	DHEA	Excessive stress
Andropause	Testosterone in men	Amyloid deposition
Cardiopause/ vasculopause	Ejection fraction and bloodflow	Stroke, coronary artery disease
Dermatopause	Collagen, vitamin D synthesis	Osteoporosis, heart disease, cancer, autoimmune disease, depression, insomnia, arthritis, psoriasis, fibromyalgia
Gastropause	Nutrient absorption, gastric acidity	Colitis, irritable bowel syndrome (IBS)
Genopause	Telomeres	Alzheimer's disease, brain tumors, brain immune disorders
Immunopause/ thymopause	Hormonal and cellular immunity	Cancer, multiple sclerosis, lupus, arthritis, allergies
Menopause	Estrogen, progesterone, and testosterone in women	Fatigue and sleep disorders, mood swings, anxiety, depression, yeast infections
Nephropause	Renal failure	Kidney disease
Osteopause/ parathyropause	Bone density	Osteoporosis
Pancreopause	Glucose tolerance	Diabetes, obesity
Pinealpause	Sleep depth, REM sleep cycle	Insomnia
Sensorypause	Touch, hearing, vision, and smell sensitivity	Hearing loss, deafness, vision loss, loss of balance
Somatopause	Growth hormone	Chronic pain, brain cell death, brain myelinization
Thyropause	Calcitonin and thyroid hormone levels	Hyperthyroidism, hypothyroidism

result in the brain becoming malnourished; neurogenesis ceases, and the existing brain cells become far less efficient.

You'll also see how many of the following are also risk factors for different diseases: They are therefore affecting your total body health as well as your cognition. In fact, many are linked to form a new diagnosis now called metabolic syndrome: a cluster of conditions—increased blood pressure, elevated insulin levels, excess body fat around the waist, abnormal cholesterol levels—that occur together, increasing your risk of heart disease, stroke, and diabetes.

The good news is that the fix for each of the following diseases, along with metabolic syndrome, is exactly the same. By following the Braverman Protocol, you can take your health into your own hands by first making small but significant lifestyle changes. If you are more than 15 pounds overweight, following the diet outlined in Chapter 9 and losing weight will naturally reduce your risk for stroke, heart disease, and diabetes. Carrying excess weight means that your body may be turning excess fat and cholesterol into plaque. Being overweight can also make your heart work harder, raising your blood pressure and decreasing the functionality of all of the important metabolic organs. By losing weight, you may reduce both risk factors at the same time. Also, because the eating plan outlined in this book reduces the amount of salt, saturated fat, and cholesterol in your diet, it may lower cholesterol levels in your blood.

Staying off alcohol, cigarettes, and other addictions will also help you reverse these diseases. Alcohol may raise the cholesterol levels in your blood and increase blood pressure, and it adds unnecessary calories to your diet. Nicotine and carbon monoxide in cigarette smoke hurt the cardiovascular system by damaging and narrowing blood vessels, and causing blood to clot, increasing your chances for stroke as well as MCI. Most important, following an exercise routine like the one I outlined in Chapter 10 not only will help you lose weight, but also helps your heart and blood vessels work better and increases your overall metabolism so that you will store less fat and reduce sugar levels in your blood.

All these lifestyle changes make it exponentially easier to continue to improve your brain and total-body health by following the right supplementation, hormone, or medication regimens. And it's very possible that the lifestyle changes might be enough so you don't need the supplements, hormones, or medications. Once you begin to see the weight come off or feel your body getting stronger, you'll be even more motivated to take care of yourself and get younger. And just as poor health begets more poor health, the opposite is also true. A recent study was performed to determine whether improvements in metabolic control could help overcome the cognitive dysfunction associated with diabetes. The results show that cognitive improvement was achievable with pharmacological interventions targeting glycemic control. Bottom line: An improvement in diabetes maintenance improves cognitive function. And an improvement in bloodflow throughout the body will affect bloodflow to the brain, diminishing your MCI.

The human body has no radar: Disease usually finds you. The key to reversing diseases remains early diagnosis. Read through the following short descriptions to determine if your health is affecting your thinking, and if you need to see a doctor to start the least invasive treatments with the most promising results.

Cancer

About 25 percent of cancer patients report post-treatment problems with mental fogginess. The hallmark symptoms include memory lapses, poorer concentration, and slower thinking. This cancer-related cognitive impairment is commonly called chemo-brain or chemo-fog. For example, up to one-third of women breast cancer survivors report difficulties with concentration, multitasking, and memory.

As suggested by its name, people originally believed these symptoms were a side effect of chemotherapy, the drug-based treatment used to shrink or destroy cancerous cells and tumors. However, the actual cause of this cognitive impairment is unclear. Some people with cancer who never had chemotherapy report similar cognitive lapses.

Regardless of the cause, chemo-brain is an unexpected, distressing, and lingering problem. Its symptoms can last for a few weeks or several years, depending on the individual. While it lasts, chemo-brain can cause you to feel unable to keep up with the demands of daily life—taking a terrible toll on self-confidence and overall quality of life.

Doctors and researchers are making huge strides every day in their battle with cancer. Researchers suspect the memory, fatigue, and sleep problems associated with chemo-brain may be hormone related or a function of stress on an already overtaxed immune system. Based on our current understanding of chemo-brain's causes and progress, cognitive therapy like the program described in this book is likely to help with it. If you are a cancer survivor, you may find that the relaxation exercises, as well as the brain training, will help restore your memory and attention.

Chronic Pain

Pain is often a symptom of a greater problem, one that is usually caused by a brain chemical deficiency. Most likely, those who experience chronic pain have a GABA deficiency. Pain can be seen as both a physical and a mental condition: It is a component of many different issues ranging from muscle strain to backache, irritable bowel syndrome to arthritis.

The mental component caused by pain can often make you irritable, anxious, or angry, which can affect your thinking. Chronic pain can bring on depression, problems with memory and concentration, and general brain fog. It can also be very distracting, making attention and focus particularly difficult. A 2007 study from the University of Alberta showed that pain may disrupt the maintenance of the memory trace that is required to hold information for processing and to later retain it for storage in longer-term memory stores.

Whatever the cause, I know that chronic pain is very real. However, once pain can be properly managed or, better yet, eliminated, you'll find that your memory and ability to concentrate return as well.

Diabetes

Diabetes is a metabolic disorder that makes the body less able to metabolize sugars, which causes chronically elevated glucose, or blood sugar levels. It begins when the body can no longer correctly process the sugars it takes in from carbohydrate-dense foods such as white rice, white flour, and potatoes. The body should be able to break down these foods into simple sugars, or glucose, and use this by-product as fuel on the cellular level. The hormone insulin should transport the glucose to the cells. However, when the body can no longer produce insulin, or becomes insensitive to it, the glucose just sits there, building up in the bloodstream, causing a condition called hyperglycemia, or high blood sugar. This condition sets up a cascade of events that contribute to inflammation and plaque deposition within the vascular system, including high blood pressure. Type 1 diabetes is also referred to as juvenile-onset diabetes because it typically occurs before the age of 20. Individuals with this kind of diabetes are usually thin. Type 1 diabetes is caused when the pancreas stops secreting the right amount of the hormone insulin. A more common type of diabetes is type 2, also known as adult-onset diabetes. People with type 2 diabetes are usually overweight. The cause of type 2 diabetes is insulin resistance: The pancreas continues to produce insulin, but the body cannot process it effectively.

Left untreated, excess sugars circulating throughout the body can change the composition of blood, making it sticky and causing it to damage the blood vessels it travels through, greatly increasing the risk of stroke and cognitive impairment. Damage to the blood vessels in the brain can impair the functioning of the hippocampus, the area responsible for consolidating memory.

Cognitive damage that's linked to diabetes can occur even for those with mildly impaired glucose levels. A 2003 study from New York University School of Medicine showed that participants with prediabetes, or mildly affected glucose levels, scored lower on short-term memory tests than their normal-blood-sugar counterparts. The connection between cognitive damage and diabetes is so clear that many now think of Alzheimer's disease as "type 3 diabetes."

Scientists at Brown University have shown that insulin production in the brain declines as Alzheimer's disease advances. The Brown team also found that a loss of insulin is related to a loss of acetylcholine, one of the hallmarks of Alzheimer's disease. These studies draw a clear conclusion that diabetes, as part of metabolic syndrome, directly affects MCI.

However, there is good news. Type 2 diabetes is completely preventable and reversible, if you can recognize your symptoms and then change your diet. Watch for the following signs that may indicate that you have diabetes:

- Blurred vision
- Dry mouth
- Excessive hunger
- Excessive thirst
- Fatigue
- Increased urination

- Itching skin, especially in the groin or vaginal area
- Nausea
- Slow-healing sores or cuts
- Unusual weight loss or gain
- Vaginal infections
- Vomiting
- Yeast infections (for men and women)

Elevated Cholesterol Levels

Cholesterol is a fatty substance, formed from hormones, that your body needs to create new cells. But when you have too much cholesterol, it builds up in the form of plaque in the walls of arteries. If your cholesterol levels are high, you are more likely to suffer from memory problems. This is because over time, plaque can reduce the blood's flow through the arteries, making it more difficult for blood to reach the brain and subsequently making the brain less efficient, affecting memory. What's more, plaques can rupture, causing blood clots to form and further block bloodflow, causing coronary artery disease. And if a clot blocks a blood vessel that feeds the brain, it causes a stroke.

A high level of LDL ("bad") cholesterol is symptomless but can be determined through routine and simple blood tests. However, high levels of HDL ("good") cholesterol may help prevent a decline in memory. Elevated triglyceride levels are another marker of damage from cholesterol. The major form of fat stored by the body, triglycerides come from the food we eat and are produced by the body. High triglyceride levels indicate a greater risk factor for heart disease and are also linked to MCI.

Heart Surgery Changes Your Thinking

Before you go for any type of heart-related surgery, make sure you have exhausted your full medical possibilities. The most common complaint following bypass surgery is memory problems that result from blood being cut off to the brain during the operation. The heart might work successfully following surgery, but the brain will be damaged.

According to a 1988 Harvard School of Dental Medicine study, high levels of triglycerides also appear to contribute to the decreased ability to perform short-term memory tasks.

Hypertension (High Blood Pressure)

Normal blood pressure moves blood smoothly throughout your body. High blood pressure damages blood vessels—including those in the brain and the carotid arteries in the neck that supply blood to your brain. High blood pressure is the top risk factor for heart disease and stroke, and it is a predictor of severe cognitive impairment later in life. Researchers have found that people with high blood pressure have more damage to their white matter than same-age peers with normal blood pressure. Left untreated, hypertension can lead to dementia. Yet hypertension is symptomless, painless, and often unexpected. For these reasons, if you have already been diagnosed with high blood pressure, or have a close family member who continues to be treated, it is critical to follow your doctor's recommendations for lifestyle changes and medications. Many people with mildly high readings (prehypertension) can lower them by simply altering diet and increasing physical activity.

Multiple Sclerosis

Multiple sclerosis (MS) is a chronic neurological disorder that is related to a deficiency in the brain chemical acetylcholine. While beginning as a series of benign symptoms, it can lead to an incapacitating condition. MS occurs when lesions or holes form on the myelin sheaths found around the nerves in the brain, causing them to erode. These sheaths are made of acetylcholine and are used as insulation. When they break down, it slows conduction of the functions of neuronal circuits in the brain and spinal cord, and the brain literally begins to burn up its neurons.

MS can induce a tingling electrical-like feeling down the back and inner thighs, as well as unsteadiness in walking. Depression is the most common psychological deficit of MS. In addition, there are frequently impairments in memory, attention, and conceptual reasoning due to the misfiring of the poorly myelinated circuits. About half of all sufferers of MS report cognitive difficulties. While there is no cure for MS, many people with MS-related cognitive problems improve with medications that increase acetylcholine production as well as those that increase attentiveness and alertness.

Classic symptoms include:

- Altered emotional responses
- Bladder dysfunction
- Double vision
- Impaired vision
- Impairment of deep sensation
- Numbness
- Trouble swallowing
- Trouble walking
- Weakness

Parkinson's Disease

The hallmark of Parkinson's disease is tremors, but up to one-half of sufferers also experience significant cognitive problems. This disease is directly related to a loss of dopamine, which damages the brain's neurons that were meant to receive this chemical message. This causes physical damage to the brain and impairs its ability to powerfully distribute its electricity. Because of this, those with Parkinson's often experience problems with memory and attention. In fact, Parkinson's is the third-most-common cause of dementia.

Parkinson's signs and symptoms may include the following. Symptoms typically begin on one side of the body and usually remain worse on that side even after symptoms begin to affect both sides.

Rigid muscles with or without pain. Muscle stiffness can occur in any part of your body. For example, you may notice that you no longer swing your arms when walking. Rigid muscles can impair posture and the ability to balance.

Slowed motion. When you walk, your steps may become short and shuffling, or your feet may freeze, making it hard to take the first step.

Speech changes. You may speak more softly, more rapidly, or in a monotone. You might also begin slurring or repeating words, or hesitating before speaking.

Tremor. The characteristic shaking associated with Parkinson's often begins in a hand. A back-and-forth rubbing of your thumb and forefinger, known as pill-rolling, is also common.

Seizures and Epilepsy

Seizures occur on a continuum: Anxiety, depression, insomnia, and panic are on one end, and epilepsy on the other. All of these symptoms are related to a GABA deficiency, as they occur when the brain has lost its natural balance. During a seizure, the brain's electrical responses are not distributed in a smooth flow. Seizures occur in the brain but can result in actions that occur anywhere on the body. For example, when tinnitus (chronic, persistent ringing in the ears) occurs, the ears are experiencing a localized seizure.

Seizures affect thinking from many different angles. The seizures themselves can cause memory loss; the medication used to control them can affect cognition; and the surgical procedures used to correct them are all contributors. Verbal memory loss (the "tip-of-the-tongue" phenomenon) is a common complaint from those suffering from seizures. The seizure may affect memory if it occurs in the temporal lobe, especially the hippocampus. Damage to the left side of the brain is more likely to cause difficulty with verbal memory, such as remembering conversations and written material. Damage to the right side can affect

Brain Training Reverses Tinnitus

In a 2011 study from Washington University School of Medicine in St. Louis, researchers found that brain exercises like the ones we've listed in Chapter 10 reverse the symptoms of tinnitus. In the study, 20 patients were sent to a "brain gym" to be trained in more accurate listening. More than 80 percent of the individuals participating in the study had substantial relief from their tinnitus. While the tinnitus's loudness had not been consistently altered, participants believed that the frequency with which tinnitus rose to consciousness in ways that disrupted their lives decreased. They also reported that the intrusive, disturbing power of the tinnitus decreased. After training, it was far easier for these patients to willfully ignore their tinnitus when it did arise. The study also reported that participants described improvements in listening and language abilities, in their attentional control, and in memory and other cognitive abilities resulting from brain training.

visual memory, such as scenes or directions. During the actual seizure, the person experiencing it will not be able to decode or learn any new information about what is going on around him or her, causing additional memory gaps. The more frequent the seizures, the more frequent the gaps in memory. Seizures can be controlled with proper medication, which is often the same as what is prescribed for memory loss.

During a seizure, you may experience any of the following:

- A sinking feeling
- Epileptic convulsions
- Increased anxiety
- Involuntary outcries
- Jerking motor movements
- Repetitive blinking
- Tongue biting
- Urinary or bowel incontinence

Sickle Cell Disease

Sickle cell disease is a genetic blood disorder caused by an abnormal form of blood cells. Unlike normal red blood cells, which are usually smooth and malleable, sickle-shaped red blood cells cannot squeeze through small blood vessels. When the sickle cells block small blood vessels, the organs are deprived of blood and oxygen, causing periodic episodes of pain and permanently damaging the vital organs.

Typically, sickle cell disease is diagnosed early in life, and until recently, it was a major cause of death for children. However, because of major advances in medicine, many Americans who have been diagnosed can now live well into middle age or beyond. Unfortunately, along with a prolonged life span come previously unrecognized complications. For example, stroke is a common complication of sickle cell disease, which often leads to learning disabilities, brain damage, long-term disability, paralysis, or death. However, new studies of brain function in children who have sickle cell disease have suggested that some children with the disease, even if they have not suffered a stroke, have experienced silent brain injury that seems to worsen with age. In a 2010 study funded by the National Heart, Lung, and Blood Institute (NHLBI), part of the National Institutes of Health, researchers found that sickle cell disease may also affect brain function in adults who have few or mild complications of the inherited blood disease. The multicenter study compared brain function scores and imaging tests in adult patients with few sickle cell complications with results in similar adults who did not have the blood disease. Researchers reported that twice as many patients as healthy adults (33 percent versus 15 percent) scored below normal levels. This study suggests that some adult patients who have sickle cell disease may develop cognitive problems, such as having difficulty organizing their thoughts, making decisions, or learning.

Sickle cell anemia is a serious disease that is present at birth. If you have been diagnosed with this disease, talk to your doctor about how it is affecting your cognition.

Stroke

A stroke occurs when the vascular system begins to fail and allows a blood clot to form. This clot can block the blood supply to the brain or cause a blood vessel in the brain to burst. These two scenarios define two different types of strokes. The first is called an ischemic stroke and is caused by a blocked artery in the brain, which stops bloodflow to surrounding areas in the brain. A hemorrhagic stroke occurs when a brain artery ruptures and there is bleeding in the brain.

When either of these occurs, oxygen is cut off and brain cells begin to quickly die around the area of the stroke. Because stroke directly affects the brain, its relationship to MCI is direct. What's more, the type of cognitive failure you will experience is determined by the location of the stroke. For example, a stroke in the brain's occipital lobe will likely lead to impaired vision, while a stroke in your motor cortex will result in

Stay Clean and Avoid Infections

It's not only the big medical issues that can affect your memory—the little ones are just as dangerous. Allergies and the medications associated with them can lead to brain fog. Chronic infections are another common cause of memory loss. What this shows is that it doesn't take much to tip the brain out of balance, which is why simple tricks like good hygiene can make a big difference in your thinking.

mobility problems. The type and severity of the impairment depends on the size of the stroke and the location in the brain. After the age of 50, many people experience lacuna infarcts, which are microstrokes that occur without your even knowing it, but their damage can be picked up on an MRI.

The five most common signs and symptoms of stroke are:

- Sudden numbness or weakness of the face, arm, or leg.
- Sudden confusion or trouble speaking or understanding others.
- Sudden trouble seeing in one or both eyes.
- Sudden dizziness, trouble walking, or loss of balance or coordination.
- Sudden severe headache with no known cause.

Having high cholesterol, high blood pressure, or diabetes can increase your risk of stroke. However, treating these conditions can reduce the risk of stroke—and you can greatly reduce your risk of stroke by following

Patient Profile: Deborah's Memory Returned When She Took Care of Her Health

By the time Deborah came to see me, she was very ill. Back in 2007 she was diagnosed with stage 4 renal failure. She had already explored many different types of treatments near her home in California, and some were very successful. However, when her doctor told her that her kidneys had dramatically recovered to the point where they were as good as they were ever going to get, Deborah was less than elated. In reality, she still felt miserable. The treatments were depleting her body and causing her to develop osteoporosis. She was always tired and had gained weight, even though she was working out all the time. And her memory was so bad that she was concerned that she was having some type of dementia. She used to forget names of people that she should know. She would have a brain fog problem, walking through the grocery store and not remembering why she was there. Other doctors couldn't understand what she was talking about and weren't making the connection between her head and the rest of her body.

the Braverman Protocol, including easy lifestyle changes and, in some cases, medication.

Thyroid Disorders

The thyroid is a small gland located in the neck that secretes thyroid hormones that control your metabolism. When this gland does not work properly, it secretes either too much or too little thyroid hormone, which either speeds up or slows down your metabolism. Slow metabolism, or hypothyroidism, is caused by an underactive thyroid and leads to weight gain as well as memory loss, poor concentration, lack of focus, fatigue, and depression. In fact, nearly 15 percent of those diagnosed with depression actually have a thyroid hormone deficiency. Along with these symptoms, a thyroid deficiency is marked by dry skin and hair, intolerance to cold, and constipation. Hypothyroidism can also contribute to heart disease and dementia. One prominent side effect of a low level of

In March 2010, Deborah came to my office to deal with her weight and her memory issues. By this point, she was barely talking about her kidneys. However, I assured her that we would be able to get to the bottom of all her health issues at once. The blood tests I ran confirmed that she was back to stage 3 kidney failure, even though she had no idea how sick she was. My testing also revealed that her MCI was significant, and I explained to Deborah how interconnected her health issues were. Renal failure can cause a decline or loss of any of the brain chemicals because there is a loss of protein in the brain. I prescribed supplements to boost her brain chemicals back to normal levels along with relaxation techniques and better diet, and I taught her how to incorporate a healthier lifestyle.

In just 3 months, her kidney problems resolved at an unprecedented rate. At 59 years old, she now has more energy than she had had in years. Her mind is sharper, and her memory is back. She has lost 30 pounds, and her bone density has improved. Now she knows that she still has room for improvement of her memory and uses the brain exercises every day.

thyroid hormone is an increased amount of LDL ("bad") cholesterol circulating in the blood.

Hyperthyroidism, on the other hand, comes from an overactive thyroid, leading to increased anxiety, poor attention, insomnia, tremors, decreased menstrual flow, weight loss, and irregular heartbeat. More people suffer from hypothyroidism than hyperthyroidism.

A blood test can determine if you are experiencing hypothyroidism or hyperthyroidism, and treatment involves balancing this hormone to normal levels.

WORK WITH YOUR DOCTOR TO REVERSE DISEASE AND RESTORE YOUR MEMORY

If you believe that you are experiencing any of these conditions, or if you already have been diagnosed, take this book to your doctor and discuss all treatment options and how they affect your cognition. Taking care of your body begins exactly the same way that I've taught you how to take care of your brain. The first step is early testing. I know that when we can detect illness at the earliest possible point, we can reverse disease and extend our ability to think clearly for years to come.

Start with the Very Best Physical

The typical American doctor's office is often ill-equipped to detect disease in its earliest stages. The traditional physical exam has not been updated for nearly 100 years: Your doctor is probably examining you the same way his or her mentor might have examined your grandparents, even though the technological world has completely changed.

I believe that a computer can do a better job than any doctor's hands in identifying all the lumps and bumps of the human body. A full-body ultrasound exam along with comprehensive blood work is the best way for doctors to see the condition and functioning of every organ, and then prioritize a treatment protocol on the predisease states that the standard American physical cannot possibly find. By using all that current medical technology has to offer, we don't need to guess when disease first strikes. Instead, doctors like me can clearly see nodules, precancers, damage, inflammation, calcifications, and dehydration. And you pay the consequences when they miss these signs—instead, the disease grows, spreads, becomes more invasive, and begins to affect other areas of the body or, worse, leads to an early death.

The tests listed here form the backbone of the type of physical you must insist on having in order to get the very best health care.

Abdominal ultrasound. This test shows an enlarged liver or spleen; allows doctors to find early changes of alcoholic hepatitis, nonalcoholic fatty liver, gallstones, gallbladder wall thickening, liver cysts, hemangiomas, other benign tumors and cancers, calcifications, cysts/calcifications of the pancreas, and enlargement or atherosclerotic changes in the abdominal aorta. Can identify damage due to drugs and infections. Can detect pancreatic cancer or previously benign cysts, sarcomas, abdominal aortic aneurysms, and spleen calcification.

Breast ultrasound. The best test to find breast cysts. Also shows nodules, masses, calcifications, and dense breast tissue. Can detect cancers and precancers.

Carotid ultrasound. Measures blood from the main artery in the neck to the brain. Can show early changes in bloodflow, intimal thickening, or advanced atherosclerotic disease blockages.

Echocardiogram. Shows heart size (all four chambers), ejection fraction, valvular disease, early changes in heart appearance, and changes in wall motion as a sign of previous or current heart attack and/or failure. Can detect early changes/enlargements in ventricles and atria. Can predict higher risk for atrial fibrillation. Can suggest coronary artery disease.

Pelvic ultrasound. Detects uterine enlargement, fibroids, changes in ovaries (increased size, cysts, or tumors), prominent endometrium, cervical cysts, sarcomas, and fluid collection due to advancing ovarian cancer. Can also identify bladder size and bladder stones.

Prostate ultrasound. Shows the size of the prostate and its nodules, calcifications, and mass; bladder size and function; and the presences of residual urine in patients with enlarged prostates.

Renal ultrasound. Shows kidney stones/cysts/tumors, fluid collections in kidneys (hydronephrosis), enlargement, or kidney atrophy.

Scrotal ultrasound. Can determine and diagnose size of testicles and epididymis, as well as presence of a varicocele, a spermatocele, or water in testicles; and can diagnose infertility, cancer, overuse of testosterone, changing size of testicles, calcifications, and tumors.

Thyroid ultrasound. Shows goitrous changes, enlarged thyroid, cancer, masses, nodules, calcifications, cysts, and atrophy for earliest possible diagnosis of disease.

Transcranial ultrasound. Measures bloodflow in the main arteries of the brain. Can detect aneurysms and damaged blood vessels, can provide information regarding migraines and possibility of dementia, and can also detect increase in velocity of bloodflow due to vascular spasm or blockage.

DEXA scan. The most effective method of determining bone density as well as body fat percentage is by using dual-energy x-ray absorptiometry, more commonly known as a DEXA (or DXA) scan. The DEXA outshines standard body mass index (BMI) charts and formulas and virtually all other methods of weight measurement.

PET scan. Besides their work in detecting early signs of Alzheimer's disease, PET scans can find tumors in their earliest stages all over the body and are extremely accurate in diagnosing cancer. A whole-body PET scan can detect tumors and precancers in any part of the body in one exam, although it is less sensitive in detecting cancers in the pancreas, bladder, and prostate. It can also accurately locate areas of radiation therapy treatments.

Treat Disease Head First

Once you've been properly diagnosed, discuss your treatment options with your physician. Unless the diagnosis is life threatening, I typically treat my patients using a "steps of care" approach. Just as in the Braverman Protocol, I start by prescribing the mildest options, such as behavioral or lifestyle changes, including diet and relaxation techniques. Then I progress to nutrient supplements. Often, the same excellent results that can be obtained with medications can be found by using bioidentical hormones or nutritional supplements with fewer side effects and less damage to your thinking. When I've exhausted all other options, I'll move to medications, with the goal being to have my patients take them for as short a time as possible. However, with many conditions, you can achieve a full reversal of symptoms by staying on the right dosage of medication indefinitely.

However, once you are on medication, you don't have to drop the other aspects of the Braverman Protocol. All of these therapies work synergistically for the best results possible. For example, I don't treat high cholesterol with only medications: My patients typically continue to follow the diet in Chapter 9, take nutrients such as niacin, exercise regularly, and take a statin. I treat anxiety with medications, nutrients, and the CES device. I treat weight loss with diet, exercise, nutrients such as carnitine and resveratrol, and also weight-loss medications. By taking a combined approach and using all the tools in our arsenal, we create leverage so that everything works better together. In fact, it's the hard work of following the program of nutrition, diet, exercise, and lifestyle that makes medications more effective.

Once your health is under control, you may find that your thinking—and your mood—become recognizably better almost instantly. However, your symptoms of MCI may persist even after your health improves. Give yourself a reasonable amount of time before you decide to move on to the next course of action.

It's also a good idea to go back and retake the Braverman Brain Advantage Test on a monthly basis. We do have inspirational "aha" moments, but for most people, getting smarter is built on day-in, day-out small increments of change. Watching your test scores improve, even if you don't feel any smarter, will give you even more motivation to stay with the program.

Chapter 14

The Daily Smarts

In my office, I see medical miracles happen every day. And so I know that you can use the tools that I have just shared with you to reverse mild cognitive impairment, or MCI, and become smarter as you get older. No matter how you feel today, you can think better tomorrow and for years to come.

You've now learned the six steps to building a better brain. Don't wait for your doctor to tell you that you have MCI to start this program. As I've said before, by the age of 40, most of us will have experienced some cognitive decline, and most doctors will not accurately make this diagnosis. That's why it is so critical for you to use what you've learned right now so that you can detect and reverse MCI at the earliest stages.

Just by reading this book, you've uncovered the many ways that your brain may have become unbalanced, and you have learned effective strategies for repair. You've mastered exercises that can make both your brain and your body more resilient, so that when you have to deal with life's obstacles, you'll be able to manage at a higher level. You've also come to understand why you need to continue the process of neurogenesis well into old age: The only way you can stay young is by restoring your health, maintaining a positive mood, and continuing to learn. That's what I call becoming healthy, happy, and wise.

These goals are not always easy to attain, and getting smarter does take work, every single day. That's why I refer to this effort as the Daily

Smarts. One easy way to follow the Braverman Protocol is to remember the acronym SMARTS, in which each letter represents one aspect of the daily program. By staying focused on this word, you'll be sure to get smarter. Make SMARTS your daily checklist to stay on track.

Stimulate brain and body with daily exercise.

Monitor diet and mood by keeping a journal.

Actively engage in life to stay mentally fit.

Read something every day to increase intelligence.

Take your medications, nutrients, and hormone therapies as prescribed.

Sleep to restore and reset your brain.

BEING SMARTER MEANS BETTER RELATIONSHIPS

The goal of this book has never been to get you to function like a smartphone, so you have the world's knowledge at your fingertips. With virtually effortless access to the world's vast collection of knowledge via the Internet, no one needs to memorize addresses and telephone numbers anymore. We don't have to master trivia or easily recall the details of our favorite movies. Instead, we can look at computers and see what they are capable of doing—and whatever they can do for us, we can learn to do something else, because we no longer need to maintain those skills. By redirecting your mental efforts, you'll be able to high-jump the performance gap.

Memory doesn't have to be limited to just feeling competent. We can use our enhanced brain functioning to become better people, develop a higher character, and have deeper, richer relationships. That is where the true joy in a younger life resides.

It's said that we use only 10 percent of our brains' power. I want to get humanity to reach a whole new level, to make big jumps and use more of our brains than we ever have before. In the past, before people were literate, they were using only 5 percent. Before that, cave people were using only 1 percent until they were able to formulate spoken language. The inevitable march of human history is the increasing utilization of the brain. If we're up from 5 percent to 10 percent, we've made progress. Standards of hygiene, social justice, and a technologically advanced world have all occurred because we have better-thinking brains. Now let's see what you can do with the other 90 percent of your brain.

The first order of business is improving character so that we all learn how to treat others with dignity and respect. Real change in character can occur only when all four brain chemicals are both balanced and enhanced. It is the culmination of all your hard work in achieving better attention and memory, and combining it with emotional IQ enhancement, common sense enhancement, and past, present, and future bandwidth. The ability to learn from the past to shape a better future will lead to greater character in the same way that literacy over the past 2,000 years has led to greater intelligence. And with increased mastery of technology, and using it to catch disease or dysfunction at its earliest possible stages, the opportunity for increased change in the way we deal with those we love is limitless.

My biggest hope is that you can imagine a world of peace, tolerance, and intelligence, and harness your better brain to help create it.

Appendix A

Answer Key for the Braverman Brain Advantage Test

Test One: VERBAL MEMORY (pages 95–100)

Answers for Story #1

1. Stephanie Appel.
2. She is 8 years old.
3. She attends Boardman Elementary School.
4. She was trying to earn her Cookie Badge.
5. A friend.
6. Thin Mints.
7. November.
8. The date the next Girl Scout meeting was held was Tuesday the 19th.
9. Stephanie was awarded the Cookie Badge.
10. They were proud of her.
11. To get ice cream.
12. Two.

Answers for Story #2

1. A man.
2. Friday.
3. He was walking to work.
4. A building.
5. Brick.
6. It was under construction (being torn down).
7. Seven men.
8. Madison Avenue.

9. Crying puppies.
10. Puppies.
11. Two.
12. Brown, like the color of coffee (½ point for only one color).

Answers for Story #3

1. Wendy and Steven Murphy.
2. The Have a Healthy Smoothie Shop.
3. On the corner of River Street and Stanwich Street.
4. 17 years.
5. No, they rented the space.
6. The building was sold to a new landlord.
7. He raised the rent.
8. February.
9. $500 a month.
10. They found a new location.
11. Yes.
12. August.

Test Six: EXECUTIVE FUNCTION ANSWERS (page 111)

1. 36 inches
2. California
3. 3,000 miles or 4,800 kilometers
4. Poet
5. 32 degrees Fahrenheit or 0 degrees Celsius
6. J. D. Salinger
7. Paris
8. Portuguese
9. George Lucas
10. Jane Austen
11. Boxer
12. Any two of the following: nitrogen, oxygen, carbon dioxide, water vapor, argon, neon, hydrogen, and helium
13. 7 billion people
14. Albert Einstein
15. Marsupials
16. Moses
17. White
18. William Shakespeare

19. Taoism
20. That it is impossible to make simultaneous measurements of both the position and the momentum of an electron (or any other subatomic particle) with absolute accuracy

Test Seven: IQ/PARADIGM PATTERN RECOGNITION ANSWERS (page 113)

1. Forms of transportation
2. Forms of measurement
3. Parts of the body
4. Signs of emotions
5. Survival activities
6. Colors
7. Animals with four feet; animals with fur; pets; mammals
8. Writing instruments
9. Methods to record/show movies at home
10. Plants
11. Citrus fruits
12. Poultry
13. Places people live
14. Flowers
15. Languages/cultures
16. Spices
17. Vegetables
18. Insects
19. Mammals
20. Forms of exercise

Test Nine: DELAYED RECALL ANSWERS (pages 117–119)
Answers for Story #1

1. Cookies and cream
2. Yes

Answers for Story #2

1. To work with him
2. He brought them to an animal shelter.

Answers for Story #3

1. No
2. Blueberry

References

Introduction

Modrego, P. J. "The Prediction of Conversion to Dementia in Mild Cognitive Impairment by Means of Magnetic Resonance Spectroscopy and Other Neuroradiological Techniques." *Directions in Psychiatry* 27, no. 22 (2007).

Chapter 1

Anderer, P., B. Saletu, D. Gruber, et al. "Age-Related Cognitive Decline in the Menopause: Effects of Hormone Replacement Therapy on Cognitive Event-Related Potentials." *Maturitas* 51, no. 3 (2005): 254–69.

Banasr, M., A. Soumier, M. Hery, et al. "Agomelatine, a New Antidepressant, Induces Regional Changes in Hippocampal Neurogenesis." *Biological Psychiatry* 59, no. 11 (2006): 1087–96.

Blige, I., et al. "Brain Calcification Due to Secondary Hyperparathyroidism in a Child with Chronic Renal Failure." *Turkish Journal of Pediatrics* 47, no. 3 (2005): 287–90.

Bloom, F. E., M. F. Beal, and D. J. Kupfer. *The Dana Guide to Brain Health.* (New York: The Free Press, 2003): 639–42.

Braverman, E., V. Arcuri, and K. Blum. "Subclinical Hyperparathyroidism, an Age Dependent Phenomenon, Is an Antecedent of Both Osteoporosis (OP) and Dementia." *Alzheimer's and Dementia* 3, no. 3 (2007): S133–34.

Braverman, E. R., and K. Blum. "P300 (Latency) Event-Related Potential: An Accurate Predictor of Memory Impairment." *Clinical Electroencephalography* 34, no. 3 (2003): 124–39.

Braverman, E. R., T. Chen, T. Prihoda, et al. "Plasma Growth Hormones, P300 Event-Related Potential and Test of Variables of Attention (T.O.V.A) Are Important Neuroendocrinological Predictors of Early Cognitive Decline in Clinical Setting: Evidence Supported by Structural Equation Modeling Parameter Estimates." *Age* 29, no. 2–3 (2007): 55–67.

Braverman, E. R., K. Perrine, U. J. Damle, et al. "Delayed P300 Latency and Voltage in 85 Patients With and Without Hypometabolic PET Scans." *Endocrine Reviews* 32 (2011): 1–552.

Bruel-Jungerman, E., C. Rampon, and S. Laroche. "Adult Hippocampal Neurogenesis, Synaptic Plasticity and Memory: Facts and Hypotheses." *Reviews in the Neurosciences* 18, no. 2 (2007): 93–114.

Bush, A. L., P. A. Allen, K. P. Kaut, et al. "Influence of Mild Cognitive Impairment on Visual Word Recognition." *Neuropsychology, Development, and Cognition. Section B, Aging, Neuropsychology and Cognition* 14, no. 4 (2007): 329–52.

Chen, S. J., C. L. Kao, Y. L. Chang, et al. "Antidepressant Administration Modulates Neural Stem Cell Survival and Serotoninergic Differentiation through BCL-2." *Current Neurovascular Research* 4, no. 1 (2007): 19–29.

Chiou, S. H., S. J. Chen, C. H. Peng, et al. "Fluoxetine Up-Regulates Expression of Cellular FLICE-Inhibitory Proliferation and Inhibits LPS-Induced Apoptosis in

Hippocampus-Derived Neural Stem Cells." *Biochemical and Biophysical Research Communications* 343, no. 2 (2006): 391–400.

Chuang, D. M. "Neuroprotective and Neurotrophic Actions of the Mood Stabilizer Lithium: Can It Be Used to Treat Neurodegenerative Diseases?" *Critical Reviews in Neurobiology* 16, no. 1–2 (2004): 83–90.

"Cognitive Defects Occur with Sickle Cell Disease." *Family Practice News*, Feb. 15, 2008.

Davis, J. D., R. A. Stern, and L. A. Flashman. "Cognitive and Neuropsychiatric Aspects of Subclinical Hypothyroidism: Significance in the Elderly." *Current Psychiatry Reports* 5, no. 5 (2003): 384–89.

Davis, S. R., S. M. Shah, D. P. McKenzie, et al. "DHEA Sulfate Levels Are Associated with More Favorable Cognitive Function in Women." *Journal of Clinical Endocrinology and Metabolism* 93, no. 3 (2008): 801–8. Published online before print Dec. 11, 2007.

Dumas, J., C. Hancur-Bucci, M. Naylor, et al. "Estrogen Treatment Effects on Anticholinergic-Induced Cognitive Dysfunction in Normal Postmenopausal Women." *Neuropsychopharmacology* 31 (2006): 2065–78.

Eisch, A. J., and C. D. Mandyam. "Adult Neurogenesis: Can Analysis of Cell Cycle Proteins Move Us 'Beyond BrdU'?" *Current Pharmaceutical Biotechnology* 8, no. 3 (2007): 147–65.

Elder, G. A., R. De Gasperi, and M. A. Gama Sosa. "Research Update: Neurogenesis in Adult Brain and Neuropsychiatric Disorders." *Mt. Sinai Journal of Medicine* 73, no. 7 (2006): 931–40.

Engesser-Cesar, C., A. J. Anderson, and C. W. Cotman. "Wheel Running and Fluoxetine Antidepressant Treatment Have Differential Effects in the Hippocampus and the Spinal Cord." *Neuroscience* 144, no. 3 (2007): 1033–44.

Ge, S., C. H. Yang, K. S. Hsu, et al. "A Critical Period for Enhanced Synaptic Plasticity in Newly Generated Neurons of the Adult Brain." *Neuron* 54, no. 4 (2007): 559–66.

Godbolt, Alison K., et al. "The Natural History of Alzheimer Disease: A Longitudinal Presymptomatic and Symptomatic Study of a Familial Cohort." *Archives of Neurology* 61 (2004): 1743–48.

Golgeli, A., F. Tanriverdi, C. Suer, et al. "Utility of P300 Auditory Event Related Potential Latency in Detecting Cognitive Dysfunction in Growth Hormone (GH) Deficient Patients with Sheehan's Syndrome and Effects of GH Replacement Therapy." *European Journal of Endocrinology* 150, no. 2 (2004): 153–59.

Huang, G. J., and J. Herbert. "Stimulation of Neurogenesis in the Hippocampus of the Adult Rat by Fluoxetine Requires Rhythmic Change in Corticosterone." *Biological Psychiatry* 59, no. 7 (2006): 619–24.

Jiang, W., Y. Zhang, L. Xiao, et al. "Cannabinoids Promote Embryonic and Adult Hippocampus Neurogenesis and Produce Anxiolytic- and Antidepressant-Like Effects." *Journal of Clinical Investigation* 115, no. 11 (2005): 3104–16.

Kawas, C. H., M. M. Corrada, R. Brookmeyer, et al. "Visual Memory Predicts Alzheimer's Disease More Than a Decade Before Diagnosis." *Neurology* 60, no. 7 (2003): 1089–93.

Kerever, A., J. Schnack, D. Vellinga, et al. "Novel Extracellular Matrix Structures in the Neural Stem Cell Niche Capture the Neurogenic Factor FGF-2 from the Extracellular Milieu." *Stem Cells* 25, no. 9 (2007): 2146–57.

Ko, H. G., S. J. Lee, H. Son, et al. "Null Effect of Antidepressants on the Astrocytes-Mediated Proliferation of Hippocampal Progenitor Cells in Vitro." *Molecular Pain* 3, no. 1 (2007): 16.

Kuhn, H. G., and C. M. Cooper-Kuhn. "Bromodeoxyuridine and the Detection of Neurogenesis." *Current Pharmaceutical Biotechnology* 8, no. 3 (2007): 127–31.

Langa, K. M., N. L. Foster, and E. B. Larson. "Mixed Dementia Emerging Concepts and Therapeutic Implications." *JAMA* 292, no. 23 (2004): 2901–08.

Lie, D. C., S. A. Colamarino, H. J. Song, et al. "Wnt Signalling Regulates Adult Hippocampal Neurogenesis." *Nature* 437, no. 7063 (2005): 1370–75.

Mangone, C. A. "Clinical Heterogeneity of Alzheimer's Disease. Different Clinical Profiles Can Predict the Progression Rate." *Revista de Neurologia* 38, no. 7 (2004): 675–81.

McCrory, P., W. Meeuwisse, K. Johnston, et al. "Consensus Statement on Concussion in Sport—The 3rd International Conference on Concussion in Sport Held in Zurich, November 2008." *Journal of Science and Medicine in Sport* 12, no. 3 (2009): 340–51.

Modrego, P. J. "The Prediction of Conversion to Dementia in Mild Cognitive Impairment by Means of Magnetic Resonance Spectroscopy and Other Neuroradiological Techniques." *Directions in Psychiatry* 27, no. 22 (2007).

Morris, J. C., M. Storandt, J. P. Miller, et al. "Mild Cognitive Impairment Represents Early-Stage Alzheimer Disease." *Archives of Neurology* 58, no. 3 (2001): 397–405.

Perera, T. D., J. D. Coplan, S. H. Lisanby, et al. "Antidepressant-Induced Neurogenesis in the Hippocampus of Adult Nonhuman Primates." *Journal of Neuroscience* 27, no. 18 (2007): 4894–4901.

Petersen, R. C. "Neuropathologic Features of Amnestic Mild Cognitive Impairment." *Archives of Neurology* 63, no. 5 (2006): 665–72.

Plassman, B. L., K. M. Langa, G. G. Fisher, et al. "Prevalence of Cognitive Impairment without Dementia in the United States." *Annals of Internal Medicine* 148, no. 6 (2008): 427–34.

Quartermain, D., et al. "Links between the Pathology of Alzheimer's Disease and Vascular Dementia." *Neurochemical Research* 29, no. 6 (2004): 1257–66.

Rabitt, P., O. Mogapi, M. Scott, et al. "Effects of Global Atrophy, White Matter Lesions, and Cerebral Blood Flow on Age-Related Changes in Speed, Memory, Intelligence, Vocabulary, and Frontal Function." *Neuropsychology* 21, no. 6 (2007): 684–95.

Randt, C. T., et al. "Brain Cyclic AMP and Memory in Mice." *Pharmacology, Biochemistry, and Behavior* 17, no. 4 (1982): 677–80.

Ransome, M. I., and A. M. Turnley. "Systemically Delivered Erythropoietin Transiently Enhances Adult Hippocampal Neurogenesis." *Journal of Neurochemistry* 102, no. 6 (2007): 1953–65.

Rosario, E. R., and C. J. Pike. "Androgen Regulation of Beta-Amyloid Protein and the Risk of Alzheimer's Disease." *Brain Research Reviews* 57, no. 2 (2008): 444–53.

Sadock, Benjamin J., and Virginia A. Sadock, ed. *Kaplan & Sadock's Comprehensive Textbook of Psychiatry,* 8th ed., vol. 1. Philadelphia: Lippincott Williams & Wilkins, 2005.

Santarelli, L., M. Saxe, C. Gross, et al. "Requirement of Hippocampal Neurogenesis for the Behavioral Effects of Antidepressants." *Science* 301, no. 5634 (2003): 805–9.

Siwak-Tapp, C. T., E. Head, B. A. Muggenburg, et al. "Neurogenesis Decreases with Age in the Canine Hippocampus and Correlates with Cognitive Function." *Neurobiology of Learning and Memory* 88, no. 2 (2007): 249–59.

Steiner, B., G. Kronenberg, S. Jessberger, et al. "Differential Regulation of Glycogenesis in the Context of Adult Hippocampal Neurogenesis in Mice." *Glia* 46, no. 1 (2004): 41–52.

Stranahan, A. M., T. V. Arumugam, R. G. Cutler, et al. "Diabetes Impairs Hippocampal Function through Glucocorticoid-Mediated Effects on New and Mature Neurons." *Nature Neuroscience* 11, no. 3 (2008): 309–17.

Sung, S. M., D. S. Jung, C. H. Kwon, et al. "Hypoxia/Reoxygenation Stimulates Proliferation through PKC-Dependent Activation of ERK and Akt in Mouse Neural Progenitor Cells." *Neurochemical Research* 32, no. 11 (2007): 1932–39. E-publication Jun. 12, 2007.

Tabert, M. H. "Neuropsychological Prediction of Conversion to Alzheimer Disease in Patients with Mild Cognitive Impairment." *Archives of General Psychiatry* 63, no. 8 (2006): 916–24.

Tilvis, R. S., M. H. Kahonen-Vare, J. Jolkkonen, et al. "Predictors of Cognitive Decline and Morality of Aged People Over a 10-Year Period." *Journals of Gerontology, Series A, Biological Sciences and Medical Sciences* 59, no. 3 (2004): 268–74.

Whitmer, R. A., S. Sidney, J. Selby, et al. "Midlife Cardiovascular Risk Factors and Risk of Dementia in Late Life." *Neurology* 64, no. 2 (2005): 277–81.

Yaffe, K. "Metabolic Syndrome and Cognitive Disorders: Is the Sum Greater Than Its Parts?" *Alzheimer Disease & Associated Disorders* 21, no. 2 (2007): 167–71.

Yue, F., B. Chen, D. Wu, et al. "Biological Properties of Neural Progenitor Cells Isolated from the Hippocampus of Adult Cynomolgus Monkeys." *Chinese Medical Journal* 119, no. 2 (2006): 110–16.

Chapter 3

Barnes, D. E., G. S. Alexopoulos, O. L. Lopez, et al. "Depressive Symptoms, Vascular Disease, and Mild Cognitive Impairment." *Archives of General Psychiatry* 63, no. 3 (2006): 273–79.

Ganguli, M. "Depression, Cognitive Impairment and Dementia: Why Should Clinicians Care about the Web of Causation?" *Indian Journal of Psychiatry* 51 (2009): S29–34.

Jorm, A. F. "Is Depression a Risk Factor for Dementia or Cognitive Decline?" *Gerontology* 46, no. 4 (2000): 219–27.

Steffens, D. C., E. Otey, G. S. Alexopoulos, M. A. Butters, et al. "Perspectives on Depression, Mild Cognitive Impairment, and Cognitive Decline." *Archives of General Psychiatry* 63, no. 2 (2006): 130–38.

Chapter 4

Celsis, P., A. Agniel, D. Cardebat, et al. "Age-Related Cognitive Decline: A Clinical Entity? A Longitudinal Study of Cerebral Blood Flow and Memory Performance." *Journal of Neurology, Neurosurgery, and Psychiatry* 62, no. 6 (1997): 601–8.

Semplicini, Andrea, and Giulia Inverso. "Cognitive Impairment in Hypertension." http://www.scitopics.com/Cognitive_impairment_in_hypertension.html. Accessed Aug. 30, 2009.

Chapter 5

Colter, A. L., et al. "Fatty Acid Status and Behavioral Symptoms of Attention Deficit Hyperactivity Disorder in Adolescents: A Case-Control Study." *Nutrition Journal* 7:8. Published online February 14, 2008.

Harding, K. L., R. D. Judah, and C. Gant. "Outcome-Based Comparison of Ritalin Versus Food-Supplement Treated Children with ADHD." *Alternative Medicine Review* 8, no. 3 (2003): 319–30.

Liu, J., and A. Raine. "The Effect of Childhood Malnutrition on Externalizing Behavior." *Current Opinion in Pediatrics* 18, no. 5 (2006): 565–70.

McCann, D., et al. "Food Additives and Hyperactive Behavior in 3-Year-Old and 8/9-Year-Old Children in the Community: A Randomized, Double-Blinded, Placebo-Controlled Trial." *Lancet* 370, no. 9598 (2007): 1560–67.

Quintero, J., et al. "Nutritional Aspects of Attention-Deficit/Hyperactive Disorder." *Revista de Neurologia* 49, no. 6 (2009): 307–12.

Chapter 7

Chowdhury, M. H., A. Nagai, H. Bokura, et al. "Age-Related Changes in White Matter Lesions, Hippocampal Atrophy, and Cerebral Microbleeds in Healthy Subjects Without Major Cerebrovascular Risk Factors." *Journal of Stroke and Cerebrovascular Diseases* 20, no. 4 (2011): 302–9.

Vermeer, S. E., W. T. Longstreth Jr., and P. J. Koudstaal. "Silent Brain Infarcts: A Systematic Review." *Lancet Neurology* 6, no. 7 (2007): 611–19.

Chapter 8

Schellenberg, E. G., T. Nakata, P. G. Hunter, et al. "Exposure to Music and Cognitive Performance: Tests of Children and Adults." *Psychology of Music* 35, no. 1 (2007): 5–19. E-publication July 15, 2010.

Chapter 9

Kleim, J. A., N. R. Cooper, and P. M. VandenBerg. "Exercise Induces Angiogenesis But Does Not Alter Movement Representations Within Rat Motor Cortex." *Brain Research* 934, no. 1 (2002): 1–6.

Lange-Asschenfeldt, C., and G. Kojda. "Alzheimer's Disease, Cerebrovascular Dysfunction and the Benefits of Exercise: From Vessels to Neurons." *Experimental Gerontology* 43, no. 6 (2008): 499–504. E-publication Apr. 6, 2008.

Swain, R. A., A. B. Harris, E. C. Wiener, M. V. Dutka, et al. "Prolonged Exercise Induces Angiogenesis and Increases Cerebral Blood Volume in Primary Motor Cortex of the Rat." *Neuroscience* 117, no. 4 (2003): 1037–46.

Van der Borght, K., D. E. Kóbor-Nyakas, K. Klauke, et al. "Physical Exercise Leads to Rapid Adaptations in Hippocampal Vasculature: Temporal Dynamics and Relationship to Cell Proliferation and Neurogenesis." *Hippocampus* 19, no. 10 (2009): 928–36.

Chapter 10

Atmaca, M., M. Kuloglu, E. Tezcan, et al. "Serum Leptin Levels in Patients with Premature Ejaculation." *Archives of Andrology* 48, no. 5 (2002): 345–50.

Carrascosa, J. M., M. Ros, A. Andrés, et al. "Changes in the Neuroendocrine Control of Energy Homeostasis by Adiposity Signals during Aging." *Experimental Gerontology* 44, no. 1–2 (2009): 20–25. E-publication May 20, 2008.

Colter, A. L., et al. "Fatty Acid Status and Behavioral Symptoms of Attention Deficit Hyperactivity Disorder in Adolescents: A Case-Control Study." *Nutrition Journal* 7:8. Published online February 14, 2008.

Fernández-Galaz, M. C., T. Fernández-Agulló, J. M. Carrascosa, et al. "Leptin Accumulation in Hypothalamic and Dorsal Raphe Neurons Is Inversely Correlated with Brain Serotonin Content." *Brain Research* 1329 (2010): 194–202. E-publication Mar. 6, 2010.

Fewlass, D. C., K. Noboa, F. X. Pi-Sunyer, et al. "Obesity-Related Leptin Regulates Alzheimer's Abeta." *FASEB Journal* 18, no. 15 (2004): 1870–78.

Genc, B. O., E. A. Dogan, U. Dogan, et al. "Anthropometric Indexes, Insulin Resistance, and Serum Leptin and Lipid Levels in Women with Cryptogenic Epilepsy Receiving Topiramate Treatment." *Journal of Clinical Neuroscience* 17, no. 10 (2010): 1256–59.

Harding, K. L., R. D. Judah, and C. Gant. Outcome-Based Comparison of Ritalin Versus Food-Supplement Treated Children with ADHD." *Alternative Medicine Review* 8, no. 3 (2003): 319–30.

Isidori, A. M., F. Strollo, M. Morè, et al. "Leptin and Aging: Correlation with Endocrine Changes in Male and Female Healthy Adult Populations of Different Body Weights." *Journal of Clinical Endocrinology and Metabolism* 85, no. 5 (2000): 1954–62.

Koh, K. K., S. M. Park, and M. J. Quon. "Leptin and Cardiovascular Disease: Response to Therapeutic Interventions." *Circulation* 117, no. 25 (2008): 3238–49.

McCann, D., et al. "Food Additives and Hyperactive Behavior in 3-Year-Old and 8/9-Year-Old Children in the Community: A Randomized, Double-Blinded, Placebo-Controlled Trial." *Lancet* 370, no. 9598 (2007): 1560–67.

Oben, J. E., J. L. Ngondi, and K. Blum. "Inhibition of *Irvingia gabonensis* Seed Extract (OB131) on Adipogenesis as Mediated via Down Regulation of the PPARgamma and Leptin Genes and Up-Regulation of the Adiponectin Gene." *Lipids in Health and Disease* (2008) 7:44.

Quintero, J., et al. "Nutritional Aspects of Attention-Deficit/Hyperactive Disorder." *Revista de Neurologia* 49, no. 6 (2009): 307–12.

Theisen, F. M., S. Beyenburg, S. Gebhardt, et al. "A Prospective Study of Body Weight and Serum Leptin Levels in Patients Treated with Topiramate." *Clinical Neuropharmacology* 31, no. 4 (2008): 226–30.

Chapter 11

Aguado, T., E. Romero, K. Monory, et al. "The CB1 Cannabinoid Receptor Mediates Excitotoxicity-Induced Neural Progenitor Proliferation and Neurogenesis." *Journal of Biological Chemistry* 282, no. 33 (2007): 23892–98. E-pub Jun. 7, 2007.

Alzheimer's Association. "2009 Alzheimer's Disease Facts and Figures." *Alzheimer's & Dementia* 5, no. 3 (2009): 234–70.

Anderer, P., B. Saletu, D. Gruber, et al. "Age-Related Cognitive Decline in the Menopause: Effects of Hormone Replacement Therapy on Cognitive Event-Related Potentials." *Maturitas* 51, no. 3 (2005): 254–69.

Banasr, M., A. Soumier, M. Hery, et al. "Agomelatine, a New Antidepressant, Induces Regional Changes in Hippocampal Neurogenesis." *Biological Psychiatry* 59, no. 11 (2006): 1087–96.

Blige, I., et al. "Brain Calcification Due to Secondary Hyperparathyroidism in a Child with Chronic Renal Failure." *Turkish Journal of Pediatrics* 47, no. 3 (2005): 287–90.

Bowen, R. L., J. P. Isley, and R. L. Atkinson. "An Association of Elevated Serum Gonadotropin Concentrations and Alzheimer Disease." *Journal of Neuro-endocrinology* 12 (2000): 351–54.

Bowen, R. L., M. A. Smith, P. L. Harris, et al. "Elevated Luteinizing Hormone Expression Colocalizes with Neurons Vulnerable to Alzheimer's Disease Pathology." *Journal of Neuroscience Research* 70, no. 3 (2002): 514–18.

Braverman, E., V. Arcuri, and K. Blum. "Subclinical Hyperparathyroidism, an Age Dependent Phenomenon, Is an Antecedent of Both Osteoporosis (OP) and Dementia." *Alzheimer's and Dementia* 3, no. 3 (2007): S133–34.

Braverman, E. R., and K. Blum. "P300 (Latency) Event-Related Potential: An Accurate Predictor of Memory Impairment." *Clinical Electroencephalography* 34, no. 3 (2003): 124–39.

Braverman, E. R., T. Chen, T. Prihoda, et al. "Plasma Growth Hormones, P300 Event-Related Potential and Test of Variables of Attention (T.O.V.A) Are Important Neuroendocrinological Predictors of Early Cognitive Decline in Clinical Setting: Evidence Supported by Structural Equation Modeling Parameter Estimates." *Age* 29, no. 2–3 (2007): 55–67.

Braverman, E. R., T. J. H. Chen, J. Schoolfield, et al. "Delayed P300 Latency Correlates with Abnormal Test of Variables of Attention (TOVA) in Adults and Predicts Early Cognitive Decline in a Clinical Setting." *Advances in Therapy* 23, no. 4 (2006): 582–600.

Bruel-Jungerman, E., C. Rampon, and S. Laroche. "Adult Hippocampal Neurogenesis, Synaptic Plasticity and Memory: Facts and Hypotheses." *Reviews in the Neurosciences* 18, no. 2 (2007): 93–114.

Carroll, J. C., E. R. Rosario, L. Chang, et al. "Progesterone and Estrogen Regulate Alzheimer-Like Neuropathology in Female 3xTg-AD Mice." *Journal of Neuroscience* 27, no. 48 (2007): 13357–65.

Carroll, Jenna C., and Christian J. Pike. "Selective Estrogen Receptor Modulators Differentially Regulate Alzheimer-Like Changes in Female 3xTg-AD Mice." *Endocrinology* 149, no. 5 (2008): 2607–11.

Casadesus, G., E. L. Milliken, K. M. Webber, et al. "Increases in Luteinizing Hormone Are Associated with Declines in Cognitive Performance." *Molecular and Cellular Endocrinology* 269, no. 1–2 (2007): 107–111.

Chakravarti, S., W. P. Collins, J. D. Forecast, et al. "Hormonal Profiles after the Menopause." *British Medical Journal* 2, no. 6039: 784–87.

Chen, S. J., C. L. Kao, Y. L. Chang, et al. "Antidepressant Administration Modulates Neural Stem Cell Survival and Serotoninergic Differentiation through BCL-2." *Current Neurovascular Research* 4, no. 1 (2007): 19–29.

Chiou, S. H., S. J. Chen, C. H. Peng, et al. "Fluoxetine Up-Regulates Expression of Cellular FLICE-Inhibitory Proliferation and Inhibits LPS-Induced Apoptosis in Hippocampus-Derived Neural Stem Cells." *Biochemical and Biophysical Research Communications* 343, no. 2 (2006): 391–400.

Chiou, S. H., H. H. Ku, T. H. Tsai, et al. "Moclobemide Upregulated BCL-2 Expression and Induced Neural Stem Cell Differentiation into Serotoninergic Neuron via Extracellular-Regulated Kinase Pathway." *British Journal of Pharmacology* 148, no. 5 (2006): 587–98.

Chuang, D. M. "Neuroprotective and Neurotrophic Actions of the Mood Stabilizer Lithium: Can It Be Used to Treat Neurodegenerative Diseases?" *Critical Reviews in Neurobiology* 16, no. 1–2 (2004): 83–90.

Cleveland Clinic Foundation. "Menopause and Osteoporosis." http://my.clevelandclinic.org /disorders/menopause/hic_menopause_and_osteoporosis.aspx.

Crosignanil, P. G., M. Meschia, F. Bruschi, et al. "Gonadotrophins and Prolactin Rise after Bilateral Oophorectomy for Benign Conditions." *Human Reproduction* 10, no. 9 (1995): 2277–79.

Davis, S. R., S. M. Shah, D. P. McKenzie, et al. "DHEA Sulfate Levels Are Associated with More Favorable Cognitive Function in Women." *Journal of Clinical Endocrinology and Metabolism* 93, no. 3 (2008): 801–8.

Dumas, J., C. Hancur-Bucci, M. Naylor, et al. "Estrogen Treatment Effects on Anticholinergic-Induced Cognitive Dysfunction in Normal Postmenopausal Women." *Neuropsychopharmacology* 31 (2006): 2065–78.

Eisch, A. J., and C. D. Mandyam. "Adult Neurogenesis: Can Analysis of Cell Cycle Proteins Move Us 'Beyond BrdU'?" *Current Pharmaceutical Biotechnology* 8, no. 3 (2007): 147–65.

Elder, G. A., R. De Gasperi, and M. A. Gama Sosa. "Research Update: Neurogenesis in Adult Brain and Neuropsychiatric Disorders." *Mt. Sinai Journal of Medicine* 73, no. 7 (2006): 931–40.

Engesser-Cesar, C., A. J. Anderson, and C. W. Cotman. "Wheel Running and Fluoxetine Antidepressant Treatment Have Differential Effects in the Hippocampus and the Spinal Cord." *Neuroscience* 144, no. 3 (2007): 1033–44.

Farrag, A. K., E. M. Khedr, H. Abdel-Aleem, et al. "Effect of Surgical Menopause on Cognitive Functions." *Dementia and Geriatric Cognitive Disorders* 13, no. 3 (2002): 193–98.

Frick, K. M. "Estrogens and Age-Related Memory Decline in Rodents: What Have We Learned and Where Do We Go from Here?" *Hormones and Behavior* 55, no. 1 (2009): 2–23. E-publication Sept. 16, 2008.

Ge, S., C. H. Yang, K. S. Hsu, et al. "A Critical Period for Enhanced Synaptic Plasticity in Newly Generated Neurons of the Adult Brain." *Neuron* 54, no. 4 (2007): 559–66.

Golgeli, A., F. Tanriverdi, C. Suer, et al. "Utility of P300 Auditory Event Related Potential Latency in Detecting Cognitive Dysfunction in Growth Hormone (GH) Deficient Patients with Sheehan's Syndrome and Effects of GH Replacement Therapy." *European Journal of Endocrinology* 150, no. 2 (2004): 153–59.

Huang, G. J., and J. Herbert. "Stimulation of Neurogenesis in the Hippocampus of the Adult Rat by Fluoxetine Requires Rhythmic Change in Corticosterone." *Biological Psychiatry* 59, no. 7 (2006): 619–24.

Jiang, W., Y. Zhang, L. Xiao, et al. "Cannabinoids Promote Embryonic and Adult Hippocampus Neurogenesis and Produce Anxiolytic- and Antidepressant-Like Effects." *Journal of Clinical Investigation* 115, no. 11 (2005): 3104–16.

Kerever, A., J. Schnack, D. Vellinga, et al. "Novel Extracellular Matrix Structures in the Neural Stem Cell Niche Capture the Neurogenic Factor FGF-2 from the Extracellular Milieu." *Stem Cells* 25, no. 9 (2007): 2146–57.

Ko, H. G., S. J. Lee, H. Son, et al. "Null Effect of Antidepressants on the Astrocytes-Mediated Proliferation of Hippocampal Progenitor Cells in Vitro." *Molecular Pain* 3, no. 1 (2007): 16.

Kuhn, H. G., and C. M. Cooper-Kuhn. "Bromodeoxyuridine and the Detection of Neurogenesis." *Current Pharmaceutical Biotechnology* 8, no. 3 (2007): 127–31.

Lee, L. V., and J. M. Foody. "Cardiovascular Disease in Women." *Current Atherosclerosis Reports* 10, no. 4 (2008): 295–302.

Lie, D. C., S. A. Colamarino, H. J. Song, et al. "Wnt Signalling Regulates Adult Hippocampal Neurogenesis." *Nature* 437, no. 7063 (2005): 1370–75.

Liqin, Zhao, and Roberta Diaz Brinton. "Select Estrogens within the Complex Formulation of Conjugated Equine Estrogens (Premarin®) Are Protective against Neurodegenerative Insults: Implications for a Composition of Estrogen Therapy to Promote Neuronal Function and Prevent Alzheimer's Disease." *BMC Neuroscience* (2006) 7:24.

Liu, Y. W., E. W. Mee, P. Bergin, et al. "Adult Neurogenesis in Mesial Temporal Lobe Epilepsy: A Review of Recent Animal and Human Studies." *Current Pharmaceutical Biotechnology* 8, no. 3 (2007): 187–94.

Nilsen, J. "Estradiol and Neurodegenerative Oxidative Stress." *Frontiers in Neuroendocrinology* 29, no. 4 (2008): 463–75. E-publication Jan. 11, 2008.

Peng, C. H., S. H. Chiou, S. J. Chen, et al. "Neuroprotection by Imipramine against Lipopolysaccharide-Induced Apoptosis in Hippocampus-Derived Neural Stem Cells Mediated by Activation of BDNF and the MAPK Pathway." *European Neuropsychopharmacology* 18, no. 2 (2008): 128–40. E-publication Jun. 11, 2007.

Perera, T. D., J. D. Coplan, S. H. Lisanby, et al. "Antidepressant-Induced Neurogenesis in the Hippocampus of Adult Nonhuman Primates." *Journal of Neuroscience* 27, no. 18 (2007): 4894–4901.

Ransome, M. I., and A. M. Turnley. "Systemically Delivered Erythropoietin Transiently Enhances Adult Hippocampal Neurogenesis." *Journal of Neurochemistry* 102, no. 6 (2007): 1953–65. E-publication Jun. 7, 2007.

Robusto-Leitao, O., and J. Ferreira. "Hormones and Dementia: A Comparative Study of Hormonal Impairment in Postmenopause Women, With and Without Dementia." *Neuropsychiatric Disease and Treatment* 2, no. 2 (2006): 199–206.

Rosario, E. R., and C. J. Pike. "Androgen Regulation of Beta-Amyloid Protein and the Risk of Alzheimer's Disease." *Brain Research Reviews* 57, no. 2 (2008): 444–53.

Rossini, P. M., C. Altamura, F. Ferreri, et al. "Neuroimaging Experimental Studies on Brain Plasticity in Recovery from Stroke." *Europa Medicophysica* 43, no. 2 (2007): 241–54.

Santarelli, L., M. Saxe, C. Gross, et al. "Requirement of Hippocampal Neurogenesis for the Behavioral Effects of Antidepressants." *Science* 301, no. 5634 (2003): 805–9.

Schussler, P., M. Kluge, A. Yassouridis, et al. "Progesterone Reduces Wakefulness in Sleep EEG and Has No Effect on Cognition in Healthy Postmenopausal Women." *Psychoneuroendocrinology* 33, no. 8 (2008): 1124–31.

Shi, X. Y., J. W. Wang, G. F. Lei, et al. "Morphological and Behavioral Consequences of Recurrent Seizures in Neonatal Rats Are Associated with Glucocorticoid Levels." *Neuroscience Bulletin* 23, no. 2 (2007): 83–91.

Short, R. A., R. L. Bowen, P. C. O'Brien, et al. "Elevated Gonadotropin Levels in Patients with Alzheimer Disease." *Mayo Clinic Proceedings* 76, no. 9 (2001): 906–9.

Siwak-Tapp, C. T., E. Head, B. A. Muggenburg, et al. "Neurogenesis Decreases with Age in the Canine Hippocampus and Correlates with Cognitive Function." *Neurobiology of Learning and Memory* 88, no. 2 (2007): 249–59.

Steiner, B., G. Kronenberg, S. Jessberger, et al. "Differential Regulation of Glycogenesis in the Context of Adult Hippocampal Neurogenesis in Mice." *Glia* 46, no. 1 (2004): 41–52.

Sung, S. M., D. S. Jung, C. H. Kwon, et al. "Hypoxia/Reoxygenation Stimulates Proliferation through PKC-Dependent Activation of ERK and Akt in Mouse Neural Progenitor Cells." *Neurochemical Research* 32, no. 11 (2007): 1932–39. E-publication Jun. 12, 2007.

Venkatesan, A., A. Nath, G. L. Ming, et al. "Adult Hippocampal Neurogenesis: Regulation by HIV and Drugs of Abuse." *Cellular and Molecular Life Sciences* 64, no. 16 (2007): 2120–32.

Webber, K. M., G. Casadesus, G. Perry, et al. "Gender Differences in Alzheimer Disease: The Role of Luteinizing Hormone in Disease Pathogenesis." *Alzheimer Disease and Associated Disorders* 19, no. 2 (2005): 95–99.

Whittle, C., M. M. Corrada, M. Dick, et al. "Neuropsychological Data in Nondemented Oldest Old: The 90+ Study." *Journal of Clinical and Experimental Neuropsychology* 29, no. 3 (2007): 290–99.

Yue, F., B. Chen, D. Wu, et al. "Biological Properties of Neural Progenitor Cells Isolated from the Hippocampus of Adult Cynomolgus Monkeys." *Chinese Medical Journal* 119, no. 2 (2006): 110–16.

Chapter 13

Ahmad, A. M., M. T. Hopkins, P. J. Weston, et al. "Effects of GH Replacement on 24-h Ambulatory Blood Pressure and Its Circadian Rhythm in Adult GH Deficiency." *Clinical Endocrinology (Oxf)* 56, no. 4 (2002): 431–37.

Arwert, L. I., J. B. Deijen, M. Muller, et al. "Long-Term Growth Hormone Treatment Preserves GH-Induced Memory and Mood Improvements: A 10-Year Follow-Up Study in GH-Deficient Adult Men." *Hormones and Behavior* 47, no. 3 (2005): 343–49.

Bosevski, M., S. Tosev, and S. Sadikario. "Premature Atherosclerosis in Patients with Growth Hormone Deficiency and Diabetes Mellitus." *Bratislavské Lekárske Listy* 109, no. 6 (2008): 279–80.

Brooke, A. M., et al. "Dehydroepiandrosterone (DHEA) Replacement Reduces Growth Hormone (GH) Dose Requirement in Female Hypopituitary Patients on GH Replacement." *Clinical Endocrinology (Oxf)* 65, no. 5 (2006): 673–80.

Colao, A., C. Di Somma, T. Cascella, et al. "Relationship between Serum IGF1 Levels, Blood Pressure, and Glucose Tolerance: An Observational, Exploratory Study in 404 Subjects." *European Journal of Endocrinology* 159, no. 4 (2008): 389–97.

Colao, A., C. Di Somma, S. Spiezia, et al. "Growth Hormone Treatment on Atherosclerosis: Results of a 5-Year Open, Prospective, Controlled Study in Male Patients with Severe Growth Hormone Deficiency." *Journal of Clinical Endocrinology and Metabolism* 93, no. 9 (2008): 3416–24.

De la Monte, S. M., et al. "Review of Insulin and Insulin-Like Growth Factor Expression, Signaling, and Malfunction in the Central Nervous System: Relevance to Alzheimer's Disease." *Journal of Alzheimer's Disease* 7, no. 1 (2005): 45–61.

De la Monte, S. M., et al. "Therapeutic Rescue of Neurodegeneration in Experimental Type 3 Diabetes: Relevance to Alzheimer's Disease." *Journal of Alzheimer's Disease* 10, no. 1 (2006): 89–109.

Drew, M. R., and R. Hen. "Adult Hippocampal Neurogenesis as Target for the Treatment of Depression." *CNS & Neurological Disorders Drug Targets* 6, no. 3 (2007): 205–18.

Falleti, M. G., P. Maruff, P. Burman, et al. "The Effects of Growth Hormone (GH) Deficiency and GH Replacement on Cognitive Performance in Adults: A Meta-Analysis of the Current Literature." *Psychoneuroendocrinology* 31, no. 6 (2006): 681–91.

Giovannini, S., E. Marzetti, S. E. Borst, et al. "Modulation of GH/IGF-1 Axis: Potential Strategies to Counteract Sarcopenia in Older Adults." *Mechanisms of Ageing and Development* 129, no. 10 (2008): 593–601.

Gunnell, D., L. L. Miller, I. Rogers, et al. "Association of Insulin-Like Growth Factor I and Insulin-Like Growth Factor-Binding Protein-3 with Intelligence Quotient among 8- to 9-Year-Old Children in the Avon Longitudinal Study of Parents and Children." *Pediatrics* 116, no. 5 (2005): e681–86.

Ho, K. K., J. Gibney, G. Johannsson, et al. "Regulating of Growth Hormone Sensitivity by Sex Steroids: Implications for Therapy." *Frontiers of Hormone Research* 35 (2006): 115–28.

Hunt, K. J., et al. "A Potential Inverse Association between Insulin-Like Growth Factor I and Hypertension in a Cross-Sectional Study." *Annals of Epidemiology* 16, no. 7 (2006): 563–71.

Johansson, I., et al. "Proliferative and Protective Effects of Growth Hormone Secretagogues on Adult Rat Hippocampal Progenitor Cells." *Endocrinology* 149, no. 5 (2008): 2191–99.

Kearney, T., et al. "Effects of Short- and Long-Term Growth Hormone Replacement on Lipoprotein Composition and on Very-Low-Density Lipoprotein and Low-Density Lipoprotein Apolipoprotein B100 Kinetics in Growth Hormone-Deficient Hypopituitary Subjects." *Metabolism* 52, no. 1 (2003): 50–59.

Kok, P., F. Roelfsema, M. Frolich, et al. "Short-Term Treatment with Bromocriptine Improves Impaired Circadian Growth Hormone Secretion in Obese Premenopausal Women." *Journal of Clinical Endocrinology and Metabolism* 93, no. 9 (2008): 3455–61.

Liu, J. M., H. Y. Zhao, G. Ning, et al. "IGF-1 as an Early Marker for Low Bone Mass or Osteoporosis in Premenopausal and Postmenopausal Women." *Journal of Bone and Mineral Metabolism* 26, no. 2 (2008): 159–64.

Lutter, M., et al. "The Orexigenic Hormone Ghrelin Defends against Depressive Symptoms of Chronic Stress." *Nature Neuroscience* 11, no. 7 (2008): 752–53.

Monaco, M. D., F. Vallero, R. D. Monaco, et al. "Serum Levels of Insulin-Like Growth Factor-I Are Positively Associated with Functional Outcome After Hip Fracture in Elderly Women." *American Journal of Physical Medicine and Rehabilitation* 88, no. 2 (2009): 119–25.

Pareren, Y. K., H. J. Duivenvoorden, F. S. M. Slijper, et al. "Intelligence and Psychosocial Functioning during Long-Term Growth Hormone Therapy in Children Born Small for Gestational Age." *Journal of Clinical Endocrinology and Metabolism* 89, no. 11 (2004): 5295–5302.

Pasarica, M., J. Zachwieja, L. DeJonge, et al. "Effect of Growth Hormone on Body Composition and Visceral Adiposity in Middle-Aged Men with Visceral Obesity." *Journal of Clinical Endocrinology and Metabolism* 92, no. 11 (2007): 4265–70.

Poljakovic, Z., N. Zurak, V. Brinar, et al. "Growth Hormone and Insulin Growth Factor-I Levels in Plasma and Cerebrospinal Fluid of Patients with Multiple Sclerosis." *Clinical Neurology and Neurosurgery* 108, no. 3 (2006): 255–58.

Ransome, M. I., and A. M. Turnley. "Growth Hormone Signaling and Hippocampal Neurogenesis: Insights from Genetic Models." *Hippocampus* 18, no. 10 (2008): 1034–50.

Rolland, Y., et al. "Frailty, Osteoporosis and Hip Fracture: Causes, Consequences and Therapeutic Perspectives." *Journal of Nutrition, Health, and Aging* 12, no. 5 (2008): 335–46.

Sathiavageeswaran, M., P. Burman, D. Lawrence, et al. "Effects of GH on Cognitive Function in Elderly Patients with Adult-Onset GH Deficiency: A Placebo-Controlled 12-Month Study." *European Journal of Endocrinology* 156, no. 4 (2007): 439–47.

Schaffer, A., et al. "Insulin-Like Growth Factor-I and Risk of High-Grade Cervical Intraepithelial Neoplasia." *Cancer Epidemiology, Biomarkers and Prevention* 16, no. 4 (2007): 716–22.

Yuen, K. C., et al. "Improvement in Insulin Sensitivity without Concomitant Changes in Body Composition and Cardiovascular Risk Markers Following Fixed Administration of a Very Low Growth Hormone (GH) Dose in Adults with Severe GH Deficiency." *Clinical Endocrinology (Oxf)* 63, no. 4 (2005): 428–36.

Index

Boldfaced page references indicate illustrations. <u>Underscored</u> references indicate boxed text.

A

Abdominal ultrasound, 249
Abstract IQ, 79–80, 184
Acetylcholine
  aerobic exercise and, 187
  aging and, 48–49
  Alzheimer's disease and, 6
  calcium-rich foods for boosting, 146
  in cholinergic system, 6
  deficiency, 6, 49, 232
  eggs and, 156
  empathy and, 52
  function of, 6
  high levels of, 48
  hormones in increasing, 196–97
  medications enhancing, 215, 220–21, <u>221</u>
  in reversing mild cognitive impairment, 21
  in right-brained individuals, 10
  speed of brain and, 58
Acetylcholinesterase, <u>221</u>
ADD disorder, 65–70, 92, 222
Addictions
  as cause of mild cognitive impairment, 25, 70–72
  cognitive decline and, 70–72
  cranial electrical stimulation and, 131
  diseases affecting cognition and, 236
  dopamine and, 70–72
  sugar, 156
Adrenaline, 6, 33
Adult-onset diabetes, 137, 239

Adult attention deficit disorder, 65–70, 92
Aerobic exercise, 187–89, 191
African culinary specialties, <u>161–62</u>
Age Print Quiz, 93–94
Aging
  acetylcholine and, 48–49
  brain and, 7, 13–14, 77
  as cause of mild cognitive impairment, 13–14, 25
  IQ and, 83
  leptin and, 137
  memory and, 13
  parathyroid hormone and, 202
  sleep and, 37–38
  speed of brain declines and, 49, 231
Alcohol. *See also* Addictions
  GABA and, 168
  health effects of excessive, 72
  one drink, defining, <u>72</u>
  resveratrol and, 168–70
  sleep and, <u>42</u>
Aldosterone, 199
Allspice, 150
Alpha waves, 5, 9
Aluminum exposure, <u>157</u>
Alzheimer's disease
  acetylcholine and, 6
  causes of, 19–20
  continuum of, **15**
  diabetes and, 239
  diagnosis of, 19
  managing
    antioxidants, 31
    medications, <u>221</u>
    physical exercise, 187

mild cognitive impairment and, 14,
15, 18–19
smell and, sense of, 29
stress and, 47
symptoms of, 20
Amino acids, 130, 147, 175
Amnestic mild cognitive impairment,
24
Amyloid B, 19, 138, 152, 170
Andropause, 210–11
Anise, 150
Anticonvulsants, 216–17, 216
Antidepressants, 218–20, 218, 219,
220
Antioxidants, 31
Anxiety
brain chemistry and, 34–35
GABA and, 233
medications for reducing, 216–17,
216–17
personality changes and, 32–34
physical exercise in managing,
188
as sign of mild cognitive impairment, early, 32
sleep and, 32
speed of bran and, 33
stress and, 33–34
test, 35
Aromatherapy, 124
Aromatherapy massage, 123, 124
Arrhythmia, brain, 34
Asian culinary specialties, 162–63
Aspartame, 148
Aspirin, 148, 220
Atenolol, 220
Attention
adult attention deficit disorder
versus declining, 65–70, 92
brain and, 17–18
changes in, 18, 18, 36, 74–75
cognitive decline and problems
with, 64
dopamine and, 63–65, 147, 232
errors, 65–66

improving
Braverman Brain Workout, 183
diet and nutrition, 147–48, 147
mental exercises, 183
nutrients, 170–71, 171–74, 173
mild cognitive impairment and,
67–68
Patient Profiles, 36, 74–75
prioritizing, 76–77
technology and, 72–73, 76–77
testing, 108–10
tips for keeping focus and,
69–70
voltage of brain and, 65
Attention deficit (ADD) disorder,
65–70, 92, 222
Auditory memory, 52
Avocado, 163
Axons, 4

B

Bad habits, breaking, 186
Balanced brain, 4–5, 82–83
Basil, 150, 165
BCAA, 175
BDNF, 188
BEAM, 36, 88
Benzodiazepines, 217, 217
Beta-amyloid protein plaques, 19
Beta waves, 5
Big Brain game, 128
Bilateralization, 11
Bioidentical hormones, 196–99
Biotin, 142
Black pepper, 150
Black tea, 152
Blood flow to brain, 20, 189
Blueberries, 164
BMI, 250
Body fat, 136–37
Body mass index (BMI), 250
Brain-derived neurotrophic factor
(BDNF), 188

Brain. *See also* Speed of brain
aging and, 7, 13–14, 77
analogies, 3
anatomy of, 8–12, 8
anxiety and chemistry of, 34–37
arrhythmia, 34
attention and, 17–18
balanced, 4–5, 82–83
bilateralization, 11
blood flow to, 20, 189
body fat in, 136–37
changes in, 16–17
chemical categories, balancing, 6–7
dysrhythmia, 34
electrical activity of, 3–5
electrochemical, 3–5
emotions and, 51
energy and, 10
erectile dysfunction medications
and metabolism of, 222
function of, 3
glucose and, 155
gray matter of, 136–37
healthy, 23
hemispheres, 8, 10–11, 115–16
insulin and, 155
IQ and, 78–79
left portion, 10–11
lobes, 8–9, 8, 11, 17, 52–54
memory and, 9, 17, 51
muscle mass and, 189
neurofibrillary tangles and, 19–20
pattern recognition and, 182
pauses, 234, 235
personality and, 9, 16
plaques in, 19, 138, 170
power of, 253–54
rebalancing, 46–47
right portion, 10–11
senile, 23–24
sleep and, 38
stress and, 34
synchrony of, 5
voltage of, 4, 63, 65
waves, 5, 9, 38
white matter of, 136–37

Brain Age game, 128
Brain Electrical Activity Mapping
(BEAM), 36, 88
"Brain fog," 6
Brain Memory formula, 171
Brain Quiz, 93
Brain stem, 8, 8, 11
Brain Youth formula, 171
Branched chain amino acids (BCAA),
175
Braverman Anxiety Test, 35
Braverman Brain Advantage Test
answer key for, 255–57
overview of, 94
score, understanding, 120, 168
Test One: Verbal Memory, 95–100
Test Two: Visual Memory, 101–2
Test Three: Immediate Memory,
103–5
Test Four: Working Memory,
106–7
Test Five: Attention, 108–10
Test Six: Executive Function,
111–12
Test Seven: IQ/Paradigm Pattern
Recognition, 113–14
Test Eight: Left Brain/Right Brain,
115–16
Test Nine: Delayed Recall, 117–19
Braverman Brain Workout
for attention improvement, 183
for IQ improvement, 184–86
for memory improvement, 181–82
overview of, 179–80
weekly schedule, 186–87
Braverman Depression Test, 43
Braverman Mini Memory Test,
60–61, 65
Braverman Protocol, 46–47, 62, 234.
See also specific step in
Breakfast, 160
Breast ultrasound, 249
Broccoli, 140, 160
Bupropion, 219
BuSpar, 220
Buspirone, 220

C

Caffeine, 64, 152–54
Calcium, 146, 154
Cancer, 237–38
Capsaicin, 150
Carbohydrates, 141, 160–61
Carotid ultrasound, 249
Catechins, 168
Catecholamine system, 6
Cayenne pepper, 150, <u>161</u>
Cell phone use, 129
Central American culinary specialties, <u>163</u>
Central nervous system, 3–4
Cerebellum, 8, **8**, 11
Cerebral cortex, 9
Cerebrospinal fluid, 12
Cerebrum, 8–9, **8**
CES, 130–34, <u>131</u>
cGMP (current good manufacturing practices), <u>175</u>
Chamomile tea, 154
Chelation cleansing, 134–35
Chemo-brain, 237
Chicken, 155
Chile pepper, 150
Cholesterol levels, 157, 240–41
Choline, 143–44, <u>144</u>
Cholinergic system, 6
Chondroitin, 175
Chronic pain, 238
Cialis, <u>222</u>
Cleaning clutter in stress management, 37
Clove, 150
CNS/VS tests, 92
Coenzyme Q10, 174
Coffee, 152
Cognitex, 171
Cognitive baseline, defining, 91–94, <u>93</u>
Cognitive decline. *See also* Alzheimer's disease; Diseases affecting cognition; Mild cognitive impairment (MCI)
addictions and, 70–72

attention problems and, <u>64</u>
depression and, 42–44
diabetes and, 239
leptin and, 138
MRI for detecting, 90–91
myelin decay and, 61
overweight and, 136–37
PET scan for detecting, 89–90
speed of brain and, 23–25, 48–52, <u>51</u>
Commission attention error, 65–66
Common sense, 80, 184
Communication and mild cognitive impairment, 68
Complex carbohydrates, 141
Concussion, 28–29
Coriander, 150
Corpus callosum, 10–11
Cortisol, 33, <u>34</u>, 195, 206
Cranial electrical stimulation (CES), 130–34, <u>131</u>
Creatine, 175
Creative IQ, 80
CT scan, 88
Culinary specialties, regional, 161, <u>161–66</u>
Cumin, 151
Current good manufacturing practices (cGMP), <u>175</u>

D

D-phenylalanine, 170–71
D2 dopamine receptors, 70–71
Daily Smarts, 252–54
Dairy products, 146. *See also specific type*
Decaffeinated tea, 154
Deep-tissue massage, 123
Degenerative disorders, 27–28
Dehydroepiandrosterone (DHEA), 197, 200, 202
Delayed Recall Test, 117–19
Delta waves, 5, 38

Dementia, 6, 12, *59*. *See also*
    Alzheimer's disease; Cognitive
    decline; Mild cognitive
    impairment (MCI)
Dendrites, 4
Depression
    cognitive decline and, 42–44
    managing
        diet and nutrition, 142, *143*
        physical exercise, 188
    personality changes and, 32–34
    serotonin and, 233
    test, *43*
    untreated, 43
DEXA scan, 250
DHA, 142, 145, *145*
DHEA-sulfate (DHEA-S), 200
DHEA, 197, 200, 202
Diabetes, 137, 238–40
Diagnostics. *See* Testing for brain
    health, early; *specific test*
Dietary fats, 144–46, 160–61
Diet and nutrition for brain health
    (Step Three). *See also specific*
    food
    attention improvement, 147–48,
        147
    body fat in brain and, 136–37
    in Braverman Protocol, 136
    Braverman's diet and, 139–41
    depression management, 142, *143*
    dopamine and, 147
    exercise performance and, 174–75,
        175
    foods in, basic daily, 140
    hunger and, beating, *160*
    leptin and, 137–41, *139*
    meal, brain-balanced, 166–67
    memory improvement, 143–46,
        144, *146*
    mood improvement, 141–42, *143*
    nutrients, 167–71, *167–68*, *171–74*,
        173
    overweight and, avoiding, 136–38
    Patient Profile, *176–77*

regional culinary specialties, 161,
    161–66
rules for younger, smarter you
    basic food groups, including all,
        160–61
    caffeine, 152–54
    fiber, 157–58
    fruits and vegetables, colorful,
        158–59
    fruits and vegetables, high-qual-
        ity, 159–60
    herbs and spices, 149–52, *151*
    overview of ten, 149
    proteins, lean, 155–56, *160*
    sugar, avoiding, 156–57
    water intake, 158
    yogurt, 154–55, *155*
    toxic exposure elimination, *157*
    weight loss and, healthy, 139–40
Dill, 151
Diseases affecting cognition
    acetylcholine deficiency and, 232
    addictions and, 236
    cancer, 237–38
    chronic pain, 238
    diabetes, 238–40
    dopamine deficiency and, 232
    epilepsy, 243–44
    GABA deficiency and, 233
    high blood pressure, 241
    high cholesterol, 240–41
    infections, *245*
    multiple sclerosis, 241–42
    order of events of, 230–31
    overview of, 234–35
    Parkinson's disease, 242
    Patient Profile, *246–47*
    preventing, 236–37
    reversing, 234, 248–51
    seizures, 243–44
    serotonin deficiency and, 233
    sickle cell disease, 244–45
    "steps of care" approach and,
        250–51
    stroke, 245–47

thyroid disorders, 247–48
tinnitus, 243
Docosahexaenoic acid (DHA), 142, 145, 145
Dopamine
addictions and, 70–72
aerobic exercise and, 187
attention and, 63–65, 147, 232
in catecholamine system, 6
cranial electrical stimulation and, 130
deficiency, 6, 63–64, 70, 232
diet and nutrition for brain health and, 147
function of, 6
high levels of, 63
hormones in increasing, 196–97
IQ and, 63
in left-brained individuals, 10
leptin and, 137
medications enhancing, 215, 221–22, 222
proteins and, lean, 155
in reversing mild cognitive impairment, 21
sinuses and production of, 76
stress and, 33
sugar and, 156
Drugs. See Medications; specific type
Dual-energy x-ray absorptiometry (DEXA) scan, 250
Dysrhythmia, brain, 34

E

"Ear control," practicing, 77
Echocardiogram, 249
Eggs, 156, 160, 164
Eicosapentaenoic acid (EPA), 145
Emotional changes, 44–47
Emotional IQ, 80, 179, 184, 189
Emotions, 51, 57
Empathy, 52
Endorphins, 6–7

Energy, 10, 64
EPA, 145
Epilepsy, 243–44
Episodic memory function, 55
EPO, 200
Equal (sugar substitute), 148
Erectile dysfunction medications, 222
Erythropoietin (EPO), 200
Estradiol, 201
Estriol, 201
Estrogen, 198–200, 207
Estrone, 201
European culinary specialties, 164–66
Executive Function Test, 111–12
Exercise. See Mental exercise for brain health; Physical exercise for brain health
Exercise performance, supplements for enhancing, 174–75, 176

F

Fat. See Body fat; Dietary fats
Fennel, 151
Fiber, 140, 157–58, 160
Fish, 134, 142, 155
Fish oil supplements, 145
Five-phase exercise program, 191–94
Flavonoids, 159
Flight-or-fight syndrome, 38
Focus. See Attention
Folic acid, 152
Follicle-stimulating hormone (FSH), 206–7
Food coloring, avoiding artificial, 148
Food flavorings, avoiding artificial, 148
Food groups, basic, 160–61
Food preservatives, avoiding artificial, 148

Foods. *See* Diet and nutrition for brain health; *specific type*
Forgetfulness. *See* Cognitive decline
French culinary specialties, 164
Frontal lobes, 8, 9, 11, 17, 53–54
Fruits, 158–60. *See also specific type*
FSH, 206–7

G

GABA
  alcohol and, 168
  anxiety and, 233
  brain arrhythmia and, 34
  cranial electrical stimulation and, 130
  deficiency, 7, 233
  emotional IQ and, 80
  endorphins and, 6–7
  function of, 6–7
  in GABAergic system, 6–7
  glutamate and, 35–37
  high levels of, 38
  hormones in increasing, 196–97
  low levels of, 38
  medications enhancing, 215–17, 216–17
  physical exercise in increasing, 188
  Pilates and, 187
  production of, 9
  in reversing mild cognitive impairment, 21
  sleep and, 37
  stress and, 33–37
  yoga and, 187
GABAergic system, 6–7
GAMA, 92
Game of Five Differences, 183
Gamma-aminobutyric acid. *See* GABA
Garlic, 151, 165
General Ability Measure for Adults (GAMA), 92
General adaption syndrome, 38

German culinary specialties, 164
Ginger, 151
Ginkgo biloba, 171
Glucosamine, 175
Glucose, 155, 238
Glutamate, 35–37
Glutamine, 142, 175
Gray matter of brain, 136–37
Greek culinary specialties, 165
Greek yogurt, 154
Green tea, 152–53

H

Habits, breaking bad, 186
HDL cholesterol, 157, 240
Heart rate monitor, 130
Heart surgery and memory, 240
Heavy metals, 30, 30, 134
Hemispheres of brain, 8, 10–11, 115–16
Herbs, 149–52, 151
HGH, 197, 201
"High-voltage dementia," 12
High blood pressure, 241
High cholesterol, 240–41
Hormones for brain health (Step Five)
  acetylcholine increases and, 196–97
  aldosterone, 199
  andropause and, 210–11
  bioidentical, 196–99
  in Braverman Protocol, 197
  dehydroepiandrosterone, 197, 200, 202
  DHEA-sulfate, 200
  dopamine increases and, 196–97
  erythropoietin, 200
  estradiol, 201
  estriol, 201
  estrogen, 198–200, 207
  estrone, 201
  GABA increases and, 196–97

human growth hormone, 197, 201
  importance of, 195–96
  increlex, 201
  insulin-like growth factor, 201
  leptin and, 203
  medical care and, 211, 214
  melatonin, 202
  memory of adolescents and, 12–13
  menopause and, 206–7
  nonbioidentical, 199
  parathyroid hormone, 202
  Patient Profile, 204–5, 212–13
  performance gap and decline in, 196, 197
  pregnenolone, 202
  production of, 195
  progesterone, 198, 202–3
  serotonin increases and, 196–97
  testosterone, 197, 203
  thyroid T3 and T4, 203–4
  types of, 195
  vasporessin and, 205–6
  vitamin D and, 206
Hot stone massage, 123
Human growth hormone (HGH), 197, 201
Hunger, beating, 160
Huperzine, 170–71
Hyperglycemia, 239
Hyperparathyroidism, 202
Hypertension, 241
Hyperthyroidism, 248
Hypothyroidism, 247–48

I

IGF, 201
Immediate memory
  function of, 52–53
  improving, 181
  testing, 103–5
Impulsivity, 68–69

Increlex, 201
Infantile amnesia, 12
Infections, 26–27, 245
Information overload, 73, 76
Inositol, 141–42
Insoluble fiber, 158
Insomnia, 29, 39
Insulin-like growth factor (IGF), 201
Insulin, 155, 238–39
Insulin resistance, 239
Intelligence quotient. See IQ
Intuitiveness, 51, 53, 185
IQ
  aging and, 83
  balanced brain and, 82–83
  Binet's definition of, 78
  brain and, 78–79
  Braverman Brain Workout for improving, 184–86
  dopamine and, 63
  increasing, 84
  mastering all four types of, 83
  mental exercises for improving, 184–86
  numbers, meaning of, 81
  speed of brain and, 79
  technology and, 128
  test, 92
  traits of high, 81–82, 83
  types of, 79–80
IQ/Paradigm Pattern Recognition Test, 113–14
Italian culinary specialties, 165

J

Juvenile-onset diabetes, 239

K

Kefir, 166
KenKen (game), 180

L

L-carnitine, 175
L-theanine, 153
Laughter, in stress management, 37
LDL cholesterol, 240
Lead exposure, 157
Learning, 46, 84, 128, 179, 187
Lecithin, 146
Left Brain/Right Brain exercises,
    184–86
Left Brain/Right Brain test, 115–16
Lemon balm, 151
Lemon balm tea, 154
Lemongrass, 151
Leptin
    aging and, 137
    cognitive decline and, 138
    determining level of, 138
    diet and nutrition for brain health
        and, 137–41, 139
    dopamine and, 137
    function of, 137
    high levels of, 137–38
    hormones for brain health and,
        203
    managing level of, 138–39
    medications enhancing, 223, 223,
        226
    nutrients affecting, 139
    obesity and, 136–38
Levitra, 222
LH, 206–7
Lifestyle changes for brain health
    (Step Two)
    aromatherapy, 124
    in Braverman Protocol, 121
    cell phone use, 129
    chelation cleansing, 134–35
    cranial electrical stimulation,
        130–34, 131
    heart rate monitor, 130
    massage, 122–23, 124
    meditation, 123–25
    music, 125–27
    overview of therapies, 121–22
Patient Profile, 132–33
technology, 128
Lingonberries, 164
Lobes, brain, 8–9, 8, 11, 17, 52–54
Long-term memory, 30, 53–55, 55
Lumosity Web site, 128
Lumos Labs Web-based software,
    128
Luteinzing hormone (LH), 206–7
Lyme disease, 27

M

Male menopause, 210–11
MAO inhibitors, 218, 218
Marijuana, medical, 226
Marinol pills, 226
Marjoram, 151
Massage, 122–23, 124
MCI. See Mild cognitive impairment
Medical care, 248–51
Medical marijuana, 226
Medications for brain health (Step
    Six). See also Over-the-counter
    medications; Prescription
    medications; specific type
    acetylcholine-enhancing, 215,
        220–21, 221
    Alzheimer's disease management,
        221
    anxiety-reducing, 216–17, 216–17
    aspirin, 220
    in Braverman Protocol, 214–16
    dopamine-enhancing, 215,
        221–22, 222
    erectile dysfunction medications,
        222
    GABA-enhancing, 215–17, 216–17
    leptin-enhancing, 223, 223, 226
    marijuana, medical, 226
    for memory improvement, 220–21,
        221
    Patient Profile, 224–25
    serotonin-enhancing, 215, 218–20

Meditation, 123–25
Melatonin, 202
Memantine, 221
Memories, making, 56–57
Memory
  acetylcholine and, 232
  of adolescents, 12–13
  in adulthood, 13
  aging and, 13
  brain and, 9, 17, 51
  changes in, 17, 27, 44–45
  emotions and, 51, 57
  functions, 55
  heart surgery and, 240
  improving
    Braverman Brain Workout,
      181–82
    diet and nutrition, 143–46, 144,
      146
    medications, 220–21, 221
    mental exercises, 179–82
    music, 125–27
    nutrients, 170–71, 171–73
    supplements, 171
  of infants, 12
  life cycle stages of, 12–13
  long-term, 30, 53–55, 55
  loss, 49–50, 57–58, 62, 62
  Lyme disease and, 27
  making memories and, 56–57
  Patient Profiles, 27, 44–45
  perception and, 57–58
  resveratrol and, 170
  retention, 12
  seizures and, 243–44
  self-improvement and, 253
  short-term, 30, 52–53, 55
  sleep and, 40, 42
  smoking and, 62
  test, 60–61, 65
  types of, 52–53
Menopause
  hormones in managing, 206–7
  male, 210–11
  perimenopause and, 209–10

stages of, 211
symptoms of, 208–9
Mental exercise for brain health
    (Step Four)
  bad habits and, breaking, 186
  in Braverman Protocol
    for attention improvement, 183
    for IQ improvement, 184–86
    for memory improvement,
      179–82
  overview of, 179–80
  weekly workout, 186–87
  importance of, 178–79
  KenKen, 180
  new things, trying, 187
  Patient Profile, 192–93
  pattern recognition, 182
  Suduko, 180
Mercury exposure, 134, 157
Merriam-Webster Web site, 128
Mild cognitive impairment (MCI)
  Alzheimer's disease and, 14, 15,
    18–19
  attention and, 67–68
  causes of
    addictions, 25, 70–72
    aging, 13–14, 25
    degenerative disorders, 27–28
    infections, 26–27
    nutritional deficiencies, 31
    over-the-counter medications,
      26
    prescription medications, 25–26
    psychiatric disorders, 29
    sleep disturbances, 29
    toxic exposures, 29–30, 30
    trauma, physical, 28–29
  checklists, 54–55, 67–68
  communication and, 68
  daily living activities and, 54–55
  emotional changes and, 44–47
  forms of, 24
  incidence of, 14
  mood and, 16–17, 32–34
  other symptoms caused by, 50

Mild cognitive impairment *(cont.)*
  personality and, 16–17, 32–34
  preclinical phase of, 14
  reversing
    acetylcholine, 21
    with brain chemistry, 21–22
    with diet, 140
    dopamine, 21
    GABA, 21
    with physical exercise, 178,
      187–91
    serotonin, 21
  signs of, 15–16, 17, 32
  tests for, 93
  vision and, 54
Mineral deficiencies, 31
Mini Mental State Exam (MMSE),
  92
Miso, 162
MMSE, 92
Monoamine oxidase (MAO)
  inhibitors, 218, 218
Monosodium glutamate (MSG),
  avoiding, 148
Monounsaturated fatty acids, 145
Mood
  changes in, 32–34, 44–45, 46
  improving
    diet and nutrition, 141–42, 143
    music, 125–27
  learning and, 46
  mild cognitive impairment and,
    16–17, 32–34
  music and, 127
  Patient Profile, 44–45
MRI scan, 88, 90–91
MS, 241–42
MSG, avoiding, 148
Multiple sclerosis (MS), 241–42
Multitasking, 73
Muscle mass, 189
Mushrooms, 163
Music, 125–27
Mustard seed, 151
Myelin, 58, 60–62

N

Namenda, 221
Nature Quiz, 94
Neurofibrillary tangles, 19–20
Neurogenesis, 12, 84, 130, 131, 158,
  200
Neuron-to-neuron synapses, 4
Neurons, 3–4, 8–9, 12
New things, trying, 187
Nintendo DS system games, 128
Non-amnestic, multiple domain mild
  cognitive impairment, 24
Non-amnestic, single domain mild
  cognitive impairment, 24
Nonbioidentical hormones, avoiding,
  199
Norwegian culinary specialties, 164
Nutmeg, 151
NutraSweet, 148
Nutrients
  for attention improvement,
    170–71, 171–74, 173
  for brain health, 167–71, 167–68,
    171–74, 173
  deficiencies in, 31
  leptin and, positive effect on, 139
  for memory improvement, 170–71,
    171–73
  for natural chelation, 134–35
  for speed of brain, increasing,
    170–71, 171–73
  for stress reduction, 170, 171
Nutrition. *See* Diet and nutrition for
  brain health

O

Obesity, 136–38
Occipital lobes, 8, 9, 52
Olives, 165
Omega-3 fatty acids, 142, 144–46,
  156
Omega-6 fatty acids, 145

Omission attention error, 65
Oophorectomy, 207
Over-the-counter medications, 26.
    See also specific type
Overweight, 136–37

P

P300 value, 88–89, <u>89</u>, 92
Pain, chronic, 238
Panic. *See* Anxiety
Parasympathetic nervous system, 11
Parathyroid hormone (PTH), 202
Parietal lobes, 8, 9, 17
Parkinson's disease, 242
Passionflower tea, 154
Path Foundation, 136, 191, 202
pathmed.com, 93–94, <u>175</u>
Patient Profiles
    attention, <u>36</u>, <u>74–75</u>
    dementia, <u>59</u>
    diet and nutrition for brain health,
        <u>176–77</u>
    diseases affecting cognition,
        <u>246–47</u>
    hormones for brain health, <u>204–5</u>,
        <u>212–13</u>
    lifestyle changes for brain health,
        <u>132–33</u>
    medications for brain health,
        <u>224–25</u>
    memory, <u>27</u>, <u>44–45</u>
    mental exercise for brain health,
        <u>192–93</u>
    mood, <u>44–45</u>
    sleep, <u>41</u>
    toxic exposure, <u>132–33</u>
Pattern recognition, 113–14, <u>182</u>
Pauses, brain, 234, <u>235</u>
Pelvic ultrasound, 249
Peppermint, 151
Perception and memory, 57–58
Perceptive IQ, 80, 184
Perimenopause, 209–10

Personality
    brain and, 9, 16
    changes in, 16–17, 32–34
    mild cognitive impairment and,
        16–17, 32–34
PET scan, 89–90, 250
Phenylalanine, 147–48, <u>147</u>
Physical exam, 248–49
Physical exercise for brain health
    (Step Four)
    aerobic, 187–89, 191
    in Alzheimer's disease manage-
        ment, 187
    anxiety management, 188
    brain-derived neurotrophic factor
        and, 188
    endorphins and, 6–7
    five-phase program of, 191–94
    GABA increases and, 188
    importance of, 178
    medical evaluation before starting,
        190–91
    in mild cognitive impairment
        reversal, 178, 187–91
    muscle mass and, 189
    serotonin increases and, 188
    sports, competitive, 189
    varying routine of, <u>190</u>
    walking, 183
Phytonutrients, 159
Pilates, 187
Plaques in brain, 19, 138, 170
Polyphenols, 168–69
Polyunsaturated fatty acids, 145
Posit Science Web site, 128
Potassium, 199
Prediabetes, 239
Prefontal cortex, 51
Pregnenolone, 202
Premarin, 198–99
Prescription medications, 25–26. *See
    also specific type*
Procedural memory function, <u>55</u>
ProCog, 171
Produce. *See* Fruits; Vegetables

Progesterone, 198, 202–3
Prospective memory function, _55_
Prostate ultrasound, 249
Proteins, 154–56, 160–61, _160_
Provera, 198
Psychiatric disorders, 29. _See also_
    Anxiety; Depression
PTH, 202
Purine, 142

Q

Q10, 174
Quercetin, 168, 170–71

R

Rationality, 185–86
Reaction time attention error, 66
Reading with background noise,
    183
Receptor sites, 5
Red wine, 168, 170
Regional culinary specialties, 161,
    _161–66_
Relationships
    building better, 253–54
    relaxation and nurturing, _126_
    stressful, _126_
Relaxation response technique,
    124–25
Relaxation techniques, 37, _38_, _42_
REM (rapid eye movement) sleep,
    38–40
Reminiscing in stress management,
    37
Renal ultrasound, 249
Resveratrol, 168–70, _169_
Rhodiola rosea, 170–71
Ringing in the ears, _243_
Rooibos tea, 154
Rosemary, 151
Rye, _164_

S

Saffron, 151
Sage, 151
Salicylate foods to avoid, 148
Salmon, 142
Saturated fats, 144
Scrabble game, 179, _180_
Scrotal ultrasound, 249
Sea vegetables, _162_
Seizures, 243–44
Selective serotonin reuptake inhibi-
    tors (SSRIs), 219, _219_
Semantic memory function, _55_
Sensitivity, 185
Serotonergic system, 7
Serotonin
    cranial electrical stimulation and,
        130
    deficiency, 7, 233
    depression and, 233
    hormones in increasing, 196–97
    medications enhancing, 215,
        218–20
    physical exercise in increasing, 188
    proteins and, lean, 155
    in reversing mild cognitive
        impairment, 21
    in serotonergic system, 7
    sleep and, 29, 38
Serotonin and norepinephrine
    reuptake inhibitors (SNRIs),
    219, _219_
Sesame seeds, 152
Sex hormones, 200
Shiitake mushrooms, _163_
Short-term memory, 30, 52–53, _55_
Sickle cell disease, 244–45
Simple carbohydrates, 141
Sinuses, dopamine production and
    clogged, _76_
Sirtuin pathway, 169
Sleep
    aging and, 37–38
    alcohol and, _42_

anxiety and, 32
brain and, 38
changes in, 41
cranial electrical stimulation and, 131
disturbances, 29, 37–40
GABA and, 37
melatonin and, 202
memory and, 40, 42
Patient Profile, 41
REM, 38–40
salty snacks and, 42
serotonin and, 29, 38
Sleep apnea, 40
Smell, sense of, 29
Smoking and memory, 62
Snacks, 42, 155, 169
SNRIs, 219, 219
Socialization, 184, 189
Sodas, 152
Sodium, 199
Soluble fiber, 157–58
South American culinary specialties, 163
Soy food, 162
Spanish culinary specialties, 165
Spearmint, 152
Speed of brain
  acetylcholine and, 58
  aging and decline of, 49, 231
  anxiety and, 33
  changes in, 14
  cognitive decline and, 23–25, 48–52, 51
  defining, 4
  increasing, 50–51
  IQ and, 79
  myelin and, 58, 60–62
  nutrients for increasing, 170–71, 171–73
  P300 value and, 88–89, 89, 92
Spices, 149–52
Sports, competitive, 189
Sports massage, 123
SSRIs, 219, 219

"Steps of care" approach, 250–51
Stimulus, 3
Stress
  Alzheimer's disease and, 47
  anxiety and, 33–34
  brain and, 34
  dopamine and, 33
  GABA and, 33–37
  glutamate and, 35–37
  management, 37, 130, 170, 171
  nutrients for reducing, 170, 171
Stress hormones, 33, 34, 195, 206
Stroke, 245–47
Substance abuse. See Addictions
Sudoku (game), 180
Sugar, avoiding, 156–57
Sun exposure in stress management, 37
Supplements
  caution about, 175
  current good manufacturing practices and, 175
  for exercise performance, 174–75, 176
  fish oil, 145
  for memory improvement, 171
  Total Health Nutrients (THN), 175
Swedish culinary specialties, 164
Swedish massage, 123
Sympathetic nervous system, 11
Synapses, 4–6
Synchrony of brain, 5

T

Tau, 19–20
Teas, 152–54
Technology
  attention and, 72–73, 76–77
  games, brain-enhancing, 128
  IQ and, 128
  lifestyle changes for brain health and, 128

Tempeh, 162
Temperament. *See* Mood
Temporal lobes, **8**, 9, 52
Tenormin, 220
Testing for brain health, early (Step
    One). *See also* Braverman
    Brain Advantage Test
  in Braverman Protocol, 87
  cognitive baseline and, defining,
    91–94
  importance of, 87–88
  technology for, 91–94, 93
Testosterone, 197, 203
Theta waves, 5
THN, 175
Thyroid disorders, 247–48
Thyroid T3 and T4, 203–4
Thyroid ultrasound, 250
Tinnitus, 243
"Tip-of-the-tongue" phenomenon,
    243
Tofu, 162
Tomato, 163
Total Health Nutrients (THN),
    175
TOVA (Test of Variable Attention),
    67, 91–92
Toxic exposures
  as cause of mild cognitive impair-
    ment, 29–30, 30
  chelation cleansing for, 134–35
  diet and nutrition for eliminating,
    157
  heavy metals, 30, 30, 134
  Patient Profile, 132–33
Traditional IQ, 79–80, 184
Transcranial ultrasound, 250
Trauma, physical, 28–29
Tricyclics, 218, 218
Trigger point massage, 123
Tryptophan, 142
Turkish culinary specialties, 166
Turmeric, 152, 163
Type 1 diabetes, 239
Type 2 diabetes, 137, 239

"Type 3" diabetes, 239
Tyrosine, 147, 147

U

Ultrasounds, 249–50
USDA Food Pyramid, 161

V

Variability attention error, 66
Vasopressin, 205–6
Vegetables, 158–60. *See also specific
    type*
Verbal memory
  function of, 52
  loss of, 243
  testing, 95–100
Viagra, 222
Vision and mild cognitive impair-
    ment, 54
Visualization, 125
Visual memory
  function of, 52
  improving, 181
  testing, 101–2
Vitamin D, 206
Vitamin deficiencies, 31
Voltage of brain, 4, 63, 65

W

WAIS, 92
Walking, 183
Water intake, 158
Watermelon, 162
Waves, brain, 5, 9, 38
Wechsler Adult Intelligence Scale
    (WAIS), 92
Wechsler Memory Scale, 92
Weight loss, healthy, 139–40, 158,
    160–61

Wellbutrin, 219
Whey protein, 175
"White foods," avoiding, 141, 158
White matter of brain, 136–37
Wii system games, 128, 189
Wine, red, 168, 170
Working memory
  function of, 53
  improving, 182
  long-memory and, 53–55
  testing, 106–7

Y

Yoga, 187
Yogurt, 154, <u>166</u>

Z

Zinc, 151